THE SHAYKH OF SHAYKHS

THE SHAYKH
OF SHAYKHS

Mithqal al-Fayiz and Tribal Leadership

in Modern Jordan

YOAV ALON

STANFORD UNIVERSITY PRESS
STANFORD, CALIFORNIA

Stanford University Press
Stanford, California

©2016 by the Board of Trustees of the Leland Stanford Junior University.
All rights reserved.

Printed in the United States of America on acid-free, archival-quality paper

Library of Congress Cataloging-in-Publication Data

Names: Alon, Yoav, author.
Title: The shaykh of shaykhs : Mithqal al-Fayiz and tribal leadership in
    modern Jordan / Yoav Alon.
Description: Stanford, California : Stanford University Press, 2016. |
    Includes bibliographical references and index.
Identifiers: LCCN 2016015966 (print) | LCCN 2016021474 (ebook) |
    ISBN 9780804796620 (cloth : alk. paper) | ISBN 9780804799324 (pbk. : alk. paper) |
    ISBN 9780804799348 (electronic)
Subjects: LCSH: Fayiz, Mithqal, approximately 1880-1967. |
    Bedouins--Jordan--Biography. | Statesmen--Jordan--Biography. | Tribal
    government--Jordan--History--20th century. | Jordan--Politics and
    government--20th century.
Classification: LCC DS154.52.F395 A46 2016 (print) | LCC DS154.52.F395
    (ebook) | DDC 956.9504/2092 [B] --dc23
LC record available at https://lccn.loc.gov/2016015966

Cover image: Painting by Fadel Abbas based on a photo of Mithqal
by Ludwig Ferdinand Clauss, 1930.
Cover design: Cassandra Chu
Typeset by Bruce Lundquist in 10/14 Minion Pro

This book is dedicated to my beloved and admired mother,
Liora Alon,
and to the memory of my dear friend and mentor
Professor Joseph Kostiner

CONTENTS

Photographs follow page 71

ACKNOWLEDGMENTS

THIS BOOK has been many years in the making and many individuals and institutions helped me along the way. My interest in Mithqal al-Fayiz began years ago at Tel Aviv University. I was fascinated then by state-tribe relation in mandatory Transjordan, and Mithqal proved a great case study. I am most grateful to the late Professor Joseph [Yossi] Kostiner at Tel Aviv University. Yossi was the person who first introduced me to the fascinating world of modern states and tribes in the Middle East. I regret that he will not be reading my work.

I continued research on Mithqal at Oxford University, where I was fortunate to meet Dr. Eugene Rogan. His unique knowledge of Jordanian history and critical eye informed my research. He opened many doors for me, which allowed me to conduct extensive research in Jordan. Without his pioneering work on Ottoman Transjordan, the early life of Mithqal under the rule of the empire could not have been adequately told.

Mithqal naturally features in my first book but I soon came to the conclusion that he deserved a book of his own. This realization came to me during conversation with my colleague Professor Amy Singer who encouraged me to pursue the project. Another dear colleague and mentor, Professor Ehud Toledano, enthusiastically supported the project and helped me in framing the research as a social biography. Professor Asher Susser, a leading authority on Jordan, followed the project closely and offered invaluable suggestions. Another dear mentor, Professor Israel Gershoni, urged me to aim high and publish the book with Stanford University Press. I am also grateful for the support and guidance of Professor Emanuel Marx, whose classic work on nomadism and tribalism in the Middle East informs my work.

I owe special thanks to Professor Andrew Shryock, whose own work on tribal Jordan has inspired my work for many years. He has supported and encouraged me from day one and always made himself available to me, generously sharing his phenomenal understanding of the subject matter. His careful reading of the manuscript and excellent criticisms and suggestions significantly improved my work.

The book could not have been written had I not received the full coopera-tion of Mithqal's family. I am grateful to Faysal al-Fayiz (Abu Ghaith), former prime minister of Jordan and currently president of the Jordanian Senate, who hosted me in his house and introduced me to other members of the family. The late shaykh of shaykhs, Sami al-Fayiz, dedicated a lot of his time to answering my questions. The interviews with family members, and the pictures I took have contributed much for a fuller portrayal of Mithqal. I am particularly grate-ful to two of Mithqal's great grandsons, Ghaith al-Fayiz and Hussein al-Fayiz, for their assistance, friendship, and generous hospitality. I am especially grate-ful to the family for not trying to influence the way I wrote about their founder. They did not ask to see the draft of this book before its publication, but I am confident that they will nonetheless enjoy reading it.

Thanks to a generous grant from the Israel Science Foundation (grant no. 264/05) I was fortunate enough to have several remarkable research assistants. I am grateful to Ayelet Rosen–Zoran and Meital Fahima for collecting a large portion of the material. Idan Barir, Yoni Furas, and Dotan Halevy worked on other projects at the same time (supported by two other grants from the ISF), but their contribution to the current one is unmistakable. I am proud of my former assistants, who are now working on their own academic projects. Other former students helped me along the way: Julien Bellaiche, Jacques Rouyer Guillet, Shay Hazkani, Samantha Sementilli, and Eli Slama. Ben Mendales and Shoshi Shmuluvitz edited the first version of the manuscript.

I began writing the book while on sabbatical in Berlin in 2012. I am grateful to Professor Gudrun Kraemer, the director of the Institute for Islamic Studies, for hosting me and offering an ideal environment for research and writing. Angela Ballaschk and Sonja Eising were extremely helpful and friendly. Alex Fahim, Katja Jung, Christian Sassmannshausen, and Katrin Simon kindly and patiently listened to my research findings and kept me good company. I also thank the Institute's librarian, Kamran Haghmoradi. While in Berlin, I was fortunate to study German with Ursula Kohler. Without her, I could not have accessed the important German sources used in the book. She has also become a dear friend, the first one I made in Berlin. I owe a great debt to Ursula and her family.

My year in Berlin, including the language course, as well as subsequent re-search trips, were all supported very generously by the Gerda Henkel Foundation. In particular, I thank Ms. Anna Kuschmann, who coordinated my grant. She has been extremely attentive, helpful, and supportive throughout my engagement with the foundation.

Before and after my sabbatical, I spent long periods abroad for research and writing. I am grateful to Jean and Ken Marks, my adoptive family in London, for hosting me during my research in the United Kingdom. Glynnis and Ron Mileikowsky welcomed me to their house in Washington, DC. My work in the Washington area was also made possible by a fellowship I received for participation in the Decolonization Seminar sponsored by the National History Center and led by Professor Wm. Roger Louis. My great friend Christine Grossmann hosted me in her home in Pulheim, Germany, over two successive summers, which I spent as writing retreats. Her limitless generosity and humorous and witty company made a significant contribution to my work.

I visited many archives and libraries and enjoyed the help of many staff members. Clare Brown, the former archivist of the Private Papers Collection at St. Antony's College, Oxford, was both a friend and a guide to the writings of British officials, and the current archivist, Debbie Usher, has always been extremely helpful and generous. I am grateful as well to Gabriele Teichmann, the archivist of the Sal. Oppenheim *Hausarchiv* in Cologne for her assistance and friendship. I also enjoyed working at the National Archives and the Imperial War Museum in London; the Bodleian Library and Rhodes House in Oxford; the U.S. National Archives at College Park, Maryland, and Library of Congress in Washington, DC; Israeli State Archives, the National Library, and the Central Zionist Archive in Jerusalem; and the Hagana Archives and the Dayan Center's newspaper collection in Tel Aviv.

The best part of the research was always in Jordan. Many Jordanians willingly engaged in my project and offered help, friendship, and hospitality. HRH Prince Hassan bin Talal and HRH Princess Basma facilitated my early research in Jordan. At the University of Jordan, I am indebted to the directors and members of staff of the Centre for Strategic Studies, the Centre for Documentation and Manuscripts, and the library. At the National Library I received tremendous help from Director Muhammad Yunis al-'Abbadi and many members of the staff. I would also like to thank the staff of the American Center of Oriental Research (ACOR), the British Institute for Archaeology and History, and the German Protestant Institute of Archaeology.

Six close friends in particular deserve mention for reading this work, pushing me to clarify some of my arguments, challenging others, and all in all sharpening the prose. Their input forms a large part of this book. I am indebted to Markus Bouillon, Romi Kaplan, Efrat Lev, Mostafa Minawi, Gordon Peake, and Kevin Rosser for their time, care, and patience.

At Stanford University Press, I have enjoyed superb professional and friendly cooperation. Editor Kate Wahl was closely involved with the project from its inception. Her careful editing of my first drafts and her insistence that I could make this book more engaging, so that it would appeal to a larger audience, drove me to rise to this challenge. Her contribution to this book has been immense. Mariana Raykov and Nora Spiegel made the sometimes strenuous process of production much more agreeable. I am grateful to them for their guidance and patience. William Nelson has carefully and creatively turned my sketches into full-fledged maps. Peter Dreyer has done a wonderful job in the copyediting of the manuscript, painstakingly cleaning up the text and making it flow better. I am truly grateful to him and to the rest of the editorial, production, marketing, and publicity staff.

I was also fortunate to enjoy the friendship, affection, and support of many friends. Some contributed directly to the book. Others have had to bear with me over the past year while I was trying to complete the writing, but nevertheless gave me much moral support: they include Ma'mun 'Abd al-Qadir, the 'Abud family from Buqay'a (Peki'in), Betty Anderson, Malena Baum, Meriam Belli, Kirsten Bilz, Yuval Binyamin, Constanze Bosecker, Franziska Brockdorff, Gidon Bromberg, Johann Buessow, Harel Chorev, Yuval Dagan, Assaf David, Yaron Deckel, Noga Efrati, Alex Elsohn, Michael Fischbach, Dima Gladkov, Mottie Golani, Jan Goldberg, Orna Harari, Ra'id Ibrahim, Clive Jones, Michael Jungreis, Munira Khayyat and Heiko Wimmen, Jimena and Saskia Klemp, Sagi Krispin, Michaela and Joerg Kropp, Stefanie Kubosch, Mohammad al-Kurdi, Yossi Kurzberg, Susanne Lang, Doron Lefler, Peter Malnak, Shai Nechemia, Lea-Friederike Neubert, Dana Rabfogel and family, Gerlinde Regenhardt, Ofek Riemer, Achim Rohde, Mohammad Sharqawi, 'Adnan al-Shibli, Batia Siegel, Ravit Tamarkin, Idit Toledano, Guy Tourlamain, Sophie Wagenhofer, Joerg Walch, the Winnacker-Spitzl family in Wuppertal and Cologne, and Eyal Zisser.

Most of the writing was done in three cafés. I am grateful to the staff of the Café Liselotte in Tel Aviv and Café Oliver in Kfar Vradim for making my hard work enjoyable. In particular, I thank the wonderful ladies of Café F. (the Frauen Café, or women's café) in Pulheim, Germany, for welcoming and taking good care of me.

Finally, I want to acknowledge my gratitude and love for my family. My mother, Liora Alon, has born the responsibilities of the family on her own for many years since the premature death of my father. Her vitality, resilience, wit, and generosity are an important source of support to me, and I dedicate this book to her. I am also fortunate enough to enjoy the support and love of my brother Uri and my sister Hilla and their respective families. Now that the book has been completed, they won't have to compete for my attention with Shaykh Mithqal any more.

THE SHAYKH OF SHAYKHS

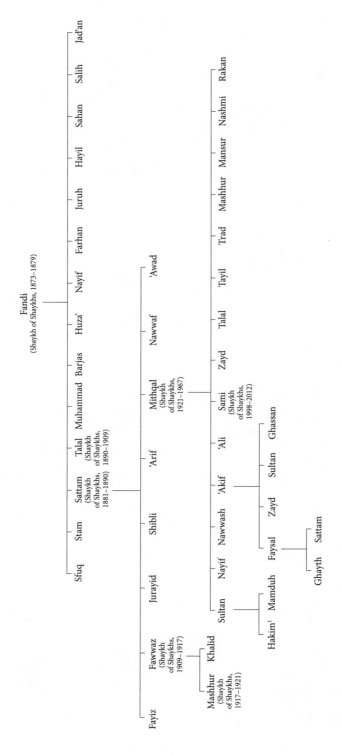

Fandi
(Shaykh of Shaykhs, 1873–1879)

Fayiz | Sfuq | Stam | Sattam (Shaykh of Shaykhs, 1881–1890) | Talal (Shaykh of Shaykhs, 1890–1909) | Muhammad | Barjas | Huza' | Nayif | Farhan | Juruh | Hayil | Sahan | Salih | Jad'an

Fawwaz (Shaykh of Shaykhs, 1909–1917) | Jurayid | Shibli | 'Arif | Mithqal (Shaykh of Shaykhs, 1921–1967) | Nawwaf | 'Awad

Mashhur (Shaykh of Shaykhs, 1917–1921) | Khalid

Sultan | Nayif | Nawwash | 'Akif | 'Ali | Sami (Shaykh of Shaykhs, 1998–2012) | Zayd | Talal | Tayil | Trad | Mashhur | Mansur | Nashmi | Rakan

Hakim[1] | Mamduh | Faysal | Zayd | Sultan | Ghassan

Ghayth | Sattam

[1] Father of MP Hind al-Fayiz.

Mithqal al-Fayiz's patrilineal family tree

INTRODUCTION

IN THE FALL OF 2012, King Abdullah II of Jordan faced his most difficult challenge since the outbreak of the Arab Spring. Over the course of the previous two years, the leaders of Egypt, Tunisia, Yemen, and Libya had been toppled, and Syria had sunk into a bloody civil war. By contrast, the small Hashemite Kingdom of Jordan had, so far, successfully coped with the limited unrest that had spread around the country. Now, however, the Jordanian monarch appeared to be more vulnerable than ever.

Demonstrators across the country, frustrated with continuing economic difficulties and the slow pace of the political and economic reforms, stepped up their protests. The slogan "Down with the Regime!" was heard more and more, and, for the first time, King Abdullah was mentioned by name. Several veteran political leaders, including one former prime minister, criticized the regime sharply and explicitly. In Amman, the main opposition party, the Muslim Brotherhood, announced what promised to be the largest rally to date, scheduled for October 5, 2012.

Under increasing pressure, King Abdullah had to react quickly. One day before the rally, he dissolved parliament ahead of new elections. The demonstration turned out some tens of thousands of participants (estimates ranged from 10,000 to 50,000 demonstrators) but was a far cry from the expectations of a massive protest of the likes of those in Cairo's Tahrir Square.[1]

Still King Abdullah continued to assert his leadership. A few days after the demonstration, he sacked his government and appointed a new prime minister to head an interim cabinet. Then, in a vigorous, direct, and candid speech in front of thousands of loyal supporters invited to his palace, he for the first time acknowledged the people calling for his overthrow, claiming that they were only a small group. The king stressed that, for him, the seat of power was not a personal privilege but a sacred duty and responsibility, one that he had inherited as a proud member of the Hashemite family and as a descendent of the Prophet Muhammad. He urged those seeking reform to do so within the framework of a new parliament and emphasized the importance of wide participation in the elections. The speech, together with the change of government and call for new elections, had a calming effect, at least temporarily.[2]

Soon, however, the pendulum swung back in favor of the regime's rivals. Faced with near-bankruptcy and mounting pressure from the International Monetary Fund to lift subsidies, the interim government raised the prices of gas and petrol on November 13 by 30–50 percent, which immediately sent tens of thousands of angry citizens across the country back into the streets. For three days, demonstrators clashed with police, blocked major roads, set fire to government offices and police stations, and vandalized and looted public property, banks, and private businesses. For the first time, photographs of King Abdullah were burned in large numbers, and daring, insolent calls for his removal, and with him, the entire regime, were heard widely. According to several reports, the volume of public resentment and the ensuing anarchy took the regime by surprise and paralyzed it completely for several days. The episode, soon known as the "November insurrection," was the worst crisis in Jordan since 1989, when widespread "bread" riots had prompted Abdullah's father, the late King Hussein, to launch a political and economic liberalization process.[3]

One of the first members of the political establishment to take the initiative in response to the challenge was the former prime minister Faysal al-Fayiz. Al-Fayiz was also the leader of the Bani Sakhr tribal confederacy, the third-largest tribal group in Jordan, numbering over 150,000.[4] A couple of days after the riots ended, he rallied his men behind the king and regime and denounced the demonstrators' violence. In a well-crafted show of power and loyalty, Faysal addressed hundreds of men in the large and elegant assembly hall of the Bani Sakhr. Faysal's uncle Sami, the ceremonial shaykh of shaykhs, or paramount shaykh, of the Bani Sakhr, sat beside the podium, clad in a long robe and traditional headgear; his presence on the stage alongside his nephew added gravitas to the event. The first row in the hall was reserved for shaykhs, clearly recognizable as tribal dignitaries by their distinctive dress. Faysal himself wore a suit and tie.

Faysal al-Fayiz's response to the rioters and to the king's critics was stern and unequivocal. He threatened that the Bani Sakhr would "cut off the hand" of those seeking to undermine the homeland and its leadership, stressing that any harm to his majesty was a red line that should not be crossed. Enthusiastic applause repeatedly interrupted Faysal's speech. The tribesmen voiced their anger at the rioters and chanted slogans in support of the king. In rallying his fellow tribesmen in this manner, reinforcing their support for the Hashemite monarchy, Faysal maintained a long-standing policy of absolute loyalty to the king, pledging on behalf of the Bani Sakhr to defend him. And Faysal and the Bani Sakhr have continued to do so in the years since.[5]

The unrest of November 2012 gradually abated. The regime made mass arrests (with a majority of those detained released quickly), but also made a number of conciliatory gestures to demonstrate its responsiveness to the "street's calls." Soon Jordanians were preoccupied with the electoral campaign. The newly elected parliamentarians, empowered by their constituencies' expectations for change, posed a greater challenge to the regime than their predecessors. They were careful to inspect the performance of ministers and scrutinize draft laws, and frequently threatened the government with votes of no confidence. But until well into 2015, the government proved successful in maintaining both the support of a majority in the house and the confidence of the palace. Prime Minister Abdullah Nsur has already exceeded three years in the office, an exceptionally long period in comparison to all but one of the previous prime ministers appointed by Abdullah since he assumed the throne in 1999. All in all, the regime has managed to quell the protest movement, at least for the time being. Occasional demonstrations continued to be staged in both the capital and the provinces for a while, but they have all but died out since.

The role played by Faysal al-Fayiz and the other tribal leaders in the kingdom in mobilizing the tribes was and remains crucial for the stability of the Hashemite monarchy. The tribal leaders enjoy much influence and respect among their tribespeople and for the most part are united in support of the monarchy. Their success in restraining their men and isolating opposition elements among them goes a long way to explaining the relatively mild manner in which Jordan experienced the wave of regional upheaval and change in the years after the so-called Arab Spring erupted in 2011. In fact, the support Faysal and the Bani Sakhr lent to the Hashemite regime stems back all the way to the early days of the creation of Jordan in 1921, and has characterized its political system ever since then. In those founding years, powerful tribes, and in particular their shaykhly families, tied their political and material fortunes to that of the Hashemites. In return for the support of the king, these tribal families enjoyed special status and received, and continue to receive, many privileges. The long-standing alliances between these tribal elites and their tribespeople, on the one hand, and the royal family, on the other, to a large extent explain the remarkable resilience of Hashemite rule in Jordan and the country's relative stability.

Faysal al-Fayiz represents the third generation of Bani Sakhr leaders to play an important role in the development of the Jordanian state and to be close allies of three generations of Hashemite kings. He inherited the status of senior representative of the Bani Sakhr tribes in the Jordanian political class from his father, 'Akif al-Fayiz, a senior politician from the 1950s until his death in 1998 and a close ally of King Hussein. 'Akif, in turn, had led the Bani Sakhr tribes since the death of his father, Mithqal al-Fayiz. Mithqal had served as the paramount shaykh of the confederacy—the shaykh of shaykhs (*shaykh al-mashayikh*) in the literal translation from the Arabic—from 1921 until his death in 1967. Over the course of his life, Mithqal was a close ally of Emir (later King) Abdullah bin Hussein, played a critical role in the events that led to the establishment of the Emirate of Transjordan, and was one of the most prominent and influential individuals in the country. Shaykh Mithqal al-Fayiz's long, eventful and fascinating life is the subject of this book.[6]

WRITING THE BIOGRAPHY OF MITHQAL AL-FAYIZ

Arab tribal shaykhs have played a central role in the Middle East for centuries. Until well into the last quarter of the twentieth century, the majority of the population in the region lived in rural areas, adhered to tribal identity and organization, and recognized the leadership of such men. The position of shaykh was a highly prized office that carried influence and power. Even the mass migration to the cities that has changed the rural-urban balance over the past few decades and the advent of modern life could not erode tribalism, which remains a key marker of identity in many Arab societies, rural and urban alike. Moreover, recent developments—notably in Jordan and the Arabian Peninsula—have shown that, far from having disappeared, tribal shaykhs remain an important and influential political elite. In Iraq and Syria, shaykhs who were side-lined for several decades have regained their power in recent years. In many countries, such as Iraq, Syria, Libya, Yemen, and even Egypt, shaykhs are now sought-after power brokers and often hold the key to stability.[7]

The life of Shaykh Mithqal al-Fayiz presents a remarkable opportunity to portray a clear and vivid picture of a tribal shaykh in modern times. For sixty years, Shaykh Mithqal (pronounced Mithgal) played a central role in imperial, regional, national and tribal politics. His long life—he was almost ninety when he died—spanned a crucial and fascinating period of Middle Eastern history: the rapid modernization of the Ottoman Empire from the middle of the nineteenth century onward, World War I and the collapse of the empire, the emergence of a new state system under colonial rule, the decolonization process in the aftermath of World War II, the establishment of the state of Israel and the Arab-Israeli conflict that ensued, as well as the rise of pan-Arabism under Gamal 'Abd al-Nasser's leadership. Mithqal al-Fayiz's life and work as a shaykh thus allow us to trace both a remarkable individual life story and the evolution of a central social, political and cultural office in an era of major social and political change.

Mithqal was born into the leading family of the Bani Sakhr. His grandfather and father led their people during the last decades of the nineteenth century and succeeded in striking an alliance with the Ottoman state, thus ensuring the prosperity and extensive autonomy of their tribes. Mithqal himself began his public career as a gifted leader of raids. He quickly rose to prominence and during World War I was the main ally of the Ottoman Empire in the Transjordanian theater of war. Astutely adapting to the new political realities after the war, he became a supporter of the Hashemites, playing a significant role in the creation and development of modern Jordan. His fierce opposition to early attempts to extend British rule east of the Jordan River paved the way for Abdullah bin Hussein to establish the Emirate of Transjordan. The alliance between the Bani Sakhr under Mithqal and Emir Abdullah contributed significantly to the process of state-formation in Jordan and made Mithqal, now the shaykh of shaykhs of the Bani Sakhr, one of the richest and most influential men in the county.

At the same time, faced with the attempts of the British-controlled government to centralize power, as well as severe economic crisis that weakened nomads such as the Bani Sakhr, Mithqal keenly sought to preserve his privileged position and the autonomy of his tribes. Looking for new allies and sources of income, Mithqal successfully cultivated contacts with the national, business and tribal elites in Transjordan, Palestine, Syria, Iraq, Saudi Arabia, and Egypt. Particularly fascinating—as well as controversial—were his open contacts with leaders of the Zionist movement and his offer to sell part of his land for the purpose of Jewish settlement east of the Jordan River.

But the success of Mithqal's endeavor to remain powerful and influential against the backdrop of the momentous changes around him also necessitated the evolution of his role into something new. From a military and political leader of an independent, autonomous community, he became part and parcel of the regime, acting as a go-between the central government and his followers. This shift was facilitated by state policies that sought to preserve the special role of tribal leaders in Jordanian society and exploit it for the good of the regime. As a result, Mithqal managed to institutionalize his position, serving as the leader of the Bani Sakhr until his death in 1967.

Mithqal's success owed much to his remarkable political skills, shrewdness, and energy. He was quick to understand changing circumstances and to recognize new opportunities. One can identify several constants in his strategy throughout the course of his long career—he was always walking a tightrope, taking calculated risks, while testing the limits of his actions and of his ability to exert pressure on the government or to profit financially. He sought a balance between cooperation and defiance, always in the hope of preserving his autonomy, and maintained relations with several, often rival, patrons, playing one off against the other in order to increase his own leverage and space for maneuvering. This strategy enabled Mithqal to maintain his leadership and privileged position, both during the colonial era and afterwards, perhaps better than any other shaykh of his stature. He also left a lasting legacy as manifested in the continuing privileged status of his family in Jordan. In this respect, Mithqal fully met the burden of expectations placed on him in his naming: Mithqal in Arabic means weight or gravitas—and he was indeed a heavyweight!

1 BORN A SHAYKH

IN THE ARABIAN DESERT a huge black goat-hair tent is surrounded by several dozen smaller tents. A herd of camels is grazing nearby, interrupting the silence with their grunting. The smells of the campfire, tobacco, and roasted coffee blend with the heavy stench of the animals. It is a miniscule island of human presence in the vast, empty desert. In this idyllic scene, the cry of a baby is heard from the big tent. It is a boy. A shaykh.

Mithqal Sattam al-Fayiz was born into the family of the leading shaykhs of the Bani Sakhr tribal confederacy around the year 1880. For two generations, his immediate family had led the confederacy, one of the largest and strongest nomadic tribal groups in the Syrian Desert. As such, his childhood was spent in preparation for the title and job of a shaykh, the tribal leader. An Arab shaykh had to demonstrate the virtues of wisdom, charisma, generosity, and courage, find victory in battle, and develop an intimate knowledge of the desert. He would hone his negotiating skills to represent the tribe vis-à-vis other tribes and government officials and would need to secure economic resources for himself and his people. At the conclusion of this long training and learning process, this boy would still be expected to compete with his brothers, cousins and nephews for the leadership of the Bani Sakhr people. It was an extremely sought after position and entailed respect, power, and wealth. It was worth killing one's own brother and even dying for.

Mithqal's childhood years occurred during a time of a great change in the desert. A decade prior to his birth, the Ottoman Empire had begun incorporating the southern regions of its Syrian province, east of the Jordan River, into its central rule. The tribes, long accustomed to their local rule and autonomy, suddenly had to adjust to sharing power with the Ottoman government. The success of Mithqal's grandfather and father in adapting to this new political reality was crucial. Their legacy paved the way for Mithqal's own greatness at a time of great geopolitical transformations. It also shaped the future leader's worldview, one that would guide him through his entire life.

THE BANI SAKHR IN THE SYRIAN STEPPE

Mithqal's family rose to prominence in the middle of the nineteenth century, during the time of his grandfather, Shaykh Fandi al-Fayiz. Fandi was born around the beginning of the century, and from at least the 1850s on led the Fayiz tribe. He gradually became the leader of the entire Bani Sakhr tribal confederacy, founding a dynasty that led it during the reminder of the Ottoman period, through the British mandate era, and into modern Jordan, till today, in fact.

During Fandi's time, the Bani Sakhr were fully nomadic, living off camel husbandry. Their cycle of life revolved around their herds. They spent the summer months in the fertile eastern parts of the Balqa' and 'Ajlun regions in present-day Jordan, as well as the southern Hawran in Syria. In winter they would dismantle their black tents and migrate hundreds of kilometers to their grazing grounds further east and south, in the Wadi Sirhan, in today's Saudi Arabia. The rich pasture and mild temperature presented ideal conditions for their camels to give birth and increased survival rates for the calves (see maps 1 and 2). Like other Arab camel herders, they laid claim to a pure, noble descent and felt superior to nomads who herded sheep and goats, to villagers, and to city folk.[1]

The Bani Sakhr constituted a tribal confederacy, the most common form of political organization in the desert. As such, it was a coalition of several smaller political entities, or tribes; Mithqal and his family belonged to the Fayiz tribe, for example. The tribe was the basic unit, offering protection to its members, who were also relatives. Tribes combined into a confederacy as a result of political alliances and unions. And while many local tribespeople believe that the tribal confederacy shares a common descent, it is more plausible that a myth of shared blood ties was created as a tool to cement the alliance and justify it ideologically. This ideology aside, the confederacy was a loose, fluid entity, each of whose constituent parts was autonomous and offered the confederacy only conditional support. Tribes or families could leave, and others could be invited to join. It was rare that the alliance acted as one body. A full union was

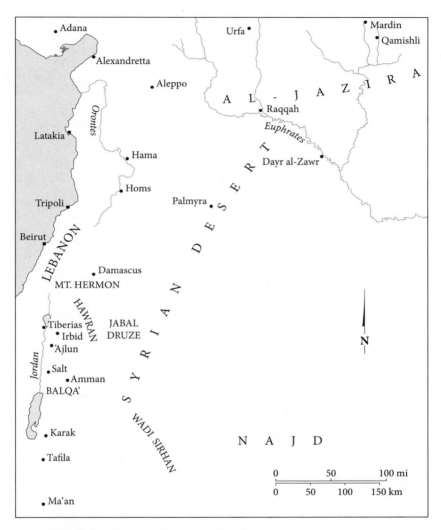

MAP 1. The Syrian Desert in the nineteenth century

achieved only on the occasions when the entire confederacy was attacked. At all other times, it was an organization that collectively controlled a territory. All members had free and safe passage within the tribal domain, or *dira*, and enjoyed the right to graze their herds and drink water from the wells.[2] A tribal confederacy also deterred aggression; enemies and rivals were fully aware of the size of the force it could mobilize.

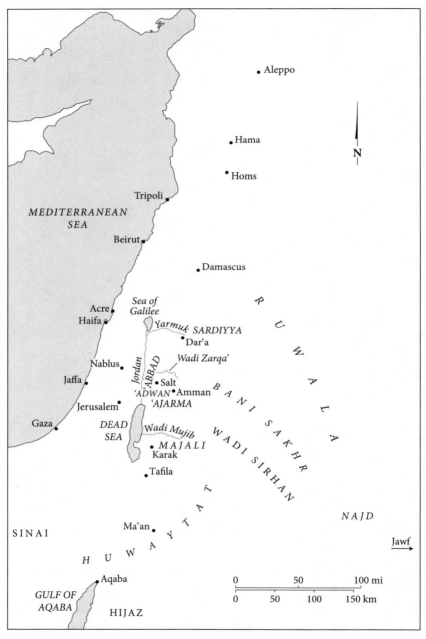

MAP 2. Tribes and migration routes

By the time Fandi became their shaykh, the Bani Sakhr were already the dominant power east of the Jordan and vast parts of the land were known to be their *dira*. Territorial hegemony had been acquired over the course of several centuries. Thought to be originally from the Hijaz, they gradually moved northwards and established their domain east of the Jordan River (see map 2).[3] The earliest written record of their presence in the region goes back to the early fifteenth century, when a classical work in Arabic noted that they were living in the Karak area, the plateau descending from the Dead Sea. Ottoman registers from the end of the sixteenth century record their presence in the northern part of what would become Jordan.[4] Over the course of the following centuries, they had to fight for their place and fame among the other tribal groups in the area. In a series of wars and quickly changing alliances, memory of which now only survives in oral histories and poetry, they managed to push the ʿAdwan and ʿAbbad tribes towards the Jordan Valley and took over the flat and fertile land in the eastern Balqaʾ region.[5] While raiding, the Bani Sakhr warriors might go further afield, west of the Jordan River all the way to Gaza or into the western desert of present-day Iraq.[6]

So by the time of Fandi's leadership, the Bani Sakhr experienced a period of nearly unprecedented strength and prosperity as a rich, powerful tribal group with thousands of members.[7] The confederacy's fighting force was formidable. One estimate refers to 6,000 fighting men. Another, probably exaggerated, puts the number at more than 4,000 men mounted on camels and horses, with a reserve force of another 4,000.[8] Since the confederacy hardly ever acted as one, these figures were only theoretical. Still, this was a considerable force in northern Arabia and enjoyed a reputation for ferocity. Visiting in 1863–64, the British clergyman and ornithologist Henry Baker Tristram wrote of the Bani Sakhr: "They have for centuries been a very strong tribe, but from some unexplained cause have increased in the last fifty years to an unexampled pitch of prosperity and wealth, both in population and cattle."[9] He evoked biblical images to illustrate their strength: "When, in 1863, they encamped in the Ghor [the Jordan Valley], just before their raid on the plain of Esdraelon, their tents, like the Midianites', covered the ground for miles, far as the eye could reach from the Mount of Beisan, and in a week there was not a green blade to be seen, where before the arrival of these locusts one stood knee-deep in the rank herbage."[10]

The Bani Sakhr domination in the region was accelerated by the withdrawal of the Ottoman presence east of the Jordan River around the beginning of the seventeenth century. For several centuries the nomadic tribes that occupied most of the Syrian Desert and its fringes were left more or less to their own devices, except when involved in the Hajj, the annual pilgrimage to the holy cities of Mecca and Medina, or the occasions on which they were contracted by the Ottomans to provide military service. Ottoman troops and officials were rarely seen in the area outside the time of the Hajj and the annual visit of the tax collectors to the permanent settlements. In the absence of central authority, the big nomadic confederacies were free to engage in intertribal wars or conduct raids. On the fringe of the desert, they extracted protection money (*khawa*), paid in the form of cash or a share in crops and other goods, from the few agricultural communities and the small and weak nomadic or semi-nomadic tribes. At the beginning of the nineteenth century Salt, the largest settlement east of the Jordan River, with several thousand inhabitants, an important marketplace for the local tribesmen, paid the Bani Sakhr *khawa*, thus acknowledging their hegemony in the region. Even after Salt stopped paying, other localities and tribes continued to do so.[11]

Likewise, the few Europeans who ventured to cross the Jordan River paid for the right to enter the tribal territory and for guidance and protection. For example, in 1818 two British Royal Navy officers visited the area east of the Jordan River and stumbled on a camp of a shaykh from the Fayiz tribe of the Bani Sakhr. When they introduced an Ottoman *firman*, or sultanic decree, assuring them safe passage, the shaykh dismissed it as useless: "The Firman was mentioned; he said he cared nothing for Firmans; that he considered them only fit for those who were weak enough to obey them; that *he* was Grand Seignior [a title applied to the sultan], and everything else here; and that we must pay."[12]

The Ottoman authorities contributed to the well-being of the Bani Sakhr in another important way. From at least 1674/75 on, the Ottoman governor in Damascus granted the confederacy's members their most important source of income, namely, the privilege of escorting and providing for the annual Hajj caravan. The tribesmen supplied camels and camel riders, food and water. They also took payment from the Ottoman authorities in return for protection and, more accurately, permission for the caravan to cross their domain safely.[13] The Hajj business not only enriched the Bani Sakhr but increased their fighting power. In the course of the nineteenth century, Arabs' spears, swords, and lances gave way to firearms, and tribesmen were able to buy rifles and ammunition with the cash it generated.[14]

Relations with the Ottoman authorities in Syria also strengthened the leadership of the Bani Sakhr. The extensive autonomy of the confederacy's constituent elements made the position of the head of the confederacy precarious: it was usually only a nominal one and was easily challenged. Only in times of war would all tribesmen recognize the leadership of the head of the confederacy. At all other times, shaykhs had great difficulty in enforcing their will. Since male egalitarianism was one of Arab tribal society's fundamental values, a shaykh at least theoretically enjoyed no more than the status of primus inter pares.[15] A shaykh had to use persuasion and reach consensus rather than seek to impose his will on his followers.[16] An additional problem for the shaykh was his inability to tax his fellow tribesmen. On the contrary, he was expected to deliver a continuous flow of goods and services to other members of the alliance. Thus, material resources available for the usage of tribal shaykhs always came from outside the tribal system, such as subjugated peasant communities, weaker tribes or the central government.[17] What is more, a shaykh constantly needed to rally the support of his followers against challenges from other able and ambitious men in his family and tribe lest he be deposed.[18] Shaykhs overcame these problems by seeking official recognition from the Ottoman authorities. The governor of Syria recognized either the shaykh he thought most influential or the one who seemed likely to be the most loyal and cooperative as the representative of the entire confederacy. This recognition, and the material gains that came with it, gave that shaykh and his immediate family an advantage over other shaykhs. It was a classic divide-and-rule policy, and without the ability to rule directly, it served as the main Ottoman strategy in the periphery.

Among the Bani Sakhr, the development of direct relations with the Ottoman authorities favored the Fayiz tribe. In 1742, the governor of Damascus contracted with Shaykh Qaʻdan al-Fayiz, the first recorded shaykh from that tribe, to escort the Hajj caravan. This privilege was probably an expression of gratitude for his military support earlier that year, when a tribal force under the leadership of Shaykh Qaʻdan had participated in the siege of Tiberias, the stronghold of Dahir al-ʻUmar, the local ruler of the Galilee, who had defied the sultan's orders.[19]

In spite of the cooperative relations that resulted, Ottoman recognition remained limited and sometimes the government failed to pay the Bani Sakhr for their services. In such cases, the tribesmen were quick to show their anger. In 1757 Qaʻdan and his men attacked with exceptional ruthlessness the *jarda*, the military escort that departed from Damascus to meet the returning pilgrims in order to supply them with fresh provisions. A few days later, the Bani Sakhr plundered the main caravan, leaving most of the helpless pilgrims to die of hunger and thirst. One victim was the sister of the sultan himself.[20] A contemporary Arab account portrays a vivid, if unsettling, account of the raid:

> When Musa Pasha, the commander of the *jarda*, arrived in Qatrana, he was attacked by the Arabs and robbed. They plundered the *jarda* and took everything in it. They went so far as to strip Musa of his clothes and take his seal [ring] from his finger. They took him down from his seat of honor [on the camel's back] and rode it instead of him. They took his drum, his flag, and his guns. Their leader was called Qa'dan al-Fayiz. The people in the *jarda* dispersed all over. Some returned to Damascus, some to the Hawran, others fled to Gaza, Jerusalem, or Ma'an . . . When the pasha was brought to Damascus, he was already dying. The next day he was buried.[21]

Mithqal's grandfather, Fandi, enjoyed more stable relations with the Ottoman authorities and in fact, these relations were critical for his leadership status among the Bani Sakhr. In the 1860s, the Ottoman governor in Syria recognized Fandi's seniority, contracting with him for the protection and provision of the Hajj caravan.[22] This recognition both reflected his emerging status among his tribes and bolstered his leadership, since it provided him with a great source of income and influence. Fandi valued his relations with the Ottomans and was careful to maintain them. He was known to be loyal to his patrons.[23]

Extensive tribal autonomy and political hegemony as enjoyed by the Bani Sakhr and the Fayiz tribe in the course of most of the seventeenth, eighteenth, and nineteenth centuries was not peculiar to Transjordan or even to Syria. The same was true with other peripheral regions of the Ottoman Empire, such as the Kurdish areas in eastern Anatolia, Iraq, the Arabian Peninsula, and most of North Africa. In all these areas, the empire's control was only nominal.[24]

UNDER THE NEW OTTOMAN ORDER

But the hegemony of the Bani Sakhr east of the Jordan did not last for long. In the late 1860s, the Ottoman government changed its attitude towards its desert periphery and decided to place it under its direct rule. Fandi and his successors had to deal with this new and unfamiliar challenge to their authority and the autonomy of their tribes.

The new Ottoman policy in the desert was one aspect of the reform movement known as the Tanzimat. In the framework of its attempts to modernize government and centralize the administration, Istanbul was determined to strengthen its control over the empire's frontier zones. Ottoman authorities singled out the nomadic tribes as the main obstacle to their exercising sovereignty in these areas. The government sought to limit the nomads' hegemony over the peasants, thereby extending cultivation, and with it the payment of taxes. Since the empire lost most of its European provinces in the course of the nineteenth century, the Arab lands grew in importance and were seen by Ottoman statesmen as their only source of new prosperity.[25]

Inconsistent measures in the 1840s and 1850s to increase Ottoman control in desert areas gave way to a more comprehensive move from the late 1860s on. In 1867, the governors of Damascus and Aleppo agreed to coordinate the administration of the desert, and a special military desert force was formed the following year. Also in 1868, the Ottomans created a new governorate of the desert.[26] These administrative reforms were also facilitated by new technology. In 1868 or 1869, the Ottoman army in Syria adopted the breach-loaded Snider rifle, which represented the state of the art at the time. Other modern models entered service in Syria in the course of the 1870s. These gave the Ottomans an initial advantage over the nomads and allowed them to begin disciplining tribes.[27]

Unfortunately for the Bani Sakhr, the application of the new Ottoman strategy east of the Jordan River proved to be a success.[28] In 1867, Mehmet Rashid Pasha, the vigorous governor of Damascus, led a large military force to 'Ajlun and the Balqa' areas. The force entered Salt without facing resistance and Rashid started to organize his rule. He cultivated close relations with local shaykhs[29] and established a permanent military garrison. The next move was to confront the powerful tribes in the area. The Ottoman force enjoyed technological superiority over the tribesmen and easily defeated an alliance of local tribes headed by Dhiyab al-Hamud, shaykh of the 'Adwan. This expedition was an unprecedented act of Ottoman penetration into the areas east of the Jordan.

Following the success of the military campaign, Rashid Pasha developed a modern administrative framework. He created two new administrative districts, one in 'Ajlun, the other in Salt. With a permanent garrison, government house, tax-collection apparatus, and, later, court and prison, the Ottomans were gradually able to consolidate their power. They established military posts and built roads, which soldiers patrolled. They encouraged the expansion of agricultural land and the arrival of new immigrants, such as merchants from Damascus and Nablus.[30] Gradually, the government checked the independence and influence of the tribes in the area.

At first, Fandi took a bystander position; he in fact enjoyed the situation. He continued to maintain good relations with the Ottoman authorities, and the governor recognized him as the representative of the region's tribes. This recognition also reflected the changing inter-tribal balance of power in the Balqa' region in favor of the Bani Sakhr after the 'Adwan, sometimes their rivals, sometimes allies, were weakened. Large parts of the latter's territory fell within the newly established direct rule of the Ottomans, whereas much of the Bani Sakhr land was still beyond the reach of the government. On top of it, Shaykh Dhiyab was imprisoned. Fandi emerged as the principal strongman of the Balqa'.[31] But when the son of Shaykh Dhiyab fled to his camp, Fandi offered him hospitality and refused to hand him over to the authorities. Doing that would have been a clear breach of the tribal custom of offering protection to fugitives.[32]

In 1869, Fandi changed his strategy and confronted the Ottomans. Under his leadership, the Bani Sakhr and 'Adwan raided a town while the governor was touring nearby. This was a clear act of defiance, provoking the governor to respond with overwhelming force. Several thousand soldiers intercepted the Bani Sakhr in a deep gorge. With no escape, the tribesmen had to give up and pay the cost of the expedition. Shaykh Fandi handed over one of his sons as a hostage, a guarantee for the payment of the fine. Another grave consequence was the loss of the right to escort the Hajj caravans.[33] Fandi's reason for rebelling might have been his realization that the Ottomans were serious in their attempts to take direct control of the steppe, and that they might threaten his position. Perhaps he found himself under pressure from his people to resist the new regime the Ottomans were creating and was prompt to act in order to keep his leadership.

But Fandi was quick to understand the new power relations between the government and his tribes and the need to adapt to this change and find a new modus vivendi with the Ottomans; he even learned how to use Ottoman rule to his advantage. In 1872, after three years of great losses, Fandi persuaded the new governor of Damascus to restore the privilege of escorting the Hajj caravans to him. The governor also recognized his leadership over the entire Bani Sakhr confederacy by conferring on him the title of *shaykh al-mashayikh*, shaykh of shaykhs, or paramount shaykh.[34] Fandi's and his family's position within the confederacy was now greatly enhanced.

Even with Ottoman support, Fandi's leadership among the Bani Sakhr did not go unchallenged.[35] In 1878, Fandi could not offer escort to a British party because he was reported to be "on bad terms" with a tribe from the Bani Sakhr that roamed the road that the travelers wanted to take.[36] A government document from the mid or late 1870s shows that the confederacy remained a loose alliance of tribes and that Ottoman recognition had its limits: "There are hostilities and conflicts among the tribes of the Bani Sakhr, and even today there are bloody battles and wars among them. Each tribe has its own shaykh, and the shaykh who is recognized by the Ottoman state is Sattam bin Fandi al-Fayiz. He rules over everybody when a war occurs between [his] tribes and foreign tribes."[37]

Fandi died in 1879 and his death resulted in a long, fierce competition among his sons for the leadership. Several years before his death, the aging shaykh had delegated some of his authority to his son Sattam, Mithqal's father, and by the late 1870s he was the de facto leader of the Bani Sakhr. But upon Fandi's death, two of his older sons challenged their younger brother. An all-out war between the siblings and their respective supporters ensued, involving others from the region's tribes. In a decisive battle in 1881, one of the brothers was killed and Sattam emerged as the victor.[38] There was nothing peculiar about these strained brotherly relations. Although solidarity with and loyalty to all kinsfolk constitute cherished values in tribal societies, competition, rivalry, and even hatred among brothers were common. This was especially true in shaykhly families, where competition between brothers was tolerated, if not even encouraged. The fact that an incumbent shaykh did not normally name his successor made this rivalry worse, since it meant that it was open to the shaykh's adult sons, his brothers, and his nephews.

It took several more months before Fandi's surviving sons reconciled their differences and Sattam's leadership was secured, not least thanks to government support. In 1881, the Ottoman governor recognized him, like his father before him, as the shaykh of shaykhs of the Bani Sakhr. It might very well be that Ottoman recognition contributed to the outcome of the power struggle among the brothers.[39] This incident was the last time the succession was contested with the use of arms. Thereafter, it was resolved peacefully with the strong intervention of the Ottoman governor (and later the Hashemite kings).

Traveling east of the Jordan for the second time nearly a decade before Sattam became leader, the British clergyman-scientist Henry Tristram hired the shaykh as his guide and was impressed by him. His descriptions of Sattam help explain why the latter became the leader of the Bani Sakhr rather than any of the other candidates. Tristram praises Sattam's intelligence, loyalty, trustworthiness, and good manners, describing him as a gentleman careful not to infringe on the foreigners' privacy. Once Sattam was in his own tent and surrounded by his own people, Tristram observes, "nothing could exceed the dignity and stateliness of the young sheik."[40] He emphasized Sattam's quiet confidence among his kin and allies.[41] Sattam was also an experienced guide and knew the country well. In 1868, he drew the attention of an Anglican missionary to the Mesha Stele (aka the Moabite Stone) and took him to see it, thus bringing about one of biblical archaeology's most important discoveries. The stele, dating from around 840 BCE, is now on display at the Louvre Museum (with a replica in the newly established Jordan Museum in Amman).[42]

The encounter between Tristram and Sattam also revealed much about the shaykh's outlook. Tristram was surprised to see a Bani Sakhr encampment near the Dead Sea, well outside their own territory, and asked Sattam to explain it. The shaykh replied "with manifest pride: 'True, the land is not ours, but our people are many, and who shall dare to prevent them from going where they please? You will find them everywhere, if the land is good for them.'" Tristram commented that this was one of the many advantages of belonging to the strongest "where might is right."[43] This modus operandi guided Sattam and was typical of the Bani Sakhr and other powerful shaykhs.

This depiction of Sattam remarkably resonates with several European descriptions of other shaykhs of the Fayiz as well as shaykhs of other tribes in the region. The collective portrait that emerges highlights characteristics such as wisdom, charisma, interpersonal skills, good manners, generous hospitality, intimate knowledge of the country, path-finding competence, and bravery.[44] Alongside these admirable qualities, foreign travelers often complained about what they saw as the shaykhs' greed, remarking on the extortionate sums of money demanded by shaykhs for offering guidance and protection.[45]

Even if slightly exaggerated, these descriptions give a fairly accurate picture of the shaykhs' characteristics. True, not all authors acquired a thorough understanding of Arab tribal culture. They also tended to portray a somewhat romantic view of Arab nomadic society.[46] Still, without these characteristics—both the ones that earned them the approval of Western observers and those condemned by them—shaykhs could not possibly have been chosen for or held on to their position of leadership. The shaykhs' difficulty in imposing their will on the tribe and the confederacy, the fact that their position was not institutionalized before modern times and was permanently insecure, and the constant fluidity of tribal alliances all called for very capable leaders. Only those who could effectively lead their confederacy, or at least gave the appearance of unified tribal power, attracted the attention of the Ottoman authorities, needed to ensure recognition of their leadership and the material profit that accompanied it. Sattam was extremely successful in both respects.

Sattam cultivated stronger relations with the Ottoman government, and during his term in office, his family became an integral part of the Ottoman administration east of the Jordan. Even before becoming the official shaykh of shaykhs, Sattam enjoyed close relations with the government. During the years 1874–77, he received large sums of money in return for imposing law and order in his sphere of influence. His role was soon formalized, and in 1879 Sattam was mentioned in Ottoman documents as head of the newly established subdistrict of Jiza, southeast of Amman. A family member held this post for the remainder of the Ottoman era, aside from the years 1885–91.[47] Sattam performed his official job dutifully. When a British party conducted an archaeological survey in the Balqa' in 1881 without Ottoman permission, Sattam reported them to the Ottoman governor, who stopped the survey.[48]

Sattam further strengthened his leadership position by initiating a pioneering strategy; he was the first ever shaykh of the Bani Sakhr to cultivate land and then register it with the government as private property. He did so while his father was still alive. Although many tribes in the Balqa' had been cultivating the land for decades, the Bani Sakhr refrained from doing so, expressing contempt for anyone who tilled the land. Sattam had to challenge such deep-rooted, old-fashioned attitudes. According to Mithqal, his father had started to cultivate land without his grandfather's knowledge. Sattam yoked himself to the plow and tilled the land himself—something unheard of for a Bani Sakhr, let alone a shaykh. "You might have big beards but not much brain," he shouted when his brothers ridiculed him.[49]

Sattam was successful in his farming venture, and when Fandi saw how profitable it was, he drove his son off the land and took it over. It is said that Sattam's wife 'Aliya advised her husband to ask his brother-in-law, Shaykh 'Ali Dhiyab al-'Adwan, then already the shaykh of the 'Adwan, for a substitute tract of land. 'Ali agreed and gave Sattam 170,000 dunam of land (just over 40,000 acres).[50] Sattam went on to cultivate land in Umm al-'Amad and other locales south and southeast of Amman, using slaves and employing peasants from Egypt or Gaza. Back then, though, the tribesmen of the Bani Sakhr, like many other nomads in Syria, still refused to work the land themselves.[51] This former 'Adwani land has remained the basis of the Fayiz shaykhs' wealth ever since.

Sattam's pioneering engagement with cultivation was probably motivated by the Ottoman push to increase cultivation of the fallow land on the empire's periphery. This was one of the main goals of the architects of the Tanzimat, who wanted to invigorate the Ottoman economy by promoting cash crops for export and increasing tax revenue. The legal framework was provided by an 1858 law that decreed land to be a commodity and landownership a universal individual right, rather than a special privilege granted by the sultan, as it had been before. Henceforth, Ottoman subjects were permitted to register their land and receive title deeds from land registry offices, which were established in the Ottoman administrative centers.[52] Registration also meant increased Ottoman control as well as the extraction of taxes. The Ottoman authorities also hoped that landownership and cultivation among nomads would lead to their permanent settlement, which would allow for increased government control. They tried to persuade tribal shaykhs in Syria and Transjordan to pursue agriculture by encouraging them to register and cultivate land that was already known to be part of their tribal *dira*, in some cases even granting them considerable additional tracts of land.[53] In both cases, the nomads had to pay taxes.

Cultivation gained momentum in the 1880s as the Ottomans settled new communities in Transjordan. During the years 1878–1906, refugees from the Caucasus fled their homeland following the wars between the Ottoman Empire and Russia. Some of them formed new settlements, most notably Amman, which was founded in 1878 as a Circassian village on the ruins of the ancient Roman city of Philadelphia. Simultaneously, the Ottomans encouraged the settlement of local Arab communities. In the ruins of Madaba, well within the Bani Sakhr territory, the government settled several Christian tribes who had been forced to leave Karak after a blood feud. When Sattam tried to challenge the Ottoman authorities' decision, he was told that uncultivated and unregistered land was the property of the sultan. Madaba was lost but Sattam rushed to register the rest of his land. By 1883, nine Bani Sakhr villages were registered and their owners paid taxes to the Ottoman government. In the 1890s, there were already twenty-five villages in the subdistrict of Jiza.[54]

Gradually, the cultivation of the land became an important source of income, not only for the shaykhs of the Bani Sakhr, but across greater Syria and Iraq. With the expansion of cultivated land and the protection the government offered to the agriculturist communities, the nomadic tribes' old sources of income became increasingly restricted. *Khawa* was abolished and the grazing fields in the fertile areas were absorbed into agricultural land. Under these circumstances, land became an important resource in its own right.[55]

The newly acquired wealth and influence that resulted from his farms and close relations with the government increased the power of Sattam and his immediate family and that of the Bani Sakhr at large. He distributed some of his land among the various shaykhs of the Bani Sakhr, in return for recognition of his leadership. He also purchased more and better arms and thus maintained a strong, perhaps superior, military position. From the late 1870s, an arms race ensued between the tribes in Syria and the Ottoman army, as well as among the tribes themselves, as the modern rifles introduced by the Ottomans spread across the deserts. This made the correlation between wealth and military power more pertinent than it had been before.[56]

New financial resources also helped Sattam in performing another of his important roles, that of giving hospitality. Shaykhs and their men would sit in the tent for hours on end, sometimes engaged in lively conversation but often in complete silence. While women and children tended to the herds and domestic chores, the men had ample free time. Although they were always on the alert to defend the tribe against enemies, they could do so while sipping coffee and smoking water pipes in the shaykh's tent.[57] What was described by European visitors as "idleness" and "masterly inactivity,"[58] was in fact crucial for the well-being of the nomadic tribe. These gatherings cemented relationships and promoted solidarity and cohesion among the tribal unit. They were also an important source of news and information, especially from passers-by and invited guests able to report on the movements of tribes and government troops, the general political situation, market prices, and where rain had fallen and pasture was to be found.[59]

With their new sources of wealth and the yield of their lands in the last third of the nineteenth century, Sattam and the Fayiz shaykhs impressed their guests with hospitality that was more lavish than ever, with overt displays of wealth. A shaykh's tent was much larger than the rest in the encampment, already reaching a length of eighty to a hundred feet at the beginning of the nineteenth century and probably earlier than that. But the interior was Spartan, even in the case of Fandi's tent.[60] Sattam's tent, however, projected luxury. Surprised at what he saw in his visit in 1872, Tristram wrote that the shaykh "conducted us to his open tent, where already carpets and cushions had been spread for us; and such carpets!—the richest Persian, quite new, into which we sunk as we sat down."[61] The food served in the tent was abundant, usually including meat, which was an expensive commodity in those days.[62]

For the shaykh, lavishing hospitality on guests was a means to assert his position and project his power among his immediate constituency. It was not only an important symbol of shaykhly legitimacy but also a means of advertising his might and enhancing his reputation as a great leader among other tribes, as well as Ottoman officials, foreign consuls and the occasional Western travelers. Hospitality was therefore a stage for the shaykh to display his virtue. More generous and luxurious hospitality meant more power and influence but wealth was needed to maintain it.[63]

As material gap between ordinary tribesmen and their shaykhs grew during the last decades of the nineteenth century, they undermined the notion of equality and unsettled the social fabric of society. Status symbols had already distinguished shaykhs from ordinary tribespeople. Apart from the size and interior of their tents, their dress was also somehow different. Like other tribesmen, shaykhs wore white or colored headscarves secured with black ropes and long-sleeved robes. Their costume was made of finer materials, such as Damascene silk, however, or was decorated with elaborate embroidery. Towards the end of the nineteenth century, these differences grew. A detailed description of one of Sattam's peers' "most picturesque costume," which included gold embroidery on the headscarf and a "beautiful abba" (robe), suggests that shaykhly fashion on the steppe had changed.[64] In addition, shaykhs owned finer weapons than other warriors, and many kept and proudly displayed expensive animals, especially thoroughbred mares.[65]

Social and cultural tensions apart, Sattam's wealth and his collaboration with the Ottoman government affected Bani Sakhr politics and even provoked opposition. His desire to satisfy the government conflicted with the interests of other members of the Bani Sakhr, who wanted to maintain their previous way of life, including raiding and the collecting of *khawa*. Tribesmen who did not enjoy privileges bestowed by the Ottoman state were not obliged to be loyal, and acts of resistance to Ottoman rule persisted.[66] The elevation of the Fayiz shaykhs also came at the expense of shaykhs of other tribes of the confederacy and probably was a cause for envy and internal conflicts. For decades, the Zaban tribe refused to recognize the leadership of Sattam and his successors,[67] and the latter had to tread a fine line between loyalty to the Ottomans and the expectations of their tribesmen that they maintain some measure of autonomy and ensure the Bani Sakhr's sources of material wealth.

MITHQAL'S COMING OF AGE

Mithqal was born to Sattam around 1880; estimates of the year of his birth range between 1875 and 1885.[68] He was the son of Thaqba, the daughter of a shaykh of one of the tribes of the Ruwala.[69] The Ruwala was the largest and most powerful group of tribes in northern Arabia and Syria, and its territory bordered on and often overlapped with that of the Bani Sakhr. Like most marriages of shaykhs, Sattam's union with the Ruwala woman seems to have been the result of political calculation; it was an attempt to improve relations between these two tribal groups, which were often rivals. Marriage and, even more important, the birth of a son, cemented political alliances, so shaykhs tended to marry many wives, up to four at a time, as permitted in Islamic law. Once a boy was conceived, some marriages had exhausted their rationale and the shaykh divorced his wife to allow him to marry another one.

The political calculation in the choice of wife does not mean that love and affection were not important. In addition to her wit and family background as the daughter of the shaykh of the 'Adwan, Sattam's wife 'Aliya was "reputed to be the belle of the country."[70] Some marriages lasted a lifetime, and Bedouin poetry is full of stories of love and romance. Shaykh Nimr al-'Adwan's love of and devotion to his wife Wadha is still legendary and was even the basis for a popular TV series in 2007.[71] Shaykh Mijwal al-Masrab from northern Syria fell in love with a British aristocrat, Jane Digby, and married her after complying with her condition that he divorce his Arab wife. They spent the next twenty-eight years together until she died.[72]

But Mithqal's mother did not fare as well and was quickly divorced by Sattam after she gave birth, or, according to another version, became a widow shortly after he was born. Either way, she took the newborn and his sister back to her family in the camp of the Ruwala, along with a herd and other property that was Mithqal's inheritance.[73] The return of a wife to her family was a common practice among some nomadic tribes. Among the Ruwala, the sons of a shaykh by his divorced wives spent the first three to four years of their lives with their mothers' families. But according to local custom, the children belonged to their father and eventually returned to him. When back in their father's camp, they were raised by their grandmother.[74] But Mithqal stayed longer with his mother, probably because his father died when he was still very young. His grandfather and later his uncle brought him up at the Ruwala camp. This upbringing had a lasting effect: Mithqal acquired the Ruwali dialect, which he spoke all his life.[75]

But even in the camp of his mother's family, Mithqal was expected, as the son of a famous shaykh, to follow the footsteps of his esteemed father. Although no credible sources are available to give us a clear picture of his childhood, it is safe to assume that Mithqal learned the ways of the desert and all aspects of tribal and pastoral life as a child, probably beginning at the age of ten, if not even younger.[76]

These included tending the herds, helping a camel to give birth, treating sick camels or horses, learning how to survive in harsh desert conditions, taking part in seasonal migration and finding his way in the desert terrain, riding, shooting, hunting, raiding, and identifying a stranger's tribal affiliation by his accent, facial features, or clothes. All these skills were required of every male member of a no-madic tribe, and sons of shaykhs were especially expected to excel in them. This was particularly true when it came to their performance in battle.

In addition, as a shaykh's son, he joined his father or his older brother—and in Mithqal's case, his grandfather and uncle—in the company of the adults. He was only allowed to drink coffee when he returned from a raid with booty. By watching them, the boy picked up the way a shaykh treated kin, guests, allies and foes, government officials, merchants, and foreign visitors. He also learnt the rich, complicated protocol of tribal customary law, a practical day-to-day guide for any member of the tribe.[77] However, a shaykh's son had to master it in a way that would allow him to act as a judge and arbitrator in due course. These were two principal roles of a shaykh and an important source of his reputation both within and outside of his immediate tribe.

Finally, the boy learnt the strict etiquette of hospitality. The host welcomed the guests into the *shigg*, or the public (and therefore male) part of the tent, and sat them according to age, rank, and importance. He made sure that their needs were provided for and that they felt comfortable. In a prime example of his hospitality, the host himself might grind and brew the coffee, which was often served before the meal that the women had prepared. Perhaps most important, the host was responsible for guiding the conversation in the tent.

Reverend Tristram provides a glimpse into this training process through his description of Mithqal's uncle, Sattam al-Fayiz's adolescent brother Sahan, who escorted his group of explorers in 1872. Though young and under the guid-ance of Sattam, Sahan took an active part in fulfilling the duties of a guide and protector. When the Europeans were intimidated by the shaykh of the southern town of Karak, the young lad "leaped up, snapped his fingers in the face of the old bully, and laughed at the notion of making his brother's friends go back."[78] His sense of duty, honor, and superiority were already fully developed. Later on, when Sattam had to leave the camp for a few days, he left Sahan and another tribesman in charge. Now Sahan carefully performed the duties of hospitality. One night he was responsible for preparing the meal, beginning with slaugh-tering and skinning a lamb, cooking it, and finally offering the best part of the meat to his guests. In another instance, in his elder brother's tent, after Tristram had apologized that they were in a hurry and could not stay for dinner, Sahan tactfully rushed out and returned with prepared cold food that they could eat quickly while waiting for the coffee to brew. Tristram was already impressed with Sahan when he witnessed the boy's first baptism by fire. One morning Sahan came to bid the Europeans farewell as he was about to join his brothers on a raid—his first military experience.[79] In some cases, sons of shaykhs participated in raids at the age of ten or even before.[80] Tristram was very impressed by the young shaykh, describing him as "bright" and adding that he was "a fine, noble-hearted, generous boy and one open to impressions."[81]

The upbringing of a shaykh's son only rarely included formal education. Nearly all the shaykhs were illiterate, although there were some exceptions. One shaykh in Syria who could read and write hired a learned man to tutor his sons. Out of nine brothers, only one took any pains to learn.[82] In 1892, the Ottoman government inaugurated the School of Tribes in Istanbul, meant for sons of shaykhs across the empire. The purpose of the school was to socialize the young boys, turning them into loyal Ottoman citizens as well as military officers and administrators.[83] But even after the opening of the school, only very few boys enjoyed formal education. One of them was Sattam al-Fayiz's son and Mithqal's brother, Fawwaz, who studied in this school and became shaykh of shaykhs in 1909.[84] Mithqal himself was illiterate all his life.

Still, in his early life, there was nothing that would predict Mithqal's rise to the leadership of the Bani Sakhr, and his future success was against all odds. He was Sattam's sixth son out of eight—daughters were generally excluded from the written sources as well as from the family's memory[85]—and therefore was too young to succeed his father. The early death of his father in 1890 also meant that Mithqal did not have a powerful father who could groom him for the job, as Fandi had done with Sattam. Moreover, when Sattam died, his brother Talal (Mithqal's uncle), and not his eldest son, replaced him. This meant that the line of succession moved away from Sattam's sons and at least potentially, the new shaykh's sons would have enjoyed an advantage in the next round of competition for the leadership. Talal enjoyed even stronger relations with the Ottoman government than his predecessors had, and this strengthened his position of leadership and that of his immediate family. The Ottoman governor not only recognized Talal as the shaykh of shaykhs (and at least according to one usually reliable source actually chose him for the job) but also conferred on him the title of pasha, a high Ottoman honor. He also received a monthly salary. The Ottomans actively supported him, and two years after his appointment, the government invited him together with his nephew, Sattam's son Fayiz, who had failed to succeed his father, to Istanbul in order to reconcile them.[86] Ultimately, Talal performed the role of leader until his death in 1909, enjoying the longest term in office as shaykh of shaykhs of the Bani Sakhr under Ottoman rule. Lastly, and most important, the fact that Mithqal lived away from his own tribe and confederacy meant that he could not make a name for himself and build the reputation necessary for a potential future leader.

But events took a different course, and around the turn of the century, when Mithqal completed his training, he rejoined the Bani Sakhr. Oral history has it that Mithqal was involved in a blood feud after killing a member of the Ruwala in revenge for the murder of one of his relatives. For his own protection, his uncle advised him to leave the Ruwala and return to the Bani Sakhr. According to another version, he left the camp after the death of his mother. He left behind his first wife from the Ruwala who had not brought him a child, married off his sister to a Ruwala man, and began a new stage in his life, making his way back to the family.[87] Given that he had lived estranged from his family for so many years, his brothers and uncles perhaps welcomed him only reluctantly at first, but they could not deny him hospitality, since he was both a relative and a fugitive who needed protection. Mithqal was soon fully integrated into the Fayiz tribe and the Bani Sakhr confederacy, however, and quickly rose to be a famous, prominent shaykh.

2 FROM MAVERICK
TO POWERFUL SHAYKH

MITHQAL REJOINED the Bani Sakhr encampment around the turn of the century. At the time, he was probably in his late teens and, at least at first, an unknown quantity to the rest of his family. But Mithqal was gifted with exceptional military skills, which he had acquired while still with the Ruwala. Now, back with the Bani Sakhr, he had plenty of opportunities to demonstrate them.

Mithqal quickly made a name for himself as a leader of raids. Though there are no concrete details on the actual battles in which he took part, a few pieces of information illustrate his military role among the Bani Sakhr and the reputation he earned as a result. One surviving poem records his participation alongside other shaykhs of the family in a fierce battle around the turn of the century, moreover referring to him as "the sweetheart of those [girls] who smile broadly."[1] A French ethnographer with thorough knowledge of the Bani Sakhr wrote in 1906 that Mithqal was an important shaykh with a significant number of men following him in battle.[2] A visitor to Mithqal's camp in 1931 recounted that Mithqal was proud of his many battle scars and wounds from bullets, swords, and lances. By that time, he had two bullets in his body.[3] A biographical list composed in 1946 by the British minister in Amman contains a short entry on Mithqal that describes him as "a raider of renown" in his youth.[4] As successful leader of raids, he marshaled many loyal warriors and enjoyed the lion's share of the booty. Ultimately, his success and courage earned him valuable credentials, as expected from a member of a respectable shaykhly family, providing him with the springboard to the position of leadership.

THE WARRIOR

Mithqal's military leadership was important for the well-being of the Bani Sakhr. At the beginning of the twentieth century, traditional raiding and tribal wars were still commonplace on the fringes of the Syrian Desert, as had been the case before the establishment of direct Ottoman rule in the last third of the nineteenth century. True, the Ottoman government succeeded in enforcing law and order in many parts of Transjordan and, gradually, the Ottoman presence in the area grew stronger. In 1894, Ottoman troops even ventured southwards, occupying and taking control of the towns of Karak, Tafila, and Ma'an, formerly independent of central rule, with the first two localities paying *khawa* to the Bani Sakhr (see map 1, p. 9). In the first years of the twentieth century, the government also introduced two technical innovations that further enhanced its ability to govern the area—the telegraph line and the Hijaz railway, stretching from Damascus to Medina along the Hajj route. Once a peripheral zone, the whole of Transjordan and other parts of the Syrian steppe were now incorporated into the Ottoman state. But even at its height, Ottoman power was not sufficient to pacify the strong nomadic confederacies and government reach was limited to a narrow strip west of the railway. Beyond it, and sometimes even within this area, tribes continued to enjoy autonomy and often fought with each other and on occasion raided peasants and clashed with Ottoman troops. In the last decade of the nineteenth century and at the beginning of the twentieth century, the Bani Sakhr were involved in a series of bloody and prolonged wars with neighboring tribes, including the Ruwala. It is possible that Mithqal fought his in-laws' tribe.

But circumstances played into Mithqal's hand in another important respect, making his combat skills even more crucial and strengthening his position of leadership. During the last years of the reign of his uncle, Talal al-Fayiz, as shaykh of shaykhs, relations between the family and the Ottoman government became strained. The main bone of contention between the tribes and the government was the construction of the Hijaz railway line, which threatened the livelihood of the Bani Sakhr as protectors of the Hajj caravans and providers of camels and supplies to the pilgrims. The number of pilgrims had already declined at the end of the nineteenth century, because the opening of the Suez Canal had introduced a quicker and safer route by sea. Still, this was an important business for the Bani Sakhr. At first, since the tribes remained potential troublemakers, Talal was able to negotiate with the provincial government in Damascus and persuade it to maintain the payment for protecting the pilgrims.

In return, he agreed not to obstruct the construction of the railway and even to guard the tracks that cut through the Bani Sakhr's territory. Still, the wages the tribesmen received to protect the railway did not make up for the losses they incurred when the Hajj caravans ended in 1908 with the completion of the line. In addition, the Ottomans did not always keep to the agreement and often withheld the promised subsidy. Moreover, the government confiscated some of the tribes' land adjacent to the railway and declared it sultanic property. Some of this land had been cultivated by peasants hired by the Fayiz shaykhs.[5]

This Ottoman policy, derived from ever-growing confidence in their ability to subjugate the tribes, undermined Talal's leadership. In late 1908, he met an old acquaintance in Jerusalem, who found him in a distressed state of mind. The shaykh was on his way back from Damascus, where he had met several Ottoman officials. He complained that the Ottomans had stopped paying his personal salary and the Hajj subsidy for his tribes, since pilgrims now took the train. This severe loss of income made the tribespeople rebellious. They threatened to destroy the railway tracks and a clash with the government over this issue led to the tribesmen's military defeat. Talal was summoned to Damascus to meet the governor with the aim of reconciliation. To Talal's detriment, the meeting coincided with the Young Turks' coup in Istanbul. The dramatic events unfolding at the center of the empire, culminating in the deposal of the reigning sultan, relegated relations with nomads in one of its peripheries to a low priority and the governor had not received any instructions as to what to do with the Bani Sakhr. The disappointed shaykh left Damascus empty-handed and worried about "what his kinsmen might yet compel him to do."[6]

But Talal's ability to execute such a threat, namely, to rebel, was very limited. Only a few decades earlier, the main role of a shaykh had been to lead his men in battle, and many shaykhs and their sons were killed in the process. Reportedly, six out of the seven sons of the shaykh of the Ruwala died in battle. Other shaykhly families endured this occupational hazard, if on a smaller scale. Many of Mithqal's elder brothers were killed in the same manner.[7] So frequent was a shaykh's death in battle that a missionary who had much experience in the region remarked that few of the shaykhs he had known in person had died of natural causes, and when they did, the tribesmen "ascribe it to poison given by the Turks."[8] All the Bani Sakhr shaykhs of shaykhs who apparently died of old age or illness, starting with Fandi al-Fayiz and including his successors Sattam, Talal, and Fawwaz, were rumored to have been poisoned by the Ottomans.[9] Nothing was more undignified than death from natural causes![10]

The fact that the four Fayiz shaykhs died naturally might have been a mere coincidence, but it is more likely that it reflects the change in the nature of the tribes' leadership. As the nineteenth century drew to a close, the likelihood of senior shaykhs living a full life increased. With the Ottoman government gradually extending its direct rule into the periphery, limiting raids on the peasantry, creating close contacts with the shaykhly families, and encouraging them to cultivate their land, the leaders of the big tribal confederacies were seen less on battlefields and more in Aleppo, Damascus, Jerusalem, Nablus, or Salt—the urban centers of Ottoman power. Maintaining cordial relations with the government gradually became the chief's main task, rather than leading the tribesmen in war. With the growing divorce between the military role of the senior shaykh and his duty to represent his people vis-à-vis the government—and in light of growing tensions with the government—capable young military leaders such as Mithqal were an asset to the shaykh of shaykhs. At the same time, they posed a threat. This was even more pertinent after Talal died in 1909 and Mithqal's brother, Fawwaz, assumed the leadership of the Bani Sakhr.

By that point in time, Mithqal was already a powerful, influential shaykh with considerable support. In 1909, he gathered a large force of his tribesmen and took over a piece of fertile land on a farm south of Amman, which Fawwaz and his brothers, including Mithqal, had sold eight years earlier. Mithqal and his tribesmen occupied the land for months, keeping the peasants from cultivating the fields. When the legal owners finally complained to the Ottoman authorities, the governor in Salt told Fawwaz al-Fayiz, in his capacity as head of the Jiza subdistrict, to address his younger brother's illegal actions. After some negotiations, Mithqal signed a document admitting that he was the aggressor and promising to allow cultivation. But he did not keep this promise and did not hesitate to challenge the authority of his older brother Fawwaz, the shaykh of shaykh of the Bani Sakhr and an official representative of the Ottoman government. Fawwaz soon reported to the governor that Mithqal continued his aggressions. Fawwaz sided with the owners and recommended that the authorities teach his brother a harsh lesson. He also requested an additional fifty soldiers to help him govern the relevant areas more effectively.[11] But the Ottoman authorities could not or did not want to intervene and risk a confrontation with the troublemaking Mithqal, who continued to hold onto the land and enjoy its yields for another year. Mithqal thus took advantage of the limits of Ottoman dominance east of the Jordan River to increase his wealth at the expense of the weak peasants.

Soon, however, the Ottomans and the Bani Sakhr were embroiled in much more serious conflict, which relegated this local dispute to a matter of no importance. After consolidating power in Istanbul, the Young Turks launched new centralizing policies that further strained relations with the tribes. Trying to enforce one unified law across the empire, they did away with the relative tolerance and acceptance of local customs that had characterized Ottoman attitudes towards local societies along the imperial periphery for centuries. Thus, in 1909, the Ottomans had to quash a rebellion by the Druze community in Syria, which was provoked by their decision to abolish long-standing Druze autonomy. The successful suppression of the Druze rebellion encouraged the commander of the Ottoman army in Syria to implement a similar policy further south. Accordingly, villagers in northern Transjordan were disarmed and conscripted. In Salt and Madaba, the administration produced identification documents and conducted personal registration in preparation for conscription. Similar attempts in the southern town of Karak led to a rebellion in December 1910, which several nomadic tribes, including some sections of the Bani Sakhr, joined. Registration, disarmament, and conscription meant severe restrictions on tribal autonomy, which the stronger tribes refused to relinquish.[12]

Although the Ottomans suppressed the Karak Revolt within ten days, they understood the limits of their power on the periphery and put a stop to the measures that had provoked such resentment. The Bani Sakhr shaykhs also realized that direct confrontation with the government was not in their best interests. They hurried to publish a declaration that denied their participation in the rebellion. Notwithstanding the doubts raised in the Syrian press regarding the sincerity of this announcement, the shaykhs made an effort to appease the government.[13] Meanwhile, the Ottomans also sought to mend ties with the tribes.

This might explain why the government did not use military force against Mithqal to expel him from the land he occupied. Finally, two years after the initial takeover of the land, the two disputing parties reached a compromise. Without government intervention, several intermediaries made peace based on local custom. The owners gave Mithqal a flock of two hundred ewes and, in return, he dropped his claim to the land.[14]

This episode demonstrates not only how powerful—and cunning—Mithqal was, but also the importance of land for an ambitious shaykh. Displays of bravery and success in battle were still crucial, but were no longer the only prerequisite to becoming a prominent shaykh. The office required vast economic resources, and raids alone were not enough, especially after the Ottoman government limited them in the areas under its rule. It was in this context that land became an important economic resource for shaykhs. That is why Mithqal went so far as to bully the peasants and then risk a confrontation with the Ottoman government and his brother in order to maintain his control of it. In addition, he benefited from the land that he and his brothers had inherited from his father. According to the Ottoman land registers from 1897, Mithqal owned land on several farms south and southeast of Amman.[15] The profits from the land helped Mithqal to provide for his men, to purchase arms and ammunitions, and to offer the traditional generous hospitality expected from a shaykh of his stature.

And Mithqal had another advantage while he was making his way. The fact that his elder brother, Fawwaz, was the leader of the Bani Sakhr greatly strengthened his political position. Even if there was some tension between the brothers at first, they soon reconciled, and Mithqal became Fawwaz's right-hand man. A newspaper report from 1913 implies that the two shaykhs were acting as partners in the leadership of the Bani Sakhr under Ottoman patronage. By that time, they were generally known for their friendship with the government and faced internal opposition for that reason. When a famous warrior of the Bani Sakhr and an outlaw wanted to defy the government, he set fire to Mithqal's and Fawwaz's threshing floors and stole their cattle.[16] Fawwaz's reliance on Mithqal may have been the result of affection for his young brother, regard for his military skills, or fear of his power and potential competition. Whatever the case, Mithqal was an asset to Fawwaz as a military leader, particularly in light of the unstable relations between the tribes and the Ottoman government and the impending threat of the Young Turks to curtail their autonomy.

WORLD WAR I AND
THE FIRST BID FOR POWER

When the Ottoman Empire entered World War I in November 1914, allying with Germany and Austria-Hungary against Britain, France, and Russia, the balance of power between the nomadic tribes and the government changed once again. Faced with the enormous war effort, the Ottomans now needed the tribes' support. This became crucial in 1916 following the outbreak of the Arab Revolt led by the head of the Hashemite family of Mecca, Sharif Hussein bin 'Ali. A direct descendant of the Prophet Muhammad and the keeper of the holy cities on behalf of the sultan, Hussein threw in his lot with the British Empire in return for a vague promise of Arab independence under his throne. He recruited nomadic tribesmen with promises for gold and booty, together with a regular army composed of Arab prisoners of war who had initially fought with the Ottomans. After fighting Ottoman troops in the Hijaz, the bulk of the rebel forces under the command of Sharif Hussein's third son, Faysal, advanced north towards Transjordan and Syria. The Ottomans made enormous efforts to maintain the loyalty of the tribes, while the Hashemites tried to win them over to their side.

The conditions of prolonged war served Mithqal's aspirations for the leadership of the Bani Sakhr well. They allowed certain shaykhs to demonstrate their military prowess, which in turn increased their fame and influence. Since their military support was in high demand, they were able to attract patrons among the rival forces operating in their theater of war and ask for high price in return for their loyalty. Shaykh 'Awda abu Taya of the Huwaytat, whose role in the revolt has been immortalized in the Hollywood classic *Lawrence of Arabia*, is one case in point; Mithqal is another. The exact role Mithqal played during the war is difficult to discern because there are gaps in the information and some conflicting evidence. What is clear is that Mithqal remained loyal to the Ottomans throughout the war and was a very valuable asset to them. Moreover, within less than a year of the beginning of the revolt, Mithqal eclipsed the official shaykh of shaykhs, Fawwaz. A British intelligence report from early 1917 stated that Mithqal was reported to be "the stronger man [compared with his brother Fawwaz], who takes command in times of war."[17]

Even before the outbreak of the revolt, the value of the tribes to the Ottoman authorities had significantly increased. In January 1915, soon after the Ottoman declaration of war, the government invited the shaykhs of the Bani Sakhr to Damascus with the hope of obtaining their assistance in transporting weapons, ammunition and provisions to Beersheba for an Ottoman attack on the Suez Canal. The government reportedly asked for five hundred camels, and promised the shaykhs money, gifts, and honors in return. The shaykhs took their money and medals, but moved their herds back to the desert, beyond the reach of the government. When the ammunition reached the meeting point and the Ottoman and German officers demanded that Fawwaz hand over the camels he had promised, he supposedly replied: "The Bedu will sacrifice himself for the sake of his camel and it is impossible that they will provide their animals for the transport of material for such a long distance. That is why they fled eastwards. I am personally loyal to the government and carry its orders but my people are rebellious."[18] If Fawwaz indeed said this, it is puzzling (and reads like a poor excuse); providing camels for transport was exactly what the Bani Sakhr had done for hundreds of years when they escorted the Hajj.

The tribes gained even more clout following the declaration of the Arab Revolt in June 1916 and especially after the advance of the Hashemite army northwards in the summer of 1917. The swift and surprising takeover of the Ottoman fort in Aqaba, at the northern edge of the Red Sea, turned Transjordan into the main theater of war and further obscured the future political configuration of the region. The shaykhs faced a dilemma: Which side to back? As the Hashemite family built the entire strategy of the revolt on the creation of a tribal coalition,[19] it was crucial for both parties to obtain the support of the tribes, especially those such as the Bani Sakhr whose territory lay along the Hijaz railway, the prime target of T. E. Lawrence's guerrilla attacks.

In order to foster and retain the tribes' loyalty, the Ottoman authorities in Syria showered the tribal shaykhs with both material and symbolic rewards. Ahmet Cemal Pasha, one of the three Young Turk leaders who effectively ruled the empire after they staged a coup in 1913, and who assumed the governorship of Syria as his wartime commission, bestowed honors and medals upon many leading shaykhs, including even former rebels. Later, another Ottoman general invited the region's tribal shaykhs to Damascus. There he hosted them in hotels at the government's expense, sometimes for weeks at a time.[20]

Despite these efforts, some shaykhs threw in their lot with the Hashemites. By the end of 1917, the takeover of Aqaba and General Edmund Allenby's victorious entrance to Jerusalem in December gave the impression that the British and their Arab allies were the winning party. In response, the Ottomans exiled or arrested certain shaykhs of the Bani Sakhr and other tribes whom they either suspected of collaboration with the enemy, or whom they wanted to intimidate in order to discourage any such development. Not everyone was deterred by these measures and some joined the revolt. Shaykh Muflih al-Qam'an of the Zaban tribe of the Bani Sakhr led his tribesmen in battle and was even wounded during a successful attack on one of the railway stations in January 1918. Forces from the Bani Sakhr (which numbered nearly five hundred men in one particular battle) under the command of their shaykhs took part in the battles in and around Ma'an. In the course of 1918, they constituted an integral part of the Arab Revolt's force that fought its way to Damascus.[21]

Despite this military contribution, the Bani Sakhr, like other Transjordanian and Syrian tribal groups, did not maintain a unified stance. Most of the confederacy's members remained loyal to the Ottomans or at least stayed aloof. A shaykh's decision to support one external force over another was primarily a reflection of the internal power struggle within the confederacy and among its leaders. Since the days of Fandi al-Fayiz, the Zaban had refused to recognize the leadership of the Fayiz shaykh of shaykhs. They traditionally acted independently, and their active support of the Arab Revolt was a bet on a new horse. In cultivating Hashemite and British patronage now, they hoped to change the balance of power within the confederacy at the expense of their rivals, who for several generations had enjoyed official Ottoman recognition.

Competing loyalties also emerged within the Fayiz family. Shaykh of shaykhs Fawwaz established secret ties with the Hashemites, whereas Mithqal maintained his loyalty to the Ottomans, cultivating a rapport with Mehmet Cemal Pasha, the commander of the Eighth Corps of the Ottoman Fourth Army. What might have begun as an orchestrated family strategy to avoid putting all their eggs into one basket soon developed into a leadership struggle.

From the outset of the war, Fawwaz al-Fayiz played a delicate game and maintained contacts with both sides. During the war, he continued to enjoy Ottoman patronage as the recognized leader of the Bani Sakhr and the recipient of salary from the state coffers. At the same time, he cautiously oscillated towards the Hashemites. Already in 1915, Fawwaz had allegedly met Faysal in Damascus to discuss the possibility of a revolt. At the end of 1916, he attended a meeting of shaykhs in which they decided to terminate their relations with the government. In January 1917, Fawwaz declared his loyalty to Sharif Hussein, but refused to join the revolt unless the sharif promised him military support. Just before the occupation of Aqaba, Fawwaz met Lawrence and assured him of his loyalty to Faysal. But Fawwaz died in the summer of 1917 before he had the chance to act upon his promises. British intelligence attributed his death to Ottoman poisoning but it is more likely that he died of natural causes, and the British officers misread the customary rumors about poisoning, which had been circulating in the desert for decades.[22]

Upon Fawwaz's death, Mithqal saw himself as the new leader and made his first bid to become the shaykh of shaykhs of the Bani Sakhr. A British intelligence report indicated that Mithqal "was mentioned as his successor."[23] However, Mithqal lost to his seventeen-year-old nephew, Mashhur, the son of the deceased leader. The tribal council preferred the young Mashhur, who was a graduate of a school in Damascus, to the illiterate Mithqal, even though the latter was more mature and experienced.[24] Perhaps the tribal elders thought that a shaykh with a modern education was better qualified to lead the tribes under the new conditions and in light of the uncertainties engendered by the war. Alternatively, they might have believed that a teenager would be easier to manipulate and control than the forceful Mithqal.[25]

Mithqal, though disappointed, did not come out of the competition empty-handed. As the succession took place immediately after the Aqaba campaign, and Hashemite forces were nearby, the Ottomans needed any help they could muster. One of the Cemal Pashas—the similarity in the names makes reading the sources confusing—who chose Mashhur (or at least approved the council's recommendation) compensated Mithqal with the precious title of pasha in order to maintain his allegiance. The shaykh was very flattered by this rare gesture. Many years later, after the establishment of the emirate of Transjordan, he would boast about this honor: Emir Abdullah bin Hussein was known to bestow honors liberally, and consequently many dignitaries were addressed as Basha (the Arabized pronunciation of the Turkish term), but Mithqal was the only person in the country to hold the original Ottoman title, sanctioned by the sultan himself.[26]

Granting Mithqal the title of pasha proved beneficial to the Ottomans: Mithqal remained loyal. It was probably owing to him that the majority of the Bani Sakhr did not join the Hashemites, as the British expected them to do, given that Mashhur was a stronger supporter of the Hashemite cause than his father had been. Mithqal also gave the Ottomans active support and in 1918 mobilized several hundred tribesmen to help the Ottomans confront the advancing forces of the Arab Revolt. Mehmet Cemal Pasha gave him large sums of money to that end, which in turn increased his influence among his tribesmen. Lieutenant Colonel Frederick Peake, a British officer who served with Lawrence and later founded and commanded the Transjordanian Arab Legion, was no fan of Mithqal's, and played down the shaykh's role, writing: "Mithqal led a force of 400 men, rode under the banner presented to his 'army' by Djemal Pasha as far as Suwaylah at the time of the second attack on Amman [see below]. Beyond looting a herd of Turkish Army camels, their war record was an undistinguished one."[27]

Regardless of the military contribution of his force, Mithqal was the strongman among the Bani Sakhr, overshadowing Mashhur's leadership. His special relationship with Cemal was of great importance to the Ottomans during the last year of the war and afforded Mithqal significant influence in Transjordan. In March 1918, General Allenby launched his first attack east of the Jordan River, attempting to cut the Ottoman forces' lines by taking over the towns of

Salt and Amman. At first, the British entered Salt unopposed as the Ottomans withdrew to regroup in Amman. Assuming the Ottoman retreat was permanent, the Saltis looted and demolished government offices and even fired at the retreating forces. However, a few days later the Ottoman forces pushed the British back west of the Jordan and resumed their presence in the town. With the British withdrawal, several thousand inhabitants, mainly Christians, fled to Jerusalem and settled there. Those remaining were spared the wrath of the returning Ottoman soldiers thanks only to Mithqal's intervention with Cemal.[28]

Perhaps the greatest contribution Mithqal and the Bani Sakhr made to the Ottomans during the war was their obstruction of the second British attack on Salt and Amman in late April early May 1918. After the first unsuccessful attack, a delegation of shaykhs came to the British army in Jerusalem and offered that the Bani Sakhr would block Ottoman reinforcements in the event of a new attack. Encouraged by this pledge and in order to meet the deadline the Bani Sakhr dictated, Allenby decided to launch the attack east of the river two weeks earlier than he had originally planned. Whether it was a well-orchestrated Ottoman ploy,[29] or simply the initiative of shaykhs who carried little influence within their tribal confederacy, coupled with the British intelligence failure to understand this,[30] the results were devastating. The Bani Sakhr's role was a major component in British planning and when their help did not materialize, the Ottomans reinforced their troops quickly and pushed the Australian and New Zealand (Anzac) forces back west of the River Jordan, inflicting 1,650 casualties.[31] Many years later Mithqal gave his own version of this affair: "The Bani Sakhr did not support the Arab Revolt. A messenger from Sharif Faysal came to me and promised me 10,000 British pounds in gold. However, I refused and told him that we were Arabs without gold, that we were loyal to the Ottoman Empire and felt indebted to them and that I was not going to be a traitor."[32]

Following the British retreat, as well as the Arab forces' defeat in Ma'an a fortnight previously, the position of the Ottomans in Transjordan, and of their main ally, Mithqal, seemed secure. British intelligence reported that Faysal's call to the shaykhs of the Balqa' to join his cause fell on deaf ears. This Ottoman-tribal alliance was sealed with money and decorations for the shaykhs, as well as rehabilitation for exiled notables.[33]

In September 1918 the pendulum swung once more, this time decisively, to the British side. Allenby pushed northwards through the coast of Palestine and surprised the Ottomans and Germans, who had reinforced their forces east of the river in anticipation of a third British attack. The dramatic collapse of the Ottoman defenses in Palestine was decisive, and their troops in Transjordan began their retreat. Although most of them had been loyal to the Ottoman Empire, the Bani Sakhr and other tribes could not resist the temptation to raid and loot the retreating Turks, who had to be protected from the Arab tribesmen by their Anzac enemies.[34]

Although his kinsmen were busy looting the Ottomans, Mithqal was still in the latter's camp. According to one report, he escorted the retreating forces all the way up to Aleppo. Another describes the shaykh's "dramatic farewell" to Cemal while they were still in Transjordan: "Mithqal was among the few Arabs who were considered loyal lieutenants and friends of Cemal Pasha. Both cried bitterly at their farewell, say the Bedouin. Until today, Mithqal speaks of his old friend with sympathy, and he is still fond of the Turks."[35]

The Ottoman retreat marked a loss of power and influence for Mithqal among the Bani Sakhr. Deprived of his patron Cemal Pasha, and having bet on a losing horse, Mithqal could not maintain his position. Accompanied by a few of his loyal men, he retreated to the desert, while Mashhur, who had supported the Hashemites, recovered his influence among the tribes. He had considerable help in doing so from Faysal, who confirmed his position as the shaykh of shaykhs.[36] For a short period after Cemal's departure, Faysal acted as the highest authority in the country, and many shaykhs depended on his goodwill. Mithqal's political career seemed doomed.

COMEBACK UNDER THE SYRIAN ARAB GOVERNMENT

In October 1918, the British and Arab forces entered Damascus and Sharif Faysal established an Arab administration as part of the temporary military government under the command of General Allenby. This administration extended its influence over Transjordan. To support the Arab government, Allenby deployed small British and imperial garrisons around the country. Since his government was new and found it difficult to establish its authority, Faysal sought to benefit from the influence of the country's tribal leaders. He forged alliances with many of them, adopting the Ottoman wartime practice of granting subsidies and honorary titles. Faysal recognized several shaykhs as shaykh of shaykhs, a position accompanied by a handsome salary.[37] Faysal forgave even the shaykhs who had supported the Ottomans rather than the Hashemites during the war. In a message to the local leaders he circulated during his first days in Damascus, Faysal expressed the wish to "end the conflicts between the Bedouin tribes who supported the revolt and the others, and to unite the ranks in order to prepare the way for independence."[38] The new leader of Syria tried to heal the wounds created by the war in order to build a new nation.

Mithqal, too, was a beneficiary of Faysal's tribal policy. Some time in the course of 1919, Mithqal managed to mend fences with Mashhur and made peace with Faysal. Faysal not only forgave pro-Ottoman shaykhs like Mithqal, but also rewarded them. Many shaykhs took advantage of the new regime's magnanimity to maintain or even recover their positions within their constituencies. Faysal reappointed the pro-Ottoman Sultan 'Ali al-'Adwan as shaykh of shaykhs of the Balqa' and recognized the leadership of Hamad bin Jazi, who led the branch of the Huwaytat that had opposed 'Awda abu Taya and the Hashemites. Nuri al-Sha'lan of the Ruwala received a handsome monthly subsidy, even though he had joined the Hashemites only in the very last phase of the war when the Ottoman troops began their retreat.[39]

Faysal's efforts paid off: many of the major Transjordanian players proclaimed their loyalty to him. Until the end of 1919, most parties in the country seemed content with the new order. The nomads and semi-nomads enjoyed the benefits of the new administration, which proved to be no more than an extension of the tribal coalition of the Arab Revolt; the Hashemites ruled with a light touch and allowed the local tribes a high degree of autonomy.[40]

The success of Faysal's regime proved short-lived, however. He failed to reach an agreement with France, which claimed Syria as its sphere of influence. It based its claim on its wartime deal with Britain to divide the post-Ottoman Fertile Crescent, known as the Sykes-Picot Agreement. Faysal also lost British support, and when the government in London decided to side with its European allies rather than their local ones, Arab independence was doomed. In November, the British and French prime ministers agreed that British troops would evacuate Syria to allow the French to deploy their army. By December 1, 1919, British forces had withdrawn, and shortly afterwards, Britain halved its financial support for the Arab government. Faysal could no longer subsidize the local leaders, and his administration's grip over its territory began to diminish.[41]

Mithqal took advantage of the weak and threatened government to stage his political comeback. He regained his popularity and influence among the Bani Sakhr, as well as his prominence outside the confederacy. From November 1919 on, Mithqal took a leading role on the political stage. Shaykhs from the regions of Salt, Amman, and Karak met several times in November and December to collect donations and arrange for volunteers to protect the new state; they elected Mithqal president of the Committee for National Defense. Such committees emerged all around Syria under the auspices of the Arab administration. Also in November, Mithqal was among the shaykhs representing the Bani Sakhr at a fete held in Damascus for shaykhs and notables from the Balqa'. What began as a celebration of reconciliation between two tribal groups soon turned into a national rally. The shaykhs published an open letter condemning the French and British governments and vowing to "defend the independence with our property, our children and our blood."[42]

Mithqal also tried to mobilize the tribes in Transjordan and Palestine in support of the government. He sent a letter to the shaykh of Karak asking him to support the independence movement and tried, though unsuccessfully, to persuade Sultan al-'Adwan to form a joint force to attack British troops across the river. According to Zionist reports, Mithqal recruited the shaykhs of the nomadic tribes of the Beersheba district in Palestine and invited them on Faysal's behalf to come to Damascus. For all these activities, Mithqal received large sums of money.[43]

Mithqal was drawn into the Damascus political theater, where he was exposed to the new ideology of Arab nationalism. However, like other shaykhs, his loyalty to Faysal and the Arab government had nothing to do with modern nationalism. Notwithstanding that the petitions they signed were phrased—probably by Faysal's men—in nationalist terms, the shaykhs did not adopt this new identity. Rather, they supported Faysal because his regime served their interests and the interests of their tribes by providing funds and allowing them extensive autonomy. Mithqal's and his peers' main ideology remained their loyalty to their families, tribes, and confederacies.

This attitude partly explains why Mithqal and the other leaders withdrew their support from the government in late December 1919 when it announced mandatory conscription—a threat to tribal autonomy.[44] Shortly thereafter, Mithqal openly defied Faysal by accepting gifts from the French, who sought to intensify the discord between the shaykhs and the government. According to reports from February 1920, Mithqal and other shaykhs went to Beirut to meet French officials, including High Commissioner of Lebanon Georges Picot, negotiator of the Sykes-Picot Agreement. Mithqal came back in a French car, and it was rumored that he had received £1,000, a hefty sum in those days.[45] By that time, the nomadic tribes had shaken off any lingering sense of obligation to the government in Damascus. Its authority in Transjordan was limited to Salt and Amman and their immediate hinterlands.[46]

Facing uncertainty over Syria's future, Mithqal was careful to cultivate good relations with other forces. According to some reports, he maintained relations with the Ottomans forces, now deployed in the north of Syria. He was also part of a group of ten shaykhs who traveled to Jericho in April 1920 to meet Chaim Weizmann, president of the World Zionist Organization, who wished to discuss an agreement that would ensure the safety of the Jews of Palestine. He hoped the shaykhs would sign a petition that called for Transjordan to become part of Palestine under the British Mandate rather than part of Syria. The draft included a demand to allow for Jewish immigration east of the Jordan River. Assaults on Jews in Jerusalem, which developed into what was known as the Nabi Musa riots and marked the beginning of the violence connected with the Arab-Jewish conflict over Palestine, prevented Weizmann from attending the meeting. After five days of waiting, the disappointed shaykhs returned home, albeit generously compensated for their time and expenses.[47]

The shaykhs' simultaneous dealings with rival forces earned them a reputation as shameless mercenaries and unscrupulous opportunists among contemporary observers. As one British officer remarked: "The Sheikhs of Trans-Jordania, almost without exception, are perfectly willing to take any amount of money from anybody and make all sorts of promises in return, and, if sufficient money were distributed, say, by the Chinese, they would sign a petition for a Chinese mandate."[48] A Zionist observer wrote in the same spirit: "A golden period arrived for the greedy and warlike Bedouin shaykhs of Trans-Jordania. A hundred hands full of gold and promises are stretched out to them, attempting to win their sympathy. The shaykhs accept all offers. . . . They, for their part, are ready to serve, are ready to fight and invade wherever there is a good booty in view."[49]

What was erroneously condemned as greediness provides a poor explanation for the behavior of Mithqal and the other shaykhs. In fact, the shaykhs conformed to the structure and dynamics of tribal society and politics and were busy accumulating economic resources to sustain their leadership. In the aftermath of the war, the shaykhs took this one step further, seeking not only to augment but also to diversify their sources of income. Hitherto, they had been dependent on Ottoman patronage, but they could now cultivate several powerful actors to expand their independence and autonomy. Given the country's unclear future, Mithqal and his peers hedged their bets, maintaining good relations with all those who sought to play a role in the region. This strategy made a great deal of sense and was rooted in political considerations rather than financial greed.

RESISTANCE TO BRITISH COLONIALISM

The state of uncertainty in Transjordan greatly intensified in the summer of 1920. The French government became exasperated with Faysal and his administration and ordered its army to take over Syria. With the overwhelming defeat of Faysal's forces near Damascus in July, the British government found itself responsible for Transjordan, in accordance with the Sykes-Picot Agreement. The prime concern of the British was to prevent the French in Syria from expanding beyond the territories allocated to them in the agreement, and to prevent tribal raids across the Jordan River. But the British were preoccupied with suppressing a massive revolt in Iraq and were reluctant to commit more troops. The government also confronted postwar austerity and the fatigue of the British public, so another military adventure was out of the question. The cabinet therefore refused to sanction the occupation and administration of the country. Instead, it ordered the government of Palestine to maintain its influence indirectly. A handful of British officers were to help the locals establish a form of self-government. This strategy proved to be a resounding failure, to a large degree due to Mithqal's resistance.

In August 1920, Sir Herbert Samuel, the newly arrived British high commissioner for Palestine, went to Salt to obtain the consent of local leaders to the British plan. He believed that he had already secured the population's unequivocal support after many shaykhs came to Jerusalem or sent friendly messages. Some went as far as to ask for a British administration in Transjordan. Samuel explained at a meeting with some six hundred Arabs that Britain sought to help them establish local governments and, to this end, offered them the assistance and guidance of British officers. He promised that Transjordan would not be placed under the Palestine administration's direct control, and assured them that there was no intention of conscripting or disarming the locals. As a gesture of goodwill, he pardoned two fugitives from Palestine at the request of local dignitaries. One of these was Amin al-Husseini, whom Samuel would soon appoint as Grand Mufti of Jerusalem, and who would eventually emerge as the leader of the Palestinian national movement. Samuel returned to Jerusalem pleased with the results.[50]

Following the meeting, Samuel dispatched six officers holding purely advisory positions to help establish three local governments, in 'Ajlun, the Balqa', and Karak. He instructed them to encourage the inhabitants to form local councils, nominate paramount chiefs, collect taxes and support the existing gendarmerie. A few weeks later, the Foreign Office decided to send a seventh officer, Frederick Peake, to take overall charge of the gendarmerie.[51]

Mithqal, who neither went to Jerusalem nor attended the Salt meeting, emerged as the main obstacle to the local government that the British tried to establish in the Balqa' region. Confident of their strength, he and his confederates felt no need to rush to the aid of the British, as some of the weaker tribes did. At the same time, they maintained several lines of communication with the British. Mithqal's younger brother called on the British officer in Jericho; and when they received a telegram from High Commissioner Samuel, the shaykhs responded in a friendly manner. Mithqal and Mashhur, together with the shaykh of the 'Ajarma tribes, even sent a letter to Samuel declaring their loyalty to and friendship with Great Britain. They also took the opportunity to ask for the appointment of a certain officer as the commander of the gendarmerie of Salt. Samuel responded in favorable, though noncommittal, terms.[52] The Bani Sakhr shaykhs realized that they could not ignore the new power. The British were perhaps weak east of the Jordan but very strong on its west bank.

The stakes were raised when the British tried to extend their influence from Salt to Amman by sending Captain Dunbar Brunton to form a government there. Now Mithqal was quick to indicate his opposition to this move. By that time, Amman had become an important part of Mithqal's sphere of influence and he was not willing to give it up so easily. Once part of the 'Adwan-led Balqa' tribal alliance's domain, it was lost in 1878 to the new Circassian community of immigrants and their patrons, the Ottoman government, who together established modern Amman. In the postwar years, the Bani Sakhr were able to extend their sphere of influence to include Amman. They had two assets in the town. The Circassians, who made up about half of the population of Amman, had had a mutual defense pact with the Bani Sakhr since the early years of the twentieth century. More important, Mithqal had just recently married 'Adul, the daughter of Amman's mayor, Sa'id Khayr. Khayr represented the other half of Amman's population: Syrian and Palestinian merchant families who had lived there since the end of the nineteenth century. The alliance between the Khayr and Fayiz families would prove to be one of the main sources of power and wealth for both parties. 'Adul and Mithqal's firstborn, 'Akif, would succeed his father.[53]

Mithqal tried to prevent the British coming to Amman and dispatched a series of "menacing telegrams," which had the effect of suggesting to the designated British representative, Captain Brunton, that he was persona non grata.[54] Fearing that local opposition would prevent him from entering the town, Brunton delayed his arrival for a few weeks. When he finally did arrive, on September 21, 1920, he was surprised by the friendly manner in which he was received. Even Khayr, who had been expressing anti-British views, entertained Brunton. Mithqal himself "sent word that he [would] come and pay his respects to Capt. Brunton at Amman."[55]

Reassured by his surprisingly warm reception in Amman, Brunton was convinced that he could adhere to the traditional imperial policy of co-opting and ruling through the local elite. He thus suggested appointing Mithqal as the president of a tribal council and making the official shaykh of shaykhs of the Bani Sakhr, Mashhur, the governor of Jiza, giving both "tribal autonomy as far as possible."[56] Writing from Salt, Major I. N. Camp corroborated his subordinate's assessment of the situation, singling out Mithqal as the main obstacle of the local government. He recommended inciting the other shaykhs in the area against Mithqal as a way to curb his power. Divide and rule was a common imperial tactic. However, Camp did not omit the possibility of using force against the shaykh "should the latter prove intractable or refuse to make amends for destroyed and looted property."[57] In another piece of correspondence, Camp wrote, "Mithgal is an awful blighter, and I should like to wipe him off the map of Trans-Jordania."[58]

This suggestion alarmed Samuel to such an extent that the civil secretary of the Palestine government replied to Camp that "the High Commissioner very much deprecates a conflict with the Beni Sakhr if it can be avoided." In an attempt to prevent such a scenario, Samuel wrote a letter to Mithqal to be delivered by Camp. The civil secretary also suggested that Camp provide Mithqal with incentive to cooperate by appointing him chief civil official in the Jiza subdistrict, with the possibility of a promotion to a district level. The intention was "to give him a post of honor, saddle him with responsibility and intimate that his services will not go without recognition." Jerusalem did authorize a confrontation with Mithqal if it could not be avoided and to that end gave Camp £5,000.[59]

Brunton and Camp's plans to co-opt Mithqal came to nothing, and the shaykh remained impervious to their attempts at courting him. He did not arrive in Amman as promised, and what followed was a power struggle between the Bani Sakhr shaykhs, led by Mithqal, and Brunton. At this point, the Bani

Sakhr had the upper hand. This was made clear in Brunton's reports to his superiors, which reflected his intense frustration: although he represented a powerful empire, he lacked the military means to control Mithqal, who remained the strongman on the ground.

Realizing that he could not successfully challenge the Bani Sakhr without adequate military support, Brunton focused on building up the local Reserve Force. The British were reluctant to send troops to Transjordan but knew it was impossible to exercise authority in the region without military backup; the Reserve Force was the product of a compromise between the two positions and became the nucleus of the Transjordanian Arab Legion. It was meant to support the local government and defend the settled populations from the nomads' raids. For these purposes, Brunton recruited ex-soldiers of the Ottoman and Arab armies who were unemployed and wandering the streets of Amman, in addition to members of the local Circassian population.[60]

The Reserve Force's baptism by fire occurred in early October and tipped the balance of power between the Bani Sakhr and the British-supported local government. The villagers of Sahab, southeast of Amman, defied government orders, refused to pay taxes, and stole several telegraph poles to boot. Although the Reserve Force was still unprepared for action, Brunton decided to use it in order to teach the villagers a lesson and to make an example of them in the region. At first, the force failed to even enter the village and suffered a humiliating defeat. The village surrendered the next day only after Brunton and his Arab deputy employed Haditha al-Khuraysha of the Bani Sakhr and several other shaykhs as mediators. The shaykhs' support came after the deputy convinced them that he had asked for aerial support from Palestine (which he had not). Having instilled a fear of the empire into the locals, the shaykhs persuaded the villagers to accept Brunton's terms.

In his account of the events, Brunton highlighted the positive role of Shaykh Haditha al-Khuraysah in bringing the affair to a peaceful conclusion. Brunton wrote that the shaykh "deserves the greatest credit for the way in which he acted as intermediary." He went on to describe him as "sensible and reliable . . . not wealthy but never begs like others and is generous to a degree. His manners are quiet and he has a great personal charm. One might term him the only real gentleman among the sheikhs of this region."[61] Haditha clearly embodied the stereotypical Bedouin gentleman so admired by the British. Mithqal did not. In later years, Britons serving in Transjordan often compared Haditha's virtues with what they saw as Mithqal's troublesome behavior.

The demonstration of power, though not decisive, had its intended effect and compelled Mithqal to change his attitude. Upon his return from Sahab, Brunton at last found the formidable shaykh waiting for him in Amman. They dined together and Brunton "treated him as coldly as politeness would permit" in response to what he interpreted as Mithqal's "grave breach of etiquette," namely, his long delay in meeting him. Henceforth, lukewarm though his attitude might be, Mithqal kept in touch with the British and the Reserve Force.[62] The shaykh was careful not to spark a full-scale confrontation with Brunton, who was, after all, a representative of a mighty empire.

While Brunton tried to reach a modus vivendi with Mithqal, the latter was more concerned with improving and consolidating his tribal political position. He canceled a lunch with Brunton because he was busy acting as a judge in a dispute between the 'Abbad tribes and their Circassians neighbors. The two communities' choice of Mithqal as a judge indicated their recognition of his leadership.[63] He also created a rift within the Balqa' tribal alliance, undermining the leadership of Sultan al-'Adwan, who enthusiastically supported the British. Since the end of 1919, but more so after the arrival of the British, Mithqal had closely cooperated with the shaykh of the 'Ajarma tribes from the southern part of the Balqa', who constituted a main pillar of that alliance.

Mithqal's meteoric rise to prominence in the Balqa' was aided by a British mistake. On October 18, 1920, a force of 150 men left Amman to deal with some nomads who had robbed the town of Madaba. As Brunton had already promised to have lunch with Mithqal, he and his men made a detour and stopped at Mithqal's house in Umm al-'Amad. Brunton was surprised to find Mithqal with an entire assembly of shaykhs from the Balqa'. They were the leaders of the very tribes that Brunton was about to punish. Mithqal asked for their pardon and guaranteed their good behavior in the future. The shaykhs also requested pardons for two recent fugitives. They all swore to restore or pay for all the looted property and also asked for a settlement of the land question, the source of the dispute between Madaba and the neighboring tribes. Owing to Mithqal's mediation and the conciliatory mood of the shaykhs, Brunton decided to agree to an amicable settlement. They all agreed to meet again the following day in Madaba, which they did, but the shaykhs failed to bring the loot. Instead, Mithqal and Brunton's deputy made the shaykhs swear on the Quran that they would be faithful to the government. Mithqal skillfully used a local dispute to assume the position of intermediary between the British and the Balqa' tribes. In doing so, he cleverly outmaneuvered Brunton. What is more, by mobilizing the tribes in the area, Mithqal improved his reputation and extended his influence within his traditional constituency and even beyond.

Mithqal's rise came at the expense of his rival Mashhur, and their relations grew increasingly hostile, since Mithqal posed a direct challenge to the authority of the shaykh of shaykhs. Brunton played into Mithqal's hands by offering him the post of governor of Jiza. Mithqal's noncommittal reply that the government "must do what is best for the general goal"[64] was enough to provoke Mashhur. Only the intervention of the gendarmerie prevented violence between the two shaykhs and their respective armed slaves. The matter was brought to a close the next day, when Brunton's deputy "made peace between them, and they kissed like brothers each hating the other like poison."[65]

Mithqal emerged from the episode much strengthened. What he did was to form a new tribal alliance, or what Brunton saw as a "large 'bloc' of Bedouins" under his leadership, which represented a threat to the order the British officer was trying to establish.[66] In his last report from Amman, Brunton candidly wrote that he was "not at all satisfied on the contrary with our visit to Madaba. Mithgal tied our hands. . . . We have settled the question through Mithgal as an intermediary and left no impression of just severity which is so necessary when dealing with Bedouin!"[67] Brunton's superior, Major Camp, admitted that "our original concession to settle the case amicably was taken as a sign of weakness by the Belka [Balqa'] Sheikhs."[68] Brunton found this, and the strong local opposition inspired by Sharif Abdullah bin Hussein's arrival in the southern town of Ma'an in November 1920, profoundly frustrating. At the beginning of December, he withdrew his force to Salt, and he resigned and left the country for good soon afterwards. Shortly before his departure, he was assigned to work under Peake, inspector of the police force and now commander of the Reserve Force.

But Peake fared no better than Brunton. Mithqal took care to demonstrate that he was a force to be reckoned with. The confrontation between Mithqal and Peake revolved around the same piece of land that Mithqal had taken over in 1909. Just as he had done a decade earlier, Mithqal again took advantage of the power vacuum to occupy the land and claim it as his own. The owners complained to the government in Salt, which then summoned Mithqal to discuss the matter. Knowing that he would be arrested if he went, Mithqal returned to his safe haven at Umm al-'Amad. Peake then pursued him with a substantial force, but upon arriving there, he discovered a large gathering of tribesmen. Fearing an open rebellion, he decided to adopt a diplomatic approach and rode unarmed to meet Mithqal.

Peake reported that they had reached an understanding, and that Mithqal had agreed to go to Salt with him the next day, but that he had changed his mind after several "politicians" arrived and persuaded him that Peake was a Jewish agent in disguise with a mission to take over the country and settle Jews in it.[69] The British had already interpreted Mithqal's anti-British stance as a symptom of his fear of Zionist colonization.[70] It is, however, difficult to imagine that Mithqal did not know who Peake was. It is also doubtful that someone who only several months earlier had wished to meet Weizmann in Jericho was preoccupied with a fear of Zionists.

Whether it was as Peake interpreted it, or simply a matter of retaining tribal autonomy and positioning himself as the leader of the Balqa', Mithqal ordered Peake's arrest. His men held the British officer in the stables for a day, while the shaykhs assembled to decide his fate. As a consequence, men from Peake's force deserted and joined the tribesmen. At some point, Peake took the initiative to warn the shaykhs that the British government would punish them if he were kept any longer. This threat proved effective and they decided to let him go. Mithqal himself brought him his horse and rode with the others to escort him back to Amman. Evidently, Mithqal was compelled to make a public apology to Peake two months later. His biographer C. S. Jarvis claims that Peake bore no grudge.[71] Once more Mithqal had acted pragmatically and was careful not to put his power to the test against the British Empire. He walked a fine line between resistance and collaboration.

An Arab nationalist who served in the Transjordan administration in the early 1920s used this episode to illustrate the state of affairs in the country before the arrival of Sharif Abdullah. He recounted a version of this story told by a friend, who said that "the government of Umm al-'Amad is stronger than the one the French established in Syria." According to this version, Mithqal told Peake that he was independent of Amman.[72]

Mithqal confronted Peake in the context of the move towards Transjordan in November 1920 of Sharif Abdullah bin Hussein, whose political canvassing further undermined the façade of British influence in the country. By that time Mithqal was undoubtedly the strongest person in the Balqa', if not in Transjordan as a whole, a position from which he played a decisive role in shaping the future of the country.

3 THE DECADE
OF POWER AND GLORY

IN SEPTEMBER 1920, Sharif Abdullah bin Hussein, the second son of the Arab Revolt's leader, Sharif Hussein, left Mecca by camel, accompanied by a handful of his Hashemite relatives and several hundred armed tribesmen. Arriving in Medina, they boarded a train for Ma'an, a small dusty desert town on the northern edge of his father's kingdom of the Hijaz, bordering the British sphere of influence in Transjordan. Abdullah had been the principal architect of the alliance between his family and the British during World War I and was a very ambitious politician. Whilst his young brother Faysal commanded the forces of the Arab Revolt in Transjordan and Syria, Abdullah was in charge of fighting the Ottoman army in the Hijaz. He hoped to rule over an Arabian kingdom as part of the great Arab empire the family was trying to establish. But Abdullah had failed to oust the Ottoman troops in Medina even after a prolonged siege. Only after the announcement of a truce at the end of World War I did the Ottoman commander surrender, ceremoniously handing over his sword to Abdullah. To add insult to injury, Abdullah suffered another humiliating military defeat just a few months later, this time by the warriors of Ibn Saud, the Hashemites' rival for hegemony in Arabia, who would soon found Saudi Arabia. This defeat torpedoed Abdullah's ambitions in Arabia, and for a time he saw himself as the future leader of Iraq. But when rumors about the British decision to make Faysal king of Iraq reached Mecca, jealousy, frustration and ambition made him turn his eyes to Syria.[1]

Abdullah's plan was to raise an army of volunteers among the tribes of

Syria and Transjordan to attack the French troops stationed there. His goal was not necessarily military victory. Even if that force could not have defeated the French army, it must have helped exert pressure on Britain and France to restore Hashemite rule in Syria and certainly bring him back to the center of political activity. After a rough and long train journey, Abdullah arrived in Ma'an in November. During the following three and a half months, he busied himself rallying support among local leaders.

Mithqal was one of the first shaykhs to show support for Abdullah. At the time, he was deeply involved in the power struggle with the British officers in the Balqa'. Now, Mithqal accepted invitation to come to Ma'an, where he met Sharif Abdullah bin Hussein and urged him to come to Amman and establish his rule there. During that first meeting, the two men sowed the seeds of a political alliance and friendship that would last their lifetimes. This alliance formed in the early 1920s was crucial to the process that would lead to the creation of modern Jordan nearly thirty years later.

THE MAKING OF AN ALLIANCE

After meeting Abdullah in Ma'an, Mithqal returned to Amman to organize support for him. The joint leadership of Mithqal and the mayor of Amman, his father-in-law Sa'id Khayr, turned the town into the focal point of Hashemite agitation east of the river Jordan. Abdullah was also in touch with Mashhur, the official shaykh of shaykhs of the Bani Sakhr, but it was Mithqal who played the leading role. When Abdullah was hesitant about moving north, Mithqal and Khayr reportedly persuaded him to send his relative and confidant Sharif 'Ali bin Hussein al-Harithi to organize support in Amman, Salt, and their surroundings. It was the mayor himself who drove the train that brought al-Harithi to Transjordan. The sharif's first stop was Jiza, where he was greeted by Mithqal and the other shaykhs of the Bani Sakhr and the Balqa' in a public demonstration of power and support. A thousand riders greeted him off the platform to escort him to Amman. There, al-Harithi established himself as the main agitator of the pro-Hashemite movement.[2]

On the face of it, Mithqal's decision to support Abdullah was the most obvious choice. Abdullah was a Hashemite sharif, a direct descendant of the Prophet Muhammad and the son of the keeper of the holy cities. This is how Mithqal's son, 'Akif al-Fayiz, explained his father's decision when asked in an interview in 1998.[3] Although his family background undoubtedly strengthened Abdullah's appeal to the Muslim public, this pedigree alone cannot sufficiently explain Mithqal's strategy; the son's explanation in fact reflects contemporary Jordanian hegemonic discourse in its emphasis on the royal family's religious and dynastic right to rule.[4] More likely, Mithqal allied himself with Abdullah to prevent a British or French takeover of the country. In Abdullah he found a patron who could serve his interests better than a European colonial power. Abdullah was savvy in tribal politics, yet lacked the military backing of an independent army and the financial means to sustain his rule. Therefore, he was dependent on the support of the strong nomadic tribes in the region. An alliance with him had the potential to strengthen Mithqal's position within the Bani Sakhr confederacy, as well as to allow him and his tribes a vast degree of autonomy—exactly what Mithqal was seeking.

With their support for Abdullah, Mithqal, Khayr, and al-Harithi enfeebled the already weak political position of the British, further undermining their minimal control in Transjordan. A demonstration they organized in early December prompted the British officer Captain Brunton to withdraw from Amman with his troops. A few days later, Mithqal and Khayr tried, albeit unsuccessfully, to frighten away the new commander of the gendarmerie who had been sent from Salt. Herbert Samuel, British high commissioner for Palestine, reported that Mithqal "swore he would bring 200 horsemen and clear him and his gendarmes out of the place."[5] The confrontational policy that Mithqal had pursued towards the British since the arrival of al-Harithi reached its apex with Lieutenant Colonel Peake's arrest in the stables.[6]

The worried British persuaded Abdullah to restrain his supporters with the help of his brother, Sharif Faysal. Abdullah promised not to confront the British officers lest he jeopardize Faysal's diplomatic efforts in Europe to save Arab independence. He gave orders to that effect to al-Harithi and invited Mithqal to see him again.[7] In a letter to the British, Abdullah blamed al-Harithi "for allowing Mithgal to behave as he did," probably referring to Peake's imprisonment.[8]

But the standoff on the ground was short-lived. In the second half of January 1921 anti-British and pro-Hashemite activity in Amman and beyond resumed in preparation for Abdullah's arrival. Khayr, with the support of the Bani Sakhr, worked to separate Amman from Salt—in other words from the British sphere of influence—and bring it under Abdullah's leadership. The mayor also sent Abdullah a letter, signed by the Bani Sakhr and other tribal shaykhs, endorsing Abdullah as a ruler. To encourage Abdullah to come to Amman, Mithqal declared that he would protect him.[9]

At the beginning of February, al-Harithi decided to raise the stakes. His spectacular entrance into Salt boldly challenged the British arrangement. Not only was he accompanied by hundreds of tribesmen on horseback and welcomed in celebration by the townspeople, but the gendarmerie and even the Reserve Force the British had established and paid for came with him, signaling whose authority they ultimately obeyed. High Commissioner Samuel's report that al-Harithi's presence in town "still further impaired the authority of the local Government,"[10] was something of an understatement: now tribes in the Salt area had stopped paying taxes, and in Karak the British-appointed governor, Shaykh Rufayfan al-Majali, finding himself in a difficult position, eventually left the town for Jerusalem. By now, the British officers had entirely lost their influence over the local leaders, and reports from Jerusalem warned London about the increasingly difficult situation and urged the employment of military force. Reportedly, Samuel even feared for the lives of his political officers.[11]

The Cairo Conference in March 1921 to which the new British colonial secretary, Winston Churchill, summoned senior officials in the Middle East to coordinate regional policy was an opportunity to reach a settlement in Transjordan. But just before it began, Abdullah decided to take a gamble by challenging the British and moving north.

Abdullah's entrance on March 2 into Amman, where he was overwhelmingly supported by the local population, was the final nail in the coffin of the British–supported local governments. On his way to Amman, Abdullah received pledges of loyalty from the shaykhs of Karak and the nearby town Tafila. The next stop was Jiza, where the Bani Sakhr and other tribes welcomed him with full pomp and ceremony. After spending the night, probably as a guest of Mithqal and the other Bani Sakhr shaykhs, Abdullah proceeded to Amman, where the town's inhabitants and delegates who had converged on the city from all parts of the country greeted him with enthusiasm. Even the northern 'Ajlun region—hitherto not much affected by Hashemite influence—swayed towards the sharif and the British officer there failed to prevent a deputation of shaykhs from going to Amman to greet Abdullah.[12]

With the facts on the ground in Transjordan changing, the delegates to the Cairo conference were thus faced with something of a fait accompli. Initially, the Palestine government had come up with a proposal to occupy the territory, to which end a military plan had been prepared. One of its working assumptions was that British troops would not meet much opposition. Abdullah's advance to Amman and his strong local support changed the situation and rendered this original design effectively null and void. Churchill favored reaching an understanding with Abdullah rather than confronting him. The conference adjourned without reaching a conclusive decision regarding Transjordan. Churchill set out for Jerusalem to meet Abdullah and sent his advisor, T. E. Lawrence, to fetch Abdullah from Amman. He hoped to arrive at an amicable solution, and that Abdullah would consent to leave the country voluntarily, making way for direct British administration.[13]

The fate of the territory was determined in Jerusalem in a series of meetings between the two men. Churchill gradually revised his position down after failing to convince Abdullah to leave the territory. The two men came to an agreement that the territory would remain part of Mandatory Palestine and that British government would support Abdullah's administration financially and militarily for a trial period of six months. Abdullah was also to receive a monthly personal subsidy of £5,000 and be assigned a British advisor. Churchill's policy at this time was limited in its objectives. He hoped that with British assistance Abdullah would keep Transjordan quiet, thus securing Palestine and preventing anti-French activity on the Syrian border, which could have embarrassed the British government. By supporting Abdullah, Churchill also wanted to maintain and strengthen what was known as the "Sharifian policy," namely, the choice of the Hashemite family as Britain's main ally in the Fertile Crescent.[14] Abdullah too had to scale back his ambitions. The agreement was far cry from his grand design to rule over a significant political entity, Syria, Iraq, or at least Palestine, east and west of the Jordan River. But he thought of Transjordan as a springboard after he was led to believe—perhaps even lulled into believing—by Churchill, that if he kept the country calm and prevented anti-French activity, he might be invited by the French to rule over Syria. Churchill's decision and Abdullah's consent set into motion the independent development of the emirate of Transjordan under Hashemite rule.

Jordan's creation is commonly viewed as little more than a strategy to serve British interests.[15] This is incorrect. Rather, the new territory emerged as a separate, and later, independent political entity as a result of both British imperial interests and the actions taken by Abdullah in conjunction with important segments of local society. Many shaykhs opposed the first British attempt to rule the country via local governments and lent their support to Abdullah. Mithqal's role in Abdullah's assumption of power was central, but it did not end there; he also helped Abdullah to consolidate his rule.

After his meetings with Churchill in Jerusalem, Abdullah returned to Amman to organize his new domain. The newly appointed ruler, now commonly known as emir (prince), dissolved the local governments formed by the British, instead establishing three administrative provinces and appointing a central government. The new state had a population of around 200,000.[16] But his jurisdiction was shaky, and government control was limited to the settled and the cultivated zone west of the Hijaz railway. The Reserve Force that Brunton had founded and Peake commanded was still nascent and dysfunctional. The sole organized, effective military force available was a Hijazi household army of no more than two hundred men under Hashemite command, the remains of the original tribal force that had come with Abdullah. This was no match for the strong nomadic confederacies. The British paid most of the government's expenses, helped to build the new administration, and sent military support from Palestine upon request. They maintained a watchful position, but hardly intervened.

The initial hands-off approach the British took during the first years after the establishment of this new polity allowed Abdullah to run the territory more like an extension of the tribal coalition of the Arab Revolt than a modern state. The weakness of his government made this strategy an imperative. Abdullah left the daily administration to his ministers and immersed himself in tribal politics. He kept busy securing support for his rule by forging personal alliances with the tribal shaykhs, on whose goodwill he was dependent. He therefore removed the nomads from government authority, allowed them extensive autonomy and gave them preferential treatment, often at the expense of the settled and semi-settled populations. Tribal affairs were governed either personally by him or by the Department of Tribal Administration headed by his cousin and confidant Emir Shakir bin Zayd.[17]

One of the first decisions concerning tribal affairs that Abdullah was to take had considerable implication for Mithqal's career. Abdullah recognized Mithqal as the new shaykh of shaykhs of the Bani Sakhr. This promotion came immediately after the death of the incumbent Mashhur in intertribal fighting and was apparently a natural and uncontested choice.[18] Finally, Mithqal's title matched his actual status. With this appointment, Mithqal attained the goal he had been striving to achieve for years.

As the leader of the most powerful tribal confederacy in the country, Mithqal was second only to Abdullah in his influence. Indeed, in some ways he was stronger than the emir himself. He was richer than the latter, owned large swaths of land, and commanded more armed men. Moreover, Amman, where Abdullah had established his government, was under Mithqal's influence. Although Mithqal was a clear asset to Abdullah, he thus also constituted a potential threat. Abdullah's edge on him was the political, military and financial backing of the British.

Mithqal's leverage vis-à-vis the emir and his government was established immediately after the creation of the emirate. He collaborated with other shaykhs and they quickly emerged as a formidable opposition to the government and to its attempts at centralization. Careful to maintain their tribal autonomy and preserve their personal influence, they resented men they regarded as "foreign Arabs" who had assumed positions of power in Abdullah's administration. The first government was composed of four Syrians, a Palestinian, and a man from the Hijaz. Only one of its members had been born in Transjordan and lived there. In particular, the shaykhs suspected that the Syrian exiles in the government compromised the interests of Transjordan to promote the independence of their homeland from France. As early as June 1921, several tribal leaders met in Amman to discuss ways in which to check the Syrian officials' influence and elected Mithqal as their spokesman. He went to Abdullah to demand that he restrain the prime minister and other members of his government. Mithqal went on to threaten that if the Syrians failed to "act more circumspectly and take a greater interest in improving the conditions in Trans-Jordan," the shaykhs would ask the emir to remove them from power, "failing which they will do that themselves."[19] A month later British Intelligence learned that Mithqal, Sa'id Khayr, and another shaykh were inciting tribesmen to take part in anti-French activity in Syria, "despite the known wishes of the Emir, to the contrary."[20]

Partly because of Mithqal's potential for undermining Abdullah's young regime and partly because of the support he could offer Abdullah, the latter made enormous efforts to satisfy Mithqal in the first two years after the establishment of the emirate. He showered him with many privileges, further increasing his wealth and influence.

Given his limited resources, the chief—and certainly the longest-lasting—gift that the emir had it in his power to bestow was land, and in 1922, Abdullah issued a special decree that allowed Mithqal to buy 10,000 dunam at Jiza for a modest symbolic price, payable in ten years. It was the same land that the Ottoman government had confiscated from the Fayiz shaykhs twenty years earlier for the construction of the Hijazi railway. An investigation by the Transjordanian government discovered several years later that the land was actually nearly 34,000 dunam, more than triple the nominal size of the grant, which meant that he had paid nothing for two-thirds of it. In addition to the land he had already owned in Umm al-'Amad and elsewhere, Mithqal's estate now amounted to 70,000 dunam (17,000 acres), making him the biggest landowner in the country.[21]

Land was Mithqal's main source of income, and he could not have exercised his shaykhly leadership and influence without it. He mainly cultivated wheat, barley, and lentils. Some of the wheat was consumed by his household, but most of it was sold to merchants. With proceeds, he could provide for the large, varied needs of his household, supporting his immediate family, maintaining his bodyguard, and entertaining his guests. The barley was used to feed the mares, and lentils were used for soup. Coffee, tea, sugar, dates, spices, clothes, mattresses, rugs, cushions, cooking utensils, medicines, weapons, ammunition, and other goods had to be purchased. Mithqal also distributed parcels of land to other shaykhs and to some of his men as gifts or as dowries, cementing loyalty and political support.[22]

One day an unusual, extravagant gift arrived from Abdullah: a car and a chauffeur.[23] Since cars were both expensive and rare, this enhanced Mithqal's image as a man of influence. Moreover, it provided the quick, easy transportation that his political role required. To communicate, he also availed himself of the government telephone at Jiza. Mithqal not only used his car when traveling to Amman to meet Abdullah, but on occasion also to lead his men in raids.[24]

Abdullah's cultivation of Mithqal's loyalty entailed many political and economic privileges. The shaykh enjoyed free access to the emir, which he exploited to further his interests and those of his tribes. Abdullah only too happily acted on Mithqal's behalf in government affairs, often bypassing and overruling government orders. For one thing, Abdullah turned a blind eye to Mithqal's takeover of the fertile plot of land that he had coveted since 1909 and that Peake had tried to retrieve from him before his arrest in 1920. With the establishment of the emirate, the deprived owners approached Abdullah and asked him to intervene. They produced the title deeds and satisfied Abdullah that the land belonged to them. But Mithqal persuaded Abdullah to delay his decision before finally referring the matter to the courts. In the meantime, Mithqal kept the land and farmed it profitably for several more years.[25] Once again, Mithqal did not miss an opportunity to enrich himself at the expense of others.

Another reason why Mithqal remained rich, and became richer, was because he didn't have to pay out much in taxes. Abdullah ordered the revenue for Mithqal's village of Umm al-'Amad to be fixed at the trifling sum of £10. In comparison, a neighboring farm had been assessed at £120 on its barley produce alone, not including the wheat yield, which had yet to be valued.[26] Taxes on Mithqal's and his confederacy's camels were also reduced, or they were even exempted altogether. On one occasion, Abdullah deliberately delayed the dispatch of tax collectors to the encampment of the Bani Sakhr, allowing them to migrate eastwards deep in the desert and avoid payment.[27]

The close relations between Abdullah and Mithqal had an important symbolic dimension. Abdullah was careful to lavish public expressions of respect on Mithqal. Only a few days after the establishment of his first administration, Abdullah, accompanied by the chief British representative and Emir Shakir, traveled from Amman to Jiza to spend two days with Mithqal. Every now and then, Abdullah would visit Mithqal's house in Umm al-'Amad or join him in his desert camp. Exchange of visits and hospitality was a way to display political alliance in a tribal society. Abdullah's visits advertised their closeness, and this served Mithqal well, enhancing his reputation among his own tribe and confederacy, as well as throughout Transjordan and even beyond. Mithqal was also a regular guest at Abdullah's summer camp—and later in his Raghdan palace—in Amman and his winter camp in the Jordan valley. Reports from the end of the decade indicate that at times he visited the palace on a daily basis. He clearly enjoyed unfettered access to Abdullah.[28]

A great privilege came Mithqal's way when he joined Abdullah in August 1923 during the royal visit of Faysal, by then king of Iraq. Mithqal had known Faysal well since the time of the Arab government in Syria and invited the new king to spend the last day of his visit as his guest in Umm al-'Amad, since he was scheduled to fly back from nearby Jiza. A great feast was prepared for lunch. When Faysal's pilot fell ill, the king postponed his return, staying the night at Mithqal's camp and dining in his big tent. A few months later, when Abdullah's father, King Hussein, visited Transjordan, Mithqal was among the emir's party that arrived at Aqaba to greet the king. In the summer of 1924, Mithqal joined Abdullah in performing the Hajj in Mecca.[29]

Mithqal's unique status in the emirate and his influential position with Abdullah was well known outside Transjordan. In 1922, Nuri al-Sha'lan, the leader of the Ruwala tribes who were threatened by Ibn Saud and his Wahhabiyya religious movement, sent letters to both Mithqal and Abdullah asking their permission to move within the borders of Transjordan.[30] In 1925, Abdullah denied a report, which appeared in several newspapers, that he had delegated Mithqal to represent him at the opening ceremony of the Hebrew University in Jerusalem, one of the earliest and most prominent Zionist flag projects in Palestine. It is not known whether Mithqal did participate in the ceremony, but it is clear that he was publicly associated with Abdullah. It is interesting to note that Mithqal is referred to by Abdullah in the official denial as "His Grace," a title reserved for royalty.[31] Mithqal was not a member of the royal family, but he was certainly the shaykh who enjoyed the closest relationship with Abdullah during the first decade of the emirate and benefitted from his largess more than anyone else.

ABDULLAH'S LIEUTENANT GENERAL

Mithqal's strong position within the emirate and the efforts Abdullah made to cultivate his friendship were a result, to a large extent, of the inability of the small military to handle external threats on its own. The biggest challenge came from the Ikhwan, a strong cross-tribal force that helped Ibn Saud expand his rule in Arabia. The Ikhwan refused to accept the international borders, which were starting to get into shape after World War I, and forcibly converted the nomadic tribes to Wahhabi Islamic doctrine.[32] The Arabian nomads practiced Islam in quite a relaxed way, very different from established orthodox religion that was practiced mainly in the cities. Islamic clergy often suspected nomads of not being true believers. The Wahhabi threat therefore led to a convergence of interests between the nomadic tribes in Transjordan and the central government in Amman. The tribes feared the new stricter ideology, which demanded a change in their way of life, whereas the government needed to protect its sovereignty against invaders. The location of the Bani Sakhr just outside the capital Amman and on the route of the Ikhwani advance made their cooperation of utmost strategic importance.

It was Mithqal who sounded the early warning on the Wahhabi threat. In early 1922, he informed the British representative, Harry St John Philby, of the Wahhabi advance into Wadi Sirhan, the Bani Sakhr winter grazing grounds, which would serve as a convenient base for attacks on Transjordan (see map 2, p. 10). He then accompanied Philby's expeditions to investigate the situation on the ground. Mithqal did so at the request of Abdullah, who entertained hopes of incorporating that territory and the strong Ruwala confederacy into his rule. Mithqal and Haditha al-Khuraysha, the other senior shaykh of the Bani Sakhr, accompanied Philby to the northern end of the Wadi, but refused to proceed out of fear of Ibn Saud. Determined to complete his mission, Philby arrived at the oasis of Jawf, where he got clear proof of the Wahhabi advance into northern Arabia, confirming Mithqal's information.[33]

Their fears materialized in August when a large Ikhwani force raided two Bani Sakhr villages only twelve miles south of Amman. In a two-day battle, the Bani Sakhr warriors defeated the raiders. It was claimed that the Ikhwan lost three hundred warriors whereas the Bani Sakhr's deaths amounted to forty-five men and women, among them Mithqal's cousin. To show his support, Abdullah hurried to the scene of the battle and pitched his temporary camp among the tribespeople.[34]

Mithqal led his men in the battle and earned fame for his performance. In his published memoirs, a former official of the government praised the bravery of Mithqal and other leaders, as well as the warriors. A verse from a poem composed by an Egyptian poet to commemorate the battle reads: "Long live the men of Mithqal [lit. weight], they weighed heavily."[35] One surviving oral poem credits Mithqal with leading the tribesmen. Perhaps referring mockingly to the British planes that joined the battle only towards its end, one verse reads: "Mithqal is like the chief of the air force, swooping down; Riding at the head of ninety-nine well-trained mounts."[36] Reportedly, Mithqal nearly lost his life in the battle and was saved by his slave, who shielded him from a sword blow.[37]

Following the raid, discussions between Abdullah, Philby, Mithqal, Haditha, and Mayor Sa'id Khayr led to the idea of creating a tribal force of five thousand men to join the Reserve Force in capturing the strategic oasis of Jawf so as to deter the Wahhabis. At first, Abdullah informed Philby that he had received enthusiastic responses from the main tribal groups of the area. According to a later and more realistic estimate, a thousand volunteers were expected. But when Abdullah's "grand Army" (as Peake somewhat snidely referred to it) finally went out to meet the enemy, the only tribal contribution was from the Bani Sakhr under the leadership of Mithqal, Haditha, and several other shaykhs. Even this limited contingent quickly disintegrated after the government issued all rations in advance, with the result that the nomads went home to share them with their families.

The outcome of the mobilization campaign was a force of twenty men under Mithqal. Peake explained that Mithqal, "being more noble-minded, marched with us the whole way."[38] London wanted open conflict with Ibn Saud to be avoided, so the operation was limited to the oasis of Kaf at the northwestern entrance of Wadi Sirhan, where Peake established a permanent garrison. The return from this expedition must have been a memorable day for Mithqal; for the first time in his life, he flew in an airplane.[39]

Planning a tribal army went on for another year with Mithqal playing a major role. In July 1923, Abdullah and Mithqal organized a military demonstration against the Wahhabis. Once again, the beginning of the operation was promising: large contingents of tribesmen under Emir Shakir arrived at Kaf, where no Wahhabi presence could be found. After a short stay and once the financial resources needed to maintain them dwindled, "the Amir's Bedouin Army had . . . vanished into thin air," Philby reported in frustration.[40] A military post in Kaf, bolstered by a hundred Huwaytat tribesmen, who would later be rotated with Bani Sakhr warriors, was the only practical result of Abdullah's attempts to prevent the Wahhabi advance towards his country.[41]

These half-successful military initiatives highlight the gap between the promises shaykhs made to government officials and the extent to which they went on to fulfil them. In the case of Mithqal, but probably in others as well, it was not the lack of goodwill on the part of the shaykh that led to the failure to mobilize his tribesmen, but the problematic nature of authority in a tribal society. Shaykhs could try and persuade their tribesmen to join them, and they could set an example by leading the operation themselves, as Mithqal did—but they could not force anybody to join. This explains why Mithqal could muster only a few dozen men and on rare occasions a few hundred. Many governments—the Ottoman, British, French, Hijazi, Transjordanian, and Syrian—failed time and again to understand this dynamic and relied too heavily on tribal support. By the same token, governments overestimated the potential threat tribes posed to them.

With the failure of the military plans, Transjordan was hit once again in August 1924 when a massive force of three to four thousand Ikhwani cameleers raided several villages of the Bani Sakhr and others in the Balqa'. This time, RAF planes and British armored cars defeated the invaders. Before the arrival of British support, the Bani Sakhr and other tribes engaged the Ikhwan. About 130 Transjordanians, mostly sharecroppers in the Bani Sakhr villages, were killed or wounded, whereas the raiders suffered as many as 500 casualties. Mithqal did not take part in the battle, which coincided with his pilgrimage to Mecca with Abdullah.[42]

The Ikhwani security threat elevated Mithqal's position within the emirate much above those of other tribal leaders. Because the Bani Sakhr were the prime target of the Ikhwan and dominated the area surrounding Amman, and because the emirate's armed forces were so weak, the confederacy constituted the country's de facto army during the early 1920s. In the summer of 1923, Abdullah conferred the rank of lieutenant general on Mithqal.[43] Philby's deputy noted: "Against the Wahhabi menace therefore the Amir has had resource [sic] to a species of feudalism and the Bani Sakhr is under fealty an armed force of the Amir sworn to resist Wahhabi incursions in return for which their taxes have been remitted . . . and the lands of Ziza village have been given as 'fief' to Shaikh Mithqal."[44]

Abdullah's reliance on Mithqal and the Bani Sakhr and the preferential treatment they enjoyed came at the expense of the Balqa' tribal alliance of semi-settled tribes. Since the establishment of the emirate, they lived under the tight grip of the government, which curtailed their autonomy. They also paid high taxes, perhaps to compensate for the exemptions of the Bani Sakhr and other nomadic tribes. These developments compromised the position of their leader, Shaykh Sultan al-'Adwan. Consequently, a local dispute over water and grazing rights turned into an all-out revolt, one of the formative events in the history of Jordan.[45]

The Balqa' revolt was triggered in August 1923 after the 'Adwan and 'Ajarma tribes refused the camels of the Bani Sakhr access to a well within the Balqa' alliance's tribal domain. The incident soon turned into personal struggle between Mithqal and Sultan al-'Adwan, whose position Mithqal was undermining, challenging his leadership in the Balqa'. Abdullah's intervention in an attempt to prevent a war between the opponents only made things worse. His decision to send a military force to Mithqal's village confirmed Sultan's suspicion that the emir sided with Mithqal. Rumors about Abdullah's decision to allow Mithqal to collect taxes from a village recognized as within Sultan's sphere of influence only inflamed the situation.

In an attempt to assert his leadership among his own people and put pressure on Abdullah, Sultan led hundreds of tribesmen on horseback to Abdullah's camp. His men surged through the center of Amman in a palpable and provocative demonstration of power. Shouting and shooting in the air, the demonstrators expressed their discontent with the regime and the way it treated them and the thousands more they represented. After hearing the shaykh's complaints and demands, Abdullah promised to pursue the matter further and to pay a visit to Sultan. But the emir had second thoughts about reconciling with Sultan. His cabinet advised him that a visit to the 'Adwan encampment would be interpreted as a sign of weakness. Abdullah was certainly also influenced by a counterdemonstration organized by the mayor of Amman, Sa'id Khayr, to protest against the 'Adwan's provocative move in the capital. In doing so, Khayr was acting on behalf of his son-in-law Mithqal.

Abdullah's failure to keep the appointment and the arrest and deportation of several educated native Transjordanians who were associated with the protest movement left Sultan without much choice, and the protest turned into an uprising against Abdullah. While Sultan rallied support in the Balqa', Abdullah was busy dissuading many of Sultan's natural allies from joining the rebellion and mobilized his loyal tribes, first and foremost the Bani Sakhr. On September 15, Sultan led about three hundred horsemen and five hundred warriors on foot towards Amman. The next morning, the military, supported by two British armored cars, defeated them in a surprisingly short one-hour battle. The shaykh of the 'Ajarma and a handful of rebels were killed, and Sultan and his sons fled to Syria.

Mithqal came out of the revolt with his position even further strengthened. He had supported the winning side in the conflict, and the emir's need of the support of the Bani Sakhr to stay in power was proven once more. The rival confederacy of the Balqa' tribes all but disintegrated, and their leaders were either killed, arrested, or went into exile. Sultan al-'Adwan and his sons were pardoned a few months later and reassumed their leadership, but this position was considerably weakened and was dependent more than ever on Abdullah's goodwill. Mithqal's elevated position vis-à-vis Sultan was exhibited symbolically when in May 1924 he hosted a large gathering of shaykhs of the Balqa' during which a peace was concluded. The fact that the ceremony was conducted in his home in Umm al-'Amad, rather than in Sultan's, or at least in a neutral venue such as the emir's camp, clearly reflected the new hierarchy of power in the Balqa'.[46]

IN THE FACE OF ENHANCED COLONIAL INTERVENTION

In the immediate aftermath of the Balqa' revolt, Mithqal enjoyed the peak of his strength. But paradoxically, the revolt also contributed to a process that would ultimately limit his autonomy and put growing pressure on him and his people. The challenge to the regime, and especially the grievance of the settled population that provoked it, reinforced a new thinking among British officials as regards administrating Transjordan. Mounting criticism of Abdullah's rule culminated in an effective British takeover of the administration in the summer of 1924.

From that point on, Britain ruled Transjordan directly and with stricter limitations on Abdullah and his government's authority. The newly arrived

British representative Henry Cox assumed control of all government expenses and reformed the administration. This included the abolition of Sharif Shakir's Department of Tribal Administration. Peake gained complete authority over all armed forces, now merged into the Arab Legion. Efficient administration and effective military force allowed the government to assert its control over the settled zone. With this reform, Britain imposed on Transjordan its own vision of a centralized, modern, Western-style state that would strive to implement the rule of law, with a strong, economical central administration and a certain degree of accountability.

This change came at the expense of the nomads' hitherto extensive autonomy. By the mid-1920s, British administrators could boast a substantial improvement in security and control of the nomadic tribes when they roamed around the settled zone during the summer. Tax collection proceeded satisfactorily even among nomadic tribes like the Bani Sakhr.[47] The central administration could now better enforce the law and execute court decisions. Not even the shaykhs of the most prominent nomadic tribal families were immune from legal sanction.[48]

Mithqal felt the repercussions of the new arrangement immediately after it was put into force. In the autumn of 1924, a 250-strong force from the Arab Legion supported by armored cars arrived at his village, where certain fugitives had been enjoying the shaykh's protection. Mithqal had no choice but to hand over the men, although tribal customary law stipulated the protection even of strangers who sought refuge. Then, Cox reported, Mithqal "ate humble pie" in Peake's office. It was no coincidence that Mithqal was the first tribal leader to face such an aggressive step. The British authorities chose to advertise the change in the rules of the game by making an example of Mithqal, the cock of the walk. They were very happy with the result: the British representative concluded in a self-congratulatory manner that "the Beni Sakhr have been brought into line."[49] This statement turned out to be premature, however.

Already a few months later, Mithqal led his men in a series of raids on a military base, stealing gasoline then valued at over £200.[50] Mithqal's action was a bold defiance of the central authority even though the base was in Jiza, his own village. Government investigation managed to find evidence against him regarding only a small portion of the stolen property but that was enough to charge him in court. After many delays, the judge sentenced him to a year in prison.

But Mithqal would not serve his sentence. In late 1926, he fled to the Hijaz and from there negotiated a settlement with the government and Abdullah. He returned to Transjordan only after Abdullah granted him a pardon and changed his sentence to a fine of £90. Mithqal's strong position and the immunity he had enjoyed until that point emerge clearly from the report by the British Resident (the new title of the senior British representative in Transjordan). Cox was very pleased even with this commuted sentence, commenting on its impact among the country's elite: "The Central Government and officials in general are at least coming to realise that they are bound by the law just as much as the people, whilst the execution of the sentence against Mithqal Pasha el Faiz of the Beni Sakhr has been a lesson that influential men must also keep within the law."[51]

The legal case against Mithqal and its settlement mark the beginning of a change in his position within the emirate. The shaykh could no longer do whatever he wished and defy the government with impunity as he could at the beginning of the decade. But although he had had to flee the country and pay the fine, Mithqal still enjoyed Abdullah's protection and the central authority's forgiveness even for such a bold act of insubordination. He was too valuable to the emir and was probably perceived as too much of a threat, so the government preferred a settlement rather than a conflict with him and his people. It's no wonder that the British authorities once again sought to make the formidable Mithqal an example to the rest of the country's shaykhs and notables.

The British administrators did not satisfy themselves with increased control of the settled and cultivated area of the country but tried to tighten their grip in the desert following geopolitical changes in northern Arabia in the mid-1920s. In 1925, King Ibn Saud occupied Mecca and brought about the end of Sharif Hussein's kingdom of the Hijaz. The leader of the Arab Revolt would spend the rest of his life in exile in British-controlled Cyprus and was buried in 1931 on Temple Mount in Jerusalem. The British immediately incorporated the southern towns Ma'an and Aqaba, which had been ruled by Hussein, into Transjordan. The quick establishment of Transjordanian administration in these two localities provoked a territorial dispute between Abdullah and Ibn Saud, long-standing archrivals.

At the end of 1925 the British brokered the Hadda Agreement in order to settle the border disputes between Transjordan and Najd and the Hijaz, the territories that were united in 1932 to become the kingdom of Saudi Arabia. Abdullah emerged as more loser than winner, being forced to give up his claim to the entire Wadi Sirhan. This was a particularly difficult concession for the champion of the nomads, because the Bani Sakhr and other Transjordanian tribes used the Wadi as their winter grazing grounds. In return, Ibn Saud gave up his demand for a territorial link to Syria at the expense of the part of the Transjordanian desert bordering with Iraq (see map 3). According to the agreement, tribes continued to enjoy their traditional grazing, habitation, and ownership rights across the new borders, but their movements were to be controlled in order to limit cross-border raids. To that end, the two governments

MAP 3. The emirate of Transjordan

undertook to inflict "severe punishment" on the perpetrators and to hold the tribal shaykhs responsible for the acts of their men. A tribunal was supposed to bring about a restitution settlement for looted property.[52] The agreement thus transformed raids from internal tribal affairs into a question affecting international relations in the area and those of the British Empire.

In order to implement the agreement, the British government instructed the authorities in Jerusalem and Amman to pacify Transjordan's borders. Since the middle of 1926, the British had made vigorous efforts to stop raiding both internally and externally. The new high commissioner, Arthur Plumer, formed the Trans Jordan Frontier Force (TJFF) with the task of defending the eastern and southern borders of Transjordan against tribal raids. RAF planes and British armored cars penetrated the desert, demonstrated their power to the roaming tribes in their encampments, and conducted reconnaissance. Roads were built in the desert to facilitate the movement of mechanized troops.[53]

But the British soon discovered that despite all their efforts, Abdullah and the tribal shaykhs proved more effective in calming the desert. Since the signing of the Hadda agreement, Abdullah had restrained the tribes from raiding Najd, asking their shaykhs to wait for the conclusion of the negotiations on the disputed claims. He forbade raiding and organized a series of meetings with the shaykhs, to which Najdi representatives were invited, but did not bother to come. Abdullah's success in pacifying his tribes earned him the growing appreciation of the British, who concluded that nobody was better qualified to handle the tribes than he and his cousin Shakir.[54]

Mithqal, together with the shaykh of shaykhs of the Huwaytat, Hamad bin Jazi, played a leading role in Abdullah's successful attempts to prevent raiding. In May 1926, the emir brokered a historic peace agreement between the two main nomadic confederacies, which had been enemies for many years. The agreement not only provided a framework for stopping mutual raids, but included their commitment to stop raiding altogether. Abdullah managed to persuade all the leading shaykhs of the two confederacies to make peace, forget ancient claims, mutually restore the loot from recent raids, put their faith in the Hadda tribunal and cease raiding into Najd.[55] The two confederacies observed the peace almost fully, and by the end of the year the Transjordanian tribes had returned all the stolen animals involved in undisputed claims from Najd. This was quite an achievement for Abdullah and the shaykhs, since in such agreements debts were not usually paid in full. For a year and a half following the accord, relative peace prevailed in the southern desert, although Najdi tribes did not fulfill their part in the agreement to return the loot.[56] Mithqal's influence among the Bani Sakhr was crucial in keeping to the agreements and preventing raids within and across the borders of Transjordan. Paradoxically perhaps, the more ambitious British policy became regarding the desert areas of Transjordan and especially along the borders, the more necessary Mithqal's cooperation became.

Mithqal was also deeply involved in intensive activity across the northern border during the Druze revolt in Syria in 1925–27. Interventionist French colonial policy in the Hawran undermined local autonomy of this important minority group and threatened the privileges of its traditional leadership. In attempting to quell opposition to his policy, the French high commissioner invited several Druze leaders to Damascus to discuss their grievances but instead arrested them. This ploy provoked the Druze to rebel in July 1925, and their initial success and hesitant French response turned the revolt into a general uprising across the country. It lasted nearly two years before the French managed to brutally suppress it, after bombarding Damascus, causing heavy casualties and physical damage.[57] During this time, Mithqal offered considerable assistance to the rebels. In 1926, the Bani Sakhr and other tribes ceased raiding across the border lest they accidentally harm the rebels who were roaming the same territory. When the French gained the upper hand and forced the revolt's leader, Sultan al-Atrash, and his followers to flee to Transjordan, Mithqal and Shaykh Haditha al-Khuraysha offered them shelter and generous hospitality. A little later, the British pushed the Druze exiles deep into the desert to prevent their involvement in Syria. Now Mithqal and the Bani Sakhr served as their main means of communication to the outside world, as well as the providers of food and other necessities. One Druze exile sat permanently at Mithqal's camp, acting as the liaison for al-Atrash.[58] Mithqal supported the rebels out of sympathy and the customary duty to offer hospitality and protect fugitives, but not least out of political considerations. He probably coordinated his activities with Abdullah closely, likely asked to do so by the emir. Abdullah was interested in encouraging resistance to the French mandate, because he had not given up his dream of the throne of Syria. But Abdullah was limited in his ability to support the rebels directly because the British officials kept a close eye on him lest he jeopardize their strategic relations with France. Mithqal and Haditha were freer to assist the rebels, however, since they could easily evade surveillance.

Shortly afterwards, a tribal war broke out in the south. In February 1928, an Ikhwan force raided the Zaban tribe of the Bani Sakhr, behaving with exceptional cruelty. They killed the tribe's leader (who happened to be one of Mithqal's fathers-in-law), his son, and dozens more, while women were raped. This sort of warfare was considered unprecedented and unacceptable even in rough desert life; it led to a spate of tribal raids across the border, which lasted for the next four years.[59] Abdullah and Shakir made enormous efforts to restrain the Zaban and other tribes from retaliating, asking them to wait for a peaceful return of the stolen goods by Ibn Saud. On several occasions, Shakir succeeded in breaking up large concentrations of tribesmen who had been preparing for a retaliatory raid. When minor raids did occur, Abdullah secured a quick and full return of the looted animals.[60]

Whereas Abdullah made efforts to calm his tribes, Ibn Saud did not live up to his promise to return the loot. The Zaban became more and more restive, and the cycle of raids and counter-raids resumed towards the end of the year.[61] In May 1929, urged by the British and utilizing his influence among the shaykhs, Abdullah sent Mithqal and Hamad to join Shakir and a military force to break up a group of Zaban and Huwaytat warriors on their way to Najd to recover their losses and to take revenge.[62] Although this remains the sole evidence for Mithqal's participation in the efforts to restrain his tribes, it is likely that in his capacity as their shaykh of shaykhs and as a close ally of Abdullah, he took part in many more such attempts.

Mithqal's involvement in the attempts to pacify the desert and stabilize the borders came also in the form of several official appointments. He frequently filled the position reserved for a shaykh in the Tribal Control Board. Headed by Shakir, who was joined by the commander of the Arab Legion and an appointed shaykh, the board was a mechanism the British introduced in 1929 to prevent raids and to impose state-sanctioned legal authority in the desert. Mithqal was also a member of Tranjordanian delegations composed of shaykhs and government officials who negotiated peace with neighboring tribes and governments. Apart from the negotiation with the Najdis, he took part in a tribal conference in Iraq in 1927, in which the two parties concluded a deal under the auspices of their respective governments. Mithqal was also party to an agreement in the same vein between the government and tribes of Syria signed in 1928.[63]

Mithqal himself had a high opinion of the central role he performed in maintaining the peace in Transjordan. Ludwig Ferdinand Clauß, a guest of his in 1930, reports that when Mithqal was summoned urgently to Amman by the emir to attend discussions with a Najdi delegation one day, he apologized for having to leave and explained that he was "Abdullah's field marshal."[64] Although this was self-aggrandizing on his part, he did in fact contribute significantly to the emirate's security until the end of the decade. To a large degree, it was thanks to this military role that he continued to enjoy Abdullah's attention, protection, and support. His importance to both Abdullah and the British in the second half of the 1920s was as considerable, as it had been in the beginning of the decade.

But Mithqal could not rest on his laurels. Although he had labored successfully to create a prominent, secure position for himself in the young emirate of Transjordan, he was concerned by the growing ability and resolve of the government to curb tribal autonomy. He tried to prevent some governmental steps to intervene in his life and those of his fellow tribespeople or at least to reduce or delay their impact.

Mithqal's concern about the central authority's growing power prompted him to be very active in a circle of opposition leaders to the government. The Transjordanian opposition emerged in response to the signing of the Anglo-Transjordanian treaty of 1928, which fell short of the locals' expectation of independence, instead formalizing the emirate's severe subordination to and dependency on Britain. But the treaty also stipulated the establishment of an elected Legislative Council to serve as a parliament. This provided the local leaders with a new mechanism to express their criticisms of the government and to check its power. Membership in the Legislative Council entailed recognition, honor, and status. Council members pocketed handsome yearly salary of £200 and enjoyed full legal immunity during the three months of the year when the council was in session.[65]

Mithqal was elected to the first Legislative Council in 1929, representing the Bani Sakhr and the northern nomadic tribes. His election reflected both his unchallenged leadership of the Bani Sakhr and Abdullah's support of him. It was Abdullah's prerogative to appoint a committee of shaykhs to select a representative for each of the two seats reserved for the nomads. This and the fact that the selection took place at his palace gave him almost complete control over the outcome.[66]

Mithqal made the most of the new platform at his disposal, and although he owed his seat on the council to Abdullah, he was not a yes-man. When the Legislative Council convened in the summer of 1929 and was requested by the government to ratify the Anglo-Transjordanian treaty, Mithqal emerged as one of the main voices against it. The Jaffa-based *Filastin* daily newspaper reported that Mithqal snubbed all Abdullah's attempts to persuade him to support the treaty, going as far as threatening Abdullah, "should you fight me I will ride my camel and migrate to the desert."[67] The newspaper went on to report that Mithqal proudly left Abdullah's palace walking on foot rather than taking the emir's car that had brought him there in the first place. At the council meeting, he denounced both the treaty and the emir's alleged attempts to buy off members of the opposition.[68]

As the newspaper's reports indicate, Mithqal's vocal opposition to the treaty earned him a reputation as a national leader outside Transjordan. But for him, the sticking point was not national ideology but government intervention in tribal affairs and the threat it posed to the autonomy of the nomadic tribes. Preserving this autonomy was one of Mithqal's main missions in his capacity as shaykh of shaykhs. And there were also personal motives behind such unusual action. Occasional defiance of the government or even Abdullah proved to his fellow tribesmen that he could still take an independent and courageous stance that involved a risk, as was expected of a tribal leader of his stature. Opposition also sent a clear message that his loyalty and good behavior could not be taken for granted and served to warn the authorities not to mess with him.

The outbreak of the Western Wall disturbances in Palestine a couple of months later presented Mithqal with another opportunity to show his independence by opposing the British administration, the government, and once again Abdullah. A religious conflict over praying rights on the Temple Mount in Jerusalem triggered attacks by Arabs on Jewish neighborhoods and settlements throughout Palestine in the last week of August 1929. The scale of the violence—hundreds were killed and wounded on both sides—made the riots a watershed in Arab-Jewish relations.[69] Soon after the news from Jerusalem reached Amman, Mithqal mobilized his tribesmen to loot Jewish settlements, which seemed like easy prey in light of the instability in Palestine and the overextension of the British security forces. In doing so, Mithqal showed disregard for Abdullah, who was working hard to persuade the tribes to stay out of the fighting. Ultimately, Abdullah succeeded in keeping Transjordan quiet, and Mithqal's plan did not come to much. He crossed the Jordan River and was arrested in Jerusalem by the British military authorities, but was released and returned home.[70] Obviously, the shaykh overestimated his power, or at least underestimated the power of the British mandate authorities even during a time of crisis.

Even if Mithqal failed to execute his plans, he certainly managed to create for himself and for his men the image of a powerful, perhaps destructive, force. Clauß was convinced that Mithqal and his men were the main impetus behind the 1929 riots, writing that Mithqal was a "great warrior who led his armed men across the river and plundered the cities in the Galilee in spite of the Mandate," and that, as a result, all Palestine "trembled with fear, including the weak English occupation forces."[71] By getting himself involved in the events in Palestine, Mithqal managed to sustain or even expand his reputation of being a leader of powerful tribes. Projecting this image of strength, he could reap many benefits: keeping the government at bay, attracting the attention of Abdullah and the British, increasing his legitimacy among the Bani Sakhr, and, overall, securing his privileged position and autonomy.

Mithqal's involvement in Palestine in 1929 allowed him to enjoy benefits across the river Jordan. Zionist observers, who feared for the safety of their settlements, viewed his potential to raise powerful tribal forces and cross the river with great concern. Palestinian leaders such as the Grand Mufti of Jerusalem, Hajj Amin al-Husseini, viewed that same potential differently, hoping to mobilize Mithqal and his men to support their cause.[72] These expectations inspired these two rival national movements to contact Mithqal in the course of the 1930s. His perceived might and the wish to quell it or to take advantage of it respectively account for his appeal to both Zionists and Palestinians.

The failed raid into Palestine was the last military initiative that Mithqal undertook. This was not so much a result of his age—he was approaching fifty at the time—but more of the changing realities in Transjordan and the region at large. Within a few years, state authority would expand into the desert, the nomadic tribes would come to live under stricter government control, and raids would cease altogether. The 1930s also witnessed a worldwide economic crisis. In dealing with these changes, Mithqal's role as the Bani Sakhr shaykh of shaykhs was dramatically transformed.

Mithqal al-Fayiz and King Abdullah I. Date unknown. Abdullah is seen in the center of the photo wearing a light-colored robe, and Mithqal is to his left, with what appears to be a cigarette in his mouth. The photo illustrates the closeness between these two men.

Mithqal and his camel, probably from the mid-1920s. Mithqal owned hundreds of camels, which were both an important source of wealth and a symbol of his power and honor as a nomadic shaykh. The camel in the picture also served him as a riding camel.

Mithqal and his eldest son Sultan in the late 1920s. Sultan was designated by his father to succeed him but died of illness in 1930 when he was around twenty years of age.

Shaykh Mithqal al-Fayiz photographed by John Glubb, commander of the Arab Legion, in March 1940. Mithqal had cordial but tense relations with Glubb Pasha, the British officer in control of the tribes. Source: Middle East Centre Archive, St Antony's College, Oxford, GB165-0118 Glubb Collection, Monthly Report Mar 1940, Photo no. 2, "Mithqal ibn Faiz, Sheikh of the Beni Sakhr."

Mithqal and King Hussein. Date unknown. The young king paid his respects to
Mithqal, just as his grandfather King Abdullah I had done before him.

Mithqal and his son 'Akif al-Fayiz around the mid-1960s. By that time the aging
shaykh had handed over most of his responsibilities to 'Akif, who became a prominent
politician.

Mithqal's grave in his village, Umm al-'Amad. Mithqal died in 1967. His son 'Akif built a mosque around his grave. Photo by the author.

Faysal al-Fayiz, Mithqal's grandson, then head of protocol at the royal palace, receiving an honorary title from King Abdullah II (right), Amman, 2000. On the left, the Royal Court chief, Fayiz al-Tarawna.

Diwan Mithqal al-Fayiz in Umm al-'Amad, the gathering hall of the Bani Sakhr tribes, which stands opposite Mithqal's dilapidated old palace. Photo by the author.

The *diwan* of Sami al-Fayiz, Mithqal's son and shaykh of shaykhs of the Bani Sakhr until his death in 2012, part of the shaykh's house in Jiza. Photo by the author.

4 BETWEEN TENT, CAMP, AND HOUSE

ONE DAY IN 1924, Mithqal was sitting in his large tent with his many guests when suddenly sounds of bustle reached him from outside. He came out of the tent and saw his trusted black slave Mansur accompanied by a foreign man of around forty years of age, close to Mithqal's own. Mithqal was expecting the guest and embraced him and kissed him on the forehead. It was a sign of welcome.[1]

This was William Seabrook, an American writer and traveler, who several weeks earlier left New York by boat on his way to Beirut, in order to visit the Middle East and write about his experience. In preparation for the journey, he began studying spoken Arabic while still in New York. Through a contact, he was introduced in Beirut to Emir Amin Arslan, a former Ottoman official who maintained good relations with the nomadic tribes of Arabia. He had known Mithqal for years and the two held each other in high regard. Arslan advised Seabrook to go to Mithqal in order to learn about the Bedouin. Seabrook heard "many fascinating things" about Mithqal from Arslan. He knew he was about to meet a wealthy and powerful man who was a close ally of Emir Abdullah.[2]

Seabrook stayed at Mithqal's camp for several months and enjoyed friendly relations with the shaykh. He sat next to Mithqal in the tent, accompanied him on visits to other shaykhs and even joined a raid deep in the desert. He held long discussions with the shaykh and his men. From Mithqal's camp Seabrook went on to study other Middle Eastern communities such as the Druze in Syria and the Yazidis of Iraq.

After returning to the United States in 1925, Seabrook published an account of his journey in a book, *Adventures in Arabia among the Bedouins, Druses, Whirling Dervishes and Yezidee Devil-Worshippers*. The better part of the book concerns Mithqal. In a style reminiscent of nineteenth-century travel writers, Seabrook portrayed a romantic, somewhat sentimental picture of Mithqal. He was impressed by his personality and charismatic leadership. He praised the generosity, kindness, wisdom, canniness and "great common sense" of Mithqal.[3] The shaykh had clearly made an impression on him.

Mithqal's fame and reputation attracted other Western travelers to visit him and reside in his camp for lengthy periods. Together with oral histories gathered from his family members and additional written sources, the accounts of these visitors offer a closer look into Mithqal's life and his worldview during the first decade after the establishment of the emirate of Transjordan, when he was at the peak of his career as the shaykh of shaykhs of the Bani Sakhr. Two men in particular produced detailed and perceptive descriptions of Mithqal that complement that of Seabrook. They allow a glimpse into the shaykh's daily routine, the structure and functioning of his camp and household, and even the relations within his immediate family.

In 1930, Ludwig Ferdinand Clauß, whose theories of "race" would become prominent under the Third Reich, arrived at Mithqal's house in Amman unannounced and without a recommendation, introducing himself somewhat bizarrely as the "shaykh of the German Bedouins."[4] Before arriving in Amman, Clauß had spent three years in Palestine working on his race research. During that time, he also converted to Islam. In Palestine, Clauß heard about Mithqal and formed an exaggerated idea of his role in the 1929 riots. He became Mithqal's guest for the next several months. His goal, as he stated in two books published after his return to Germany, was to live as a "Bedouin among the Bedouin."[5]

Clauß's initial admiration for Mithqal quickly evaporated. Unlike Seabrook, Clauß did not enjoy much time in Mithqal's company. The shaykh seems to have been annoyed by his guest's bold and demanding behavior and prevented him from observing his dealings. Still, Mithqal was obliged under strict rules of hospitality to bear with his guest. He left Clauß in one of his camps and saw him rarely. This long sojourn allowed Clauß to observe Mithqal's family. He also employed as his research assistant a German Jewish woman named Margarete Landé from Jerusalem whom he introduced as his wife. This trick provided him with good access to the day-to-day life of Mithqal's harem.

Shortly after Clauß left Mithqal's camp, Eliyahu (later Eilat) Epstein, a Zionist student at the Oriental Institute of the Hebrew University of Jerusalem, and later at the American University in Beirut, came to see him. Subsequently he became a diplomat, serving as the first Israeli ambassador to Washington. During his university studies, Epstein developed a special interest in the nomadic tribes of the Syrian Desert and became an expert on the subject. In February–March 1931, he spent five weeks as Mithqal's guest. The visit was organized through several Druze exiles who were in close touch with the shaykh following their revolt against the French in Syria. The shaykh dressed Epstein in Arab clothes and introduced him as a German guest. Epstein's visit was part of his own research but coincided with the Jewish Agency's growing interest in Transjordan's affairs and especially its tribes. Epstein's portrayal of Mithqal in a secret report he prepared for the Agency and in his published work is extremely positive. Of the many tribal leaders he met during the first half of the 1930s, Mithqal impressed him the most.[6]

BETWEEN DESERT AND TOWN

When Seabrook arrived in Amman, he looked for a way to contact Mithqal, who "might be anywhere within a circle of three hundred miles or more."[7] As was to be expected of a nomadic shaykh, Mithqal's life was characterized by high mobility. He seldom spent more than a few days in one place. In the mid-1920s he was mostly to be found at three locations—his mobile desert camp, his village of Umm al-'Amad, and a house in Amman.

The center of gravity of Mithqal's life was his camp and tent. The shaykh's personal camp consisted of 50–60 tents, with hundreds more tents of the Bani Sakhr clustered in groups of 40–50 tents within a radius of up to five miles. All in all, more than a thousand warriors resided in the area, ready to respond to a call from their leader.[8] Mithqal's own tent was set apart from the rest of the tribe and was much larger—"huge" the British representative said—at approximately 90 by 30 feet.[9]

The tent was decorated simply with colorful rugs, on which was laid a German-made mattress. This was covered with softer rugs, with camel saddles on both its sides for Mithqal and his guests to recline upon. Seabrook explained that for his arrival and on special occasions, "a wealth of luxurious carpets and tapestries had adorned the tent."[10] Clauß speaks of a magnificent huge carpet laid specially for a visit by Emir Abdullah.[11] Seabrook comments that, apart from this rare display of luxury, "our common daily life was of Spartan simplicity."[12]

The same simplicity characterized Mithqal's dress, which did not differ much from that of the other tribesmen and projected his status only through the finer quality of the garments. Mithqal wore a white headscarf and a long sleeved under-robe of fine muslin beneath a black camel-hair robe.[13] Fashion in the Syrian Desert had not changed much since the middle of the nineteenth century. Even today, similar attire sets shaykhs apart from other men across the Arab world.

Apart from the sheer size of the tent, the only items inside to indicate wealth and power were the coffee paraphernalia. These included five brass pots of graduated sizes, the largest of which could hold ten gallons. It was so big that it towered above a man sitting. Additional items were a heavy iron ladle for roasting the beans, an elaborately carved wooden mortar with a pestle, and a brass box of tiny cups.[14]

Apart from providing residence and defense, a major function of the camp was to cater to an important source of Mithqal's wealth and prestige—his herd of five hundred "superbly beautiful," pure white racing camels.[15] The herd went out to graze in the morning and returned to the shelter of the camp in the evening, accompanied only by an old man and a boy. Seabrook reports that Mithqal was "tremendously proud" of his camels. He had one favorite male camel, to which he showed great affection. When its name was called, this camel left the herd and came to Mithqal, nuzzling against his cheek, while the shaykh stroked the camel's neck and fed it bread.[16]

Once the camels had consumed all the grazing in the area, or when a looming threat in the form of an enemy raid or tax collectors presented itself, Mithqal led his people to a new location. The shaykh's duty was to guide his tribe towards good grazing grounds by the safest and quickest route. He took into account the information he gathered about rainfall and available grazing grounds, together with political considerations such as relations with tribes whose *dira* his people had to cross.[17] One desert explorer gave a vivid description of how in 1909 the shaykh of one of the tribes of the Bani Sakhr led his people while moving eastward to find pastures for their animals:

> It was a spectacular sight to see the whole tribe on the move. First went the camel herds driven by the lads and the asses, then followed the laden-beasts bearing the tents, the household goods, and small children. The harem walked, or rode perched high on the top of the loads, singing wild Bedouin songs, or gossiping with their neighbours. The men rode armed and on horseback, scouting far in advance, or at the rear, on the look-out for enemies . . .

> When the Sheikh found a suitable camping ground he lit a fire as a signal
> to the rest of the tribe, who were by now scattered far and wide over a large ex-
> panse of desert. The smoke of the fire showed them the position of their chief's
> tent, and they gathered around and pitched in groups . . . the black booths were
> raised, and each household started afresh its own domestic life, just as if it had
> never moved, nor was ever going to move again.[18]

Though Mithqal was constantly on the move, he maintained a permanent
residence at the village of Umm al-'Amad, about twenty miles south of the capital, where he owned a huge private estate (see map 4). In fact, he owned the
entire village, which he had inherited from his father. It was his main source
of income. Although he owned land in other nearby localities, Umm al-'Amad
was the most fertile of his properties and where most of his cultivated land was.
The farm also supported his huge herd of sheep.

During the mid-1920s, Mithqal kept his eldest wife and a retinue of slaves
at this complex.[19] His laborers were lodged in around a hundred stone houses
built around what was known as his palace, a large structure resembling a for-
tress or barracks. It was surrounded by a heavy wall with a courtyard connected
to a chamber that looked like a large guardroom, and it could host more than
a hundred men. A massive door led to Mithqal's reception hall. The stone floor
and walls were bare, but a slightly elevated platform at the far end was spread
with rugs and piled with cushions. Along the two lateral walls ran a long row of
seats, also covered with rugs. There were additional adjacent rooms.[20] Seabrook
was under the impression that Mithqal never actually lived in his palace and
rarely visited it, keeping it mainly to entertain official guests. In between these
receptions, the palace "seemed musty and unused."[21] Indeed, there was not
much sense in a nomadic shaykh staying in a stone house for long. Most probably, Mithqal used the house for storing grain, weapons, and other valuables.
Clauß echoed Seabrook and described Umm al-'Amad as a military stronghold.
He characterized it as a castle and made much of some imposing old German
machine guns in which Mithqal took pride.[22]

The palace in Umm al-'Amad served as a symbol of Mithqal's power within
the Transjordanian state: maintaining an independent military stronghold only
miles from the capital was an unequivocal political statement. This was both
for domestic consumption, to project Mithqal's position and affirm his superiority, and to impress his guests, particularly state officials.[23] In fact, these two
purposes could not have been separated, inasmuch as the visits of state officials

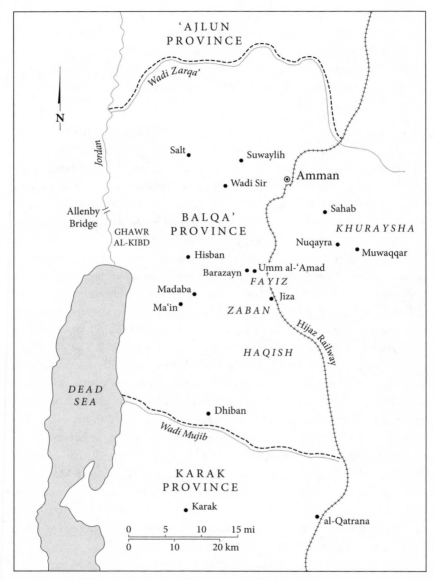

MAP 4. Balqa' Province and internal divisions of the Bani Sakhr

were an ideal opportunity for the shaykh to display his power and influence to his own people.

When Emir Abdullah came to visit Mithqal in Umm al-'Amad he was received with lavish ceremony. Mithqal guided Abdullah to the elevated platform "piled with gorgeous rugs and cushions"[24] in the center of the big hall, where the esteemed guest took a seat cross-legged with a bubble pipe at his side. Mithqal sat at his right hand to acknowledge his guest's seniority. A hundred members of the Bani Sakhr squatted in rows on the stone floor in front of the platform. Scores of other tribesmen gathered in the guardroom, anxious to enter but held back by trepidation. Gradually, new arrivals entered the room, approached the platform, dropped to one knee before the emir and kissed his hand before rising to rejoin the other men in the room. In addressing Mithqal, Abdullah was careful to demonstrate respect for the shaykh. Referring to him as "my cousin" indicated friendship, intimacy, and equality. Seabrook got the impression that the visit "had nothing to do with politics, big or little. It was merely for friendship's sake and private business affairs of their own."[25] It was probably true that friendship prevailed between these two allies, but politics constituted an important facet of their relationship. At minimum, both men made sure to put their friendship on display, since it served both their interests to do so.

Toward the end of the 1920s, Mithqal moved his center of activity from the desert to the town and his village and he rearranged his household accordingly. He pitched a permanent tent camp in Umm al-'Amad, where two of his wives lived and the sheep were tended. He handed over his huge tent as well as responsibility for the camels and the desert camp to his eldest son, Sultan, whom he was grooming for succession. This allowed him to spend more time in Amman rather than in the desert, though he rotated between the different camps and kept a watchful eye on their proceedings.[26]

Mithqal also purchased a house in Amman that served mainly as the home of his wife 'Adul, daughter of the mayor, Sa'id Khayr. It is plausible that in the first few years of their marriage around 1920, she stayed with her family. Perhaps it was only after she bore Mithqal a child or when his visits to town became more frequent that he purchased the house. Seabrook does not mention the wife or the house, possibly indicating how little time Mithqal spent there in the mid-1920s. But by 1930, Mithqal spent most of his time in the capital rather than in the desert.[27] His increasingly frequent visits resulted mainly from his growing contacts with state agencies, his membership in the Legislative Council after 1929 and his involvement in national politics. Similarly, the decline of raiding as an economic pursuit and the parallel emergence of his land as his main source of income necessitated his presence at the farm in Umm al-'Amad.

Despite these fundamental changes in his life, Mithqal remained highly mobile. Epstein wrote that while accompanying the shaykh he was "moving almost non-stop"; Mithqal spent most of his time visiting his tribesmen, who were scattered over a vast area from the Saudi border in the southeast up to the shore of the Dead Sea in the west.[28] He also inspected his farm and visited other shaykhs and tribes. He spent some of his time in Amman, either at his house, at the palace, or at the Legislative Council.[29] Epstein's evidence may be a reflection of the timing of his visit during the migration season, when the Bani Sakhr typically moved eastwards deep into the desert. Mithqal needed to move from one camp to another in order to maintain contacts with the different components of his confederacy.

The way Mithqal moved around in the desert was another sign of the changing times. In 1930, he still rode his mare on occasion, but to travel long distances, he had a car—perhaps the one Abdullah had given him in the early 1920s—and a driver.[30] In the course of the 1920s, cars gradually became commonplace in the desert. Both the military and powerful shaykhs used cars, which did not only signal prestige; the Ruwala kept six mounted with machine guns for purposes of raiding.[31]

THE HOUSEHOLD AND FAMILY LIFE

In order to perform his many duties as the paramount shaykh of the Bani Sakhr, Mithqal kept a large household. This was a complex and well-orchestrated organization consisting of the shaykh's wives, slaves, bodyguards, and immediate relatives. Every member had a well-defined role, all working together to aid Mithqal and ensure his success and that of the tribe and the confederacy at large.

The private part of Mithqal's tent, the harem, was the domain of the shaykh's wives, their female slaves, and young children. The women were responsible for the domestic affairs of the camp, particularly childcare and cooking. Accordingly, the harem had two parts—the living quarters and the cooking area. It was separated from the men's part of the tent, the *shigg*, by a curtain. On occasions such as when Emir Abdullah and his entourage came to visit Mithqal in the desert, the women moved to the cooking area in order to enlarge the public space. Two wives shared the tent harem, and this cohabitation was not always easy. Mithqal also had two other wives elsewhere.[32]

As was the custom with most important shaykhs, Mithqal married many wives during his long life, maintaining up to four wives at a time, as permitted by Islamic law. It is impossible to reconstruct Mithqal's married life precisely and to identify all his wives and offspring. As a matter of course, only the sons' names are recorded. When asked during a newspaper interview in 1994 how many wives his father had had, 'Akif al-Fayiz laughed, saying he could not remember the exact number but asserted with understatement that "it was not a small number."[33] More than fifty years previously, in 1941, the young 'Akif told a Jewish mechanic working for Mithqal that his father had married thirty-three wives. In a contemporary interview with Mithqal's sons and grandson, the number eighteen was suggested.[34]

Indeed, Mithqal married, divorced, and was widowed many times throughout his long life. Many of these marriages served political purposes, cementing alliances with important families. Others were motivated by love and affection. Some were concluded on a whim and did not last long. Mithqal's surviving sons recounted that one day their father accompanied Emir Abdullah to Ma'an by train, which broke down. Since he did not have a place to stay, Mithqal married a local girl, only to divorce her a few days later when the train was able to return.[35]

Several of Mithqal's marriages lasted longer and were much more meaningful, especially if the wife gave birth to a baby boy. Around the turn of the century, following his departure from the Ruwala camp, where he left his first wife after her failure to bear children, Mithqal married Shaha. She bore him first a daughter and then, around 1910, his eldest son, Sultan. From then on Mithqal was known as Abu Sultan, the father of Sultan. Shaha came from the Bakhit lineage of the Fayiz tribe. Mithqal needed to cement his relations within his own tribe first at the outset among the Bani Sakhr. Perhaps his reputation had not spread far enough for him to take a wife from outside the immediate tribe. Perhaps he took a liking to her. Clauß, who met Shaha in her son's camp in the desert, notes that when Mithqal arrived, he did not bother to greet her. Epstein tells a different story altogether, speaking of the great respect Mithqal had for his senior wife. He would converse with her at length and consult her. Epstein formed the impression that she enjoyed much influence in the family, and that the other wives respected her and were careful to honor her wishes.[36]

Mithqal and Shaha's eldest son, Sultan, did not live to succeed his father. When Clauß met him in 1930, he suffered from an unspecified illness, but refused to rest or to receive medical treatment apart from the first aid Clauß was able to offer him. A short time later, Sultan passed away, survived by his two wives, daughters of shaykhs from the Bani Sakhr. They bore him two boys, Hakim and Mamduh, and after his death they returned to their respective families. The boys remained with Mithqal and were raised and treated as if they were his own sons. Many years later one of the boys, Mamduh, related that Mithqal was devastated by Sultan's death. After the funeral, only Emir Abdullah could persuade him to leave the grave. Mithqal then sat in a tent next to the grave for the relatively long period of one week, accepting condolences. Mamduh goes as far as to say that when Sultan's mare died a while later, Mithqal insisted that it be buried in a grave like a human being, lest its flesh be eaten by the dogs.[37]

Following Sultan's death, Nayif, who may also have been Shaha's son, became Mithqal's "heir presumptive." But Nayif, too, died prematurely in 1934. He seems to have been forgotten by the family. In interviews, none of the family members mentions Nayif by name, nor does he appear in the family tree displayed in the guest room of Mithqal's grandson, Faysal al-Fayiz, in Amman.[38]

Sometime in the course of the 1920s, Mithqal took another wife from a neighboring tribe; she bore him a son, Nawwash. According to the family, Nawwash's mother was given to Mithqal as a present after he intervened with Abdullah to prevent her brothers' death sentences being carried out. As the story goes, Mithqal was invited to dinner, married the girl, and divorced her the next morning. One day when he arrived at the girl's tribe's camp, a man suddenly entered the tent with a baby, told the surprised Mithqal that this was his son, and handed it over. Mithqal put two gold sovereigns on the baby and left.[39] According to a version of that story from 1941, Mithqal divorced Nawwash's mother sometime during her pregnancy. Immediately after the birth, he took the baby from her, so that Nawwash never knew his mother.[40] When Nawwash grew up, Mithqal sent him to receive a modern education at a Quaker school in Lebanon, where he learned English. Mithqal molded him, he said, to become his "foreign minister." Later on, probably after Nayif's death, Nawwash became Mithqal's intended heir.[41]

'Akif, the first son of Mithqal and 'Adul Khayr, the Amman mayor's daughter, was about the same age as Nawwash. He was born no later than 1924, and possibly a few years earlier. He lived with his mother in Amman and received a formal primary education in the local schools.[42] The political importance of Mithqal's marriage to 'Adul is obvious, but it is also evident that Mithqal loved her dearly. Clauß opined that she was Mithqal's favorite wife and that he took any opportunity to visit her in Amman.[43] 'Adul bore Mithqal a larger number of boys than any of his other wives. Apart from 'Akif, she had four more boys: Zayd, Tayil, Talal, and Trad. 'Adul was Mithqal's wife for over forty years. According to his son's testimony, Mithqal was profoundly saddened by her death in 1962, saying: "Yesterday I was fifty years old, today I am hundred."[44] Mithqal also proved his devotion to 'Adul when he cut his hair for her. Tayil Mithqal al-Fayiz recounted that when his mother was introduced to Mithqal, she was intimidated by his fierce looks. It was the custom among nomads to grow their hair long and wear it in braids. 'Adul agreed to marry Mithqal provided he gave up his long braids. That he was willing to do so shows how he felt about her. Clauß reports that Mithqal was proud of his hair and would cuddle in his older sister's lap while she brushed it.[45]

When Clauß visited, Sat'a, the daughter of shaykh Hatmal al-Zaban, presided over Mithqal's harem. This was a political marriage and evidently a loveless one. The Zaban did not accept the precedence of the Fayiz among the Bani Sakhr, and in the nineteenth century they had refused to recognize the leadership of Mithqal's father, Sattam.[46] Instead, the Zaban often pursued an independent line of action, for example, supporting the Hashemites during the Arab Revolt. Mithqal hoped his marriage to Sat'a would help him exert greater influence over the Zaban. Clauß says that Sat'a "hated Mithqal from the beginning: she hates Mithqal as the enemy of her tribe, to whom she was given as a prize and a sign of reconciliation, and she hates him as her oppressor and tyrant."[47] Nevertheless, she gave birth to his son 'Ali around 1926, and in 1932, she bore him Sami. She was the senior wife in Mithqal's camp in Umm al-'Amad and was in charge of all domestic operations.

During Clauß's stay, there was a tense atmosphere in the harem. Sat'a and Tarfa, Mithqal's youngest and newest wife, quarreled constantly. Sat'a did all the work, and Tarfa did not lift a finger. To add insult to injury, she was Mithqal's favorite of the two, and both of them envied 'Adul. Mithqal loved Tarfa, Clauß says. The fact that Mithqal's elder sister supported Tarfa did not help matters either. The situation deteriorated to the point where Mithqal was forced to intervene.

One of the women's quarrels prompted Mithqal to discipline Sat'a. Raging with anger, he cursed her bitterly, pulled her by the hair, and beat her with his whip until she bled. He then drove her from the camp and back to her family. Clauß learned that Mithqal had already done this twice before, and without a reasonable pretext. Sat'a had inevitably been permitted to return each time, because nobody could run the camp as well as she did, and indeed she was back a few days later this time too.[48]

Whereas Sat'a enjoyed the help of women slaves, the day-to-day running of Mithqal's operation was entrusted largely to his black male slaves, who formed a personal guard charged with protecting him and carrying out his orders. According to Seabrook, Mithqal's camp included a personal guard numbering between thirty and forty. Writing later, Epstein puts their number at around a hundred men. If the two visitors' counts were accurate, the sharp increase in the guard might indicate that Mithqal felt less secure in 1931 than he had a few years earlier. Epstein explains that Mithqal was concerned with the challenge to his leadership posed by his nephew, Khalid bin Fawwaz, the brother of the previous shaykh of shaykhs, Mashhur. By now, Khalid had grown up, made a name for himself, and gained influence among the Bani Sakhr.[49]

So important were the slaves to Mithqal that the most senior of them, Mansur, was his right-hand man. Mansur could be found next to Mithqal at all times, assisting the shaykh in welcoming a guest or conducting a trial, or fighting next to him in battle. At other times, Mansur was sent as Mithqal's personal representative, such as when he came to fetch Seabrook from his hotel in Amman or when he was sent ahead to Umm al-'Amad to prepare the house for Emir Abdullah's visit.[50]

Thanks to his proximity to the shaykh, Mansur enjoyed high status in Mithqal's camp. Apart from status, he possessed wealth and even owned land, which Mithqal gave him as a reward for saving his life during the battle with the Wahhabis in 1922. Several years later, Clauß found another slave, Muhammad, in charge of Mithqal's camp in Umm al-'Amad while the shaykh was away. Other slaves were entrusted with mundane but necessary chores such as tending the herd or pitching the tent. One slave's sole task was to prepare the coffee.[51]

The importance and high status of slaves in a shaykh's camp was not unique to Mithqal or to the Bani Sakhr. Every shaykh in Arabia who could afford it employed slaves, who made trustworthy aides, bodyguards, or servants and often lived quite comfortably despite their inferior social status. In 1922, Shaykh Nuri al-Sha'lan of the Ruwala, probably the most powerful shaykh in Arabia during the first decades of the twentieth century, entrusted control of a strategic oasis to one of his senior slaves. Shaykh Nuri had two hundred slaves in his household.[52] The employment of slaves helped shaykhs to overcome the basic weakness of their leadership position, namely, their inability to enforce their will on their tribespeople. The slaves did not possess a genealogical connection to the tribe and owed their allegiance entirely to the individual shaykh who owned them and provided for them and for their families. In return, he could expect complete loyalty and obedience.

In this context, the term "slave," can be misleading, conjuring up images of people who endured miserable conditions of servitude in other parts of the world. In the Middle East many slaves, especially of light complexion, held a prominent status among the elite of Ottoman society. Black slaves owned by powerful shaykhs in Arabia enjoyed a similar status. They could have families of their own, though usually they married black women slaves, and they could also be manumitted.[53] As an official British document from 1924 notes: "The Shaykhly Families of the Bedouin Tribes [in Transjordan] maintain considerable numbers of slaves as personal attendants, who include among their duties that of acting as body-guard to their masters. The slaves are, more often than not, born into the service and are, as a rule, much better off than ordinary tribesmen."[54]

The tension between servitude and power that characterized many forms of slavery in the Middle East[55] was also manifested in Mithqal's camp. Despite his relative status and wealth, Mansur was clearly socially inferior to the tribesmen. When Mansur quarreled over a horse with his brother, who was another of Mithqal's slaves, and shot him, Mithqal beat both of them "most terribly," not even sparing the wounded brother. Only slaves, children, and wives could be beaten. Despite his anger, Mithqal later gave Mansur one of his own horses.[56]

Another invaluable functionary in the shaykh's household was his secretary. Like most tribal shaykhs, Mithqal was illiterate and needed someone to handle his correspondence. In the mid-1920s, Mithqal's secretary was one of his warriors who happened to be literate in Arabic as well as elementary French. Two to three times a month, Mithqal dictated a letter to the scribe and then affixed his seal to the paper as a signature. In later years, the volume of correspondence grew considerably, and Mithqal employed an educated Transjordanian as his secretary. Mithqal exchanged written correspondence in his dealings with state officials, local notables, and merchants, as well as other shaykhs.[57] He also learned to sign his name and stopped using the seal around the mid-1930s.[58]

THE DAILY LIFE OF
THE SHAYKH OF SHAYKHS

As the shaykh of shaykhs of the Bani Sakhr, Mithqal was a public figure. He performed many duties and rarely enjoyed much privacy. Whilst tradition dictated his duties, he managed to perform them with his personal touch. He was

also careful to use them to enhance his position. In fact, he was constantly exercising his leadership.

During the better part of the 1920s, Mithqal spent most of his time in his
large tent entertaining his guests. He sat in the company of dozens of his men
and occasional guests drinking endless cups of coffee, chatting, gossiping, or
smoking water pipes or cigarettes. Occasionally, Mithqal rode to visit the encampments of neighboring friends or vassal shaykhs, but more often they came
to visit him.[59] This was a clear sign of his status. A shaykh of his rank was expected to be hospitable, and most of the time, he was.

When Mithqal held court, he presided according to strict rules of etiquette
and formality dictated by clear hierarchies. When fresh coffee was made,
Mithqal was the first to be served. When members of the camp came in, they
simply touched hand to forehead, muttered a low greeting of *salam 'alaykum*
(peace upon you) and seated themselves. When a person of importance entered
or departed all rose and returned his greeting touching fingers to forehead. If
the guest was a friend and equal, Mithqal would embrace and kiss him, as he
did when he first saw Seabrook. People of humbler background dropped to one
knee in front of Mithqal and kissed his hand.[60]

Despite the elaborate etiquette of hospitality, Mithqal showed flexibility.
This was his prerogative. Seabrook was moved by Mithqal's concession to this
etiquette in order to show consideration for his foreign guest and accommodate
Western sensibilities. During their first meeting, Mithqal refused a cup of coffee and hinted to his slave Mansur to offer the first cup to his guest. Seabrook
comments that both master and slave were very pleased when he refused the
offer, insisting that Mithqal be served first, according to custom.[61]

A bolder example of Mithqal's ability to bend social and cultural rules at will
was his decision to allow Clauß to enter his harem. On the first day of Clauß's
visit, Mithqal invited him to glimpse his two wives. Grateful but nonplussed,
Clauß at first questioned Mithqal's motives. Later he realized the shaykh had
granted him this unique opportunity "just so, because he fancied doing it."[62]

Another important shaykhly duty was procreating. Shaykhs were expected
to produce many sons to secure the well-being of the family and tribe; the larger
the number of adult fighting men the tribal group could muster, the stronger
it was. Consequently, procreation was a public duty no less important than
hospitality, and a shaykh could suddenly interrupt his role as host to this end.
Seabrook records that one afternoon, when Mithqal and scores of people were
sitting in the tent as usual, the shaykh arose quietly, signaled to those present to

remain seated, stretched, and said nonchalantly, "I go to my wife." The others replied casually, "Praise be to Allah, and may power come to you." Mithqal was gone for about an hour, then reappeared at the tent and called for a kettle of water, soap, and a towel. After washing, he returned and quietly resumed his seat.[63] A shaykh's sexual life was a factor in the common good of the tribe and therefore not entirely a private, intimate matter.

Another anecdote about Mithqal's sex life also reveals its connection with the public domain. One evening, while Mithqal and his guests sat in the tent as usual, drinking coffee and chatting, they heard a disturbance behind the curtain and smelled perfume. Soon afterwards, the ceiling of the tent sank in. This was Tarfa's signal to Mithqal that she was ready for him—and a signal to the guests to leave. The men immediately vacated the tent, while one slave remained on guard.[64]

The most obvious sign of a shaykh's wealth and might was the food he offered in his tent. Seabrook reports that the food in Mithqal's tent was "wholesome, abundant, but without variety."[65] Three meals a day were served. A modest and unceremonious breakfast consisted of cinnamon tea and flatbread. Towards noon, Mithqal and his men ate dried dates and more of the same bread, and drank fermented camel milk. Dinner was a more elaborate affair. On his first night at Mithqal's camp, Seabrook enjoyed full hospitality as the guest of honor. A great brass platter (*mansaf*), five feet in diameter and six to eight inches deep, was carried in by five men. In it, the meat of two sheep (including their severed heads) lay atop a "mountain of rice" and gravy, with freshly baked flatbreads arranged around the rim of the platter. Mithqal then called by name five or six of the men sitting in the tent; they went outside, scrubbed their hands with sand (the equivalent of soap) and then washed them in water poured by a slave. Back in the tent, the men squatted around the dish and ate, while Mithqal selected pieces of liver and other choice cuts and served them to his guest. After they had finished and cleaned their hands in the sand, the rest of the men, divided into groups, had their share. After the men had had their fill, the leftovers were taken to the women's part of the tent. They had dinner this way every night, although Seabrook ceased to be treated as a special guest and was served like any other member of the household.[66]

Laying on this constant hospitality required abundant material resources. This was partly sustained by Mithqal's huge herds of sheep and camels, as well as his harvest. But since he did not produce rice, dates, coffee, tea, sugar, and spices, he had to buy or trade for these. Either way, this was a heavy financial burden. The annual cost of the coffee consumed in his desert camp was an astronomical £21.[67] This was just over 10 percent of his salary from the Legislative Council. Mithqal could afford to be so generous only because he was so rich.

Yet his hospitality was also about showing genuine concern for guests. At night, when it became chilly, it was the shaykh himself who brought his American guest a quilt. Later, after he went to sleep, Seabrook woke to find Mithqal checking on him, carefully pulling the quilt up around his shoulders. He commented that "it was the first time I had been 'tucked into bed' since my mother had done it when I was a little boy."[68]

Aside from providing hospitality, Mithqal was also on occasion called upon to lead his tribesmen in battle. He had been famous from early age as a fierce warrior, and he continued to engage in raiding during the 1920s. Seabrook claims to have taken part in one such raid.[69]

One night, Seabrook tells us, a tribesman unrelated to the Bani Sakhr rode a camel into the camp, shouting to indicate his arrival. He rushed into Mithqal's tent, dropped to one knee and kissed Mithqal's hand. He then warned Mithqal of the Sardiyya tribe's intent to launch a raid and seize Mithqal's herd of camels the following day while they were grazing outside the camp. Mithqal promised him a reward for this information and offered him food and drink.

Dispatching five horsemen to alert the Bani Sakhr's encampments and mobilize his tribesmen, Mithqal devised a plan. Despite the excitement, he remained calm and sat smoking his water pipe, taking the time to explain to the puzzled American what was going on. He could have simply kept the camels in the camp or sent them to pasture with a guard, he explained. Instead, with the benefit of early warning, he planned to set a trap and profit from it. The herd would go to pasture as usual, led only by an old man and a boy, but four hundred warriors would ambush the raiders, protect the camels, and capture the attackers' mares.

After a while, some eighty warriors arrived at the camp, whooping in excitement. The women of the camp chanted to encourage them. Dismounting, they gathered around the tent, where Mithqal addressed them and gave then his orders. Having received these, the riders then galloped away, shouting. This occurred several times in the next hour as new groups of men arrived to get their orders.

The operation began just before sunrise. The camels were led outside the camp as usual. Half an hour later, Mithqal set out with his slave Mansur, his personal guard of twenty men, and Seabrook to join one of the groups who had already set up the ambush. Most of the men held their scimitars in their right hands and a pistol in their left. During hand-to-hand combat, they controlled their horses using their knees and by shifting their bodyweight. The best fighters, who comprised about a third of the warriors, including Mithqal, carried swords. Mithqal made Seabrook promise to keep away from hand-to-hand fighting. He clearly wanted to protect his unskilled guest.

At dawn Mithqal, Mansur, and Seabrook dismounted, crawled to a ridge and looked down to the valley where the camels grazed. Through his binoculars, Mithqal spotted three Sardiyya scouts. He realized that most of the attackers were not taking the bait. The three scouts began to ride into the camels' grazing grounds. When they drew closer, Mithqal gave the order to start shooting. The scouts turned back and a hot pursuit began.

One of the attackers' horses was hit, and Mithqal took the rider prisoner. Still armed, the man, impudently but with good humor, tried to goad Mithqal, boasting that the Bani Sakhr would fail to catch the Sardiyya. Mithqal coolly returned his insults. He then gave him the choice of either remaining with the camel herdsman and the boy and returning with them to Mithqal's camp that night or going there escorted by one of his men in exchange for his rifle. He chose the first. Seabrook was astonished at Mithqal's trusting an enemy like this.

After this short exchange, Mithqal and his escort caught up with the rest of the warriors and continued the pursuit. They rode all day and most of the night but failed to find their rivals. Mithqal and his men became worried when they realized the trail was going east rather than north, towards the Sardiyya's *dira* in the Hawran. They stopped and Mithqal sent six men forward, watching them through binoculars. Half an hour later, two of the scouts came riding back, pursued by a band of thirty, who were firing at them.

For thirty men to attack four hundred could only be a trap, Mithqal realized. He shouted a command, and all four hundred sprang back into their saddles, returning fire as they retreated. "[C]lever fox that he was," Mithqal had "guessed the trick with uncanny accuracy," Seabrook observes.[70] The Sardyyia had led Mithqal's men eastward because the Ruwala were raiding there and they hoped to team up with them against the Bani Sakhr. The thirty men were in fact the Ruwala's advance guard, who had been sent as bait to engage the Bani Sakhr until the arrival of their main force. The Bani Sakhr lost three men before the Ruwala halted the pursuit. Thirty hours later they reached the safety of their camp back within the undemarcated borders of Transjordan.

Although Mithqal's plan did not work as he had hoped and not all the men returned safely, one does not get a sense that the raid was seen as a failure. Raiding was a way of life, as well as an exciting, if dangerous, sport. It allowed the men to display their courage and earn names for themselves. Seabrook himself remarks that raiding was not a war but a rough game, with camels as the prize and clear rules to prevent killing, although "lives were a part of the score."[71] Even if nothing had been gained, the fact that the Bani Sakhr managed to avoid the Sardiyya and Ruwala's trap was perhaps seen as a sufficient achievement. If this was the case, Mithqal could have been credited with skillful leadership.

Mithqal led another raid, this time in retaliation for the Ikhwan attack on the Bani Sakhr villages in 1924.[72] In an attempt to recoup the losses, Mithqal targeted not the perpetrators from Najd, but their relations who lived some five hundred miles away in Iraq. For five days and nights, Mithqal and his men rode their camels one hundred miles a day, avoiding the routes along the wells lest they be discovered. As they neared their destination, their guide led them on a longer route, delaying their arrival. Rather than attacking at dawn, they sprung their raid later in the morning after their enemies' camels were scattered over the pastures. The battle was fierce. Mithqal's party lost five men and killed the shaykh of the rival tribe. It was a victory for the Bani Sakhr, who succeeded in rounding up more than two thousand camels.

Mithqal was not, however, satisfied with this victory and the valuable booty obtained. He proceeded to lead the party into Syria to raid the Ruwala, who were also related to the Ikhwani attackers. First he had to convince the raiding band that he had a good plan. Hamad Salim, who participated in the raid, quoted Mithqal saying, "'Let us raid them pretending we are *Ikhwan*, not singing or shouting our usual war-cries but only the war-cry of the *Ikhwan*, which is *La Illaha ill' Allah*—there is no God but God.'" According to Salim "'the idea seemed good to us'" and on the dawn of the next day they launched their attack.[73] The trick was successful. Hearing the war cry and believing that they were under attack by the notoriously brutal Ikhwan, the Ruwala fled, leaving behind many of their camels. Now the Bani Sakhr party rode swiftly day and night back to their *dira* at the northern end of Wadi Sirhan. They arrived safely with three thousand new camels.

Salim went on to recount how the Ruwala had then allied with their Ikhwani rivals to attack the Bani Sakhr, who lost not only their loot but also their own camels. Salim further recounted that fifty of the Bani Sakhr were killed, including women and children. It seems that Salim was alluding to the Ikhwan attack on the Zaban branch of the Bani Sakhr in 1928. Perhaps events that took place in the course of three to four years were conflated in his memory into one raid.

Notwithstanding deficiencies in Salim's memory of events thirty years in the past, several conclusions can be drawn from his story. Mithqal was a skillful leader of raids who took risks, trying to press his advantage whenever the opportunity presented itself. Mithqal's success in raids was owing not only to his courage as a fighter, but also to his careful planning and ability to outwit his enemies. He was a natural leader, mobilizing his warriors behind him and pushing them to endure long, difficult expeditions. Ultimately, Mithqal led raids as he led the Bani Sakhr in other respects: by projecting charisma, setting an example, and reaching a consensus rather than giving orders. Indeed, shaykhly leadership was characterized by moral authority rather than the ability of the leader to impose his will on the other tribesmen.

These raids deep into Syria and Iraq were some of the last that Mithqal led. At the time of Clauß's visit, the practice of raiding was rapidly becoming defunct. From his first day on, Clauß pressed Mithqal to allow him to take part in a raid, apparently unaware that raiding was increasingly an object of nostalgia. One day, when they were on a journey in the desert, Mithqal told Clauß of his days as a leader of battles and showed him his scars. Clauß came away with the impression that the shaykh regarded these bygone days as the best of his life. Epstein likewise stresses how proud Mithqal was of his martial past, but by 1931, he writes, Mithqal preferred politics to the sword.[74]

A role that remained relevant throughout Mithqal's life was that of judge, a duty he performed countless times during his long career. Members of the Bani Sakhr as well as other tribes often asked him to act as judge or mediator. At other times, Emir Abdullah or other state officials enlisted his good offices in this respect.[75] Many sources mention the trials he judged, but Seabrook is the only witness who reports on one in detail.[76]

The case involved a family dispute between Mithqal's nephew, Jarid, a twenty-year-old shaykh with his own encampment of fifty warriors, and his wife Thirya. The couple had married two years earlier and had one child. Thirya was pregnant with another. She insisted that Jarid take a second wife, which he refused to do. They decided to refer their dispute to Mithqal. Although this was supposedly an intimate family affair, the hearing took place in public. Dozens of men sat in a circle in Mithqal's tent, while the women sat in their section of the tent, and dozens more gathered just outside it to listen to the proceedings. With such an audience, the trial presented another opportunity for Mithqal to play the role of the wise leader.

Mithqal's slave tapped three times on the sand with a camel stick and the hearing began. Mithqal turned to Jarid, who was sitting before him in the center of the circle, and asked him if he would present his case first. Jarid refused, explaining that he was content and had no complaint. Mithqal then turned to Thirya, who sat next to her husband, and asked if she would present her case for herself or request someone to speak on her behalf. She chose to speak for herself and explained that Jarid should marry again for three reasons. She did not want to bear the burden of having to produce all of Jarid's children, and thereby lose her figure and youth. A second wife would keep her company in the secluded and "stupid" life in the harem. Finally, it was undignified and unnatural for one wife to carry the responsibilities of running a shaykhly tent. In response to his wife's lengthy speech, Jarid replied briefly, proposing to take a second wife in due course but refusing to be rushed into it and criticizing his wife for nagging him.

Mithqal took a moment to ponder the case as he puffed his water pipe, and then delivered his judgment:

> Every man wants many sons, if it is the will of Allah, but it is not good for a sheikh's wife to bear burdens, like a camel, all her life. Yet a complaining and discontented wife is also a heavy burden, and if one wife fills the *hareem* with discordant quarrelling, how shall the husband wish to take another? Let Jarid and Thiriya return to their *beit-shaar* [tent made of goat hair] in peace, and let her reproaches cease. And at the end of Ramadan [the following spring], when we are returned again from the south, Jarid shall take a second wife. I have spoken.[77]

The slave tapped the stick three times and the trial was adjourned. Thirya returned to the harem "pretending she had triumphed, but really piqued."[78] The men resumed their chat and coffee drinking.

In keeping with tribal customary law, Mithqal's verdict was meant to restore the peace and mend social relations rather than deliver absolute justice. This necessitated a compromise, a commonsense solution, which both sides could live with. Mithqal's judgment combined the conventions and precedents of the law with societal norms and his own views. This allowed him much leeway in finding the best solution to the problem. Mithqal's decision reflected the superior position of the man over the woman, reaffirming it by ruling in favor of Jarid. The verdict also derived from his understanding of the relations between the sexes, and the role, status, and duties of a shaykh's wife. Mithqal himself married many women who shared the burden of bearing children, kept two wives in his camp, and as seen in the case of Sat'a, did not tolerate a discontented wife.

Mithqal also functioned in a religious capacity as shaykh. In this regard, Seabrook reports seeing him arise from the coffee circle in the tent one day at noon, take off his headscarf, and spread it on the sand in the shadow of the tent like a prayer rug. A black slave brought a bowl of water for him to rinse his mouth, nostrils, hands, and feet as prescribed by the Islamic code of ablution. Mithqal then performed the noon prayer. Meanwhile, the conversation in the tent continued uninterrupted. Seabrook explains that the shaykh customarily performed prayers on behalf of his people among the Bani Sakhr.[79]

Contrary to the pervasive perception of Arab nomads as lax in their observance,[80] Seabrook depicts Mithqal as possessing a strong, though quite moderate and accommodating belief. In the course of a discussion between the two men about Islam and Christianity Mithqal declared: "I believe myself to be a true Moslem; yet it seems to me that you and I worship the same God. It seems to me, therefore, that you must also be a Moslem in your heart, though you do not keep the observance, and have never made the pilgrimage to Mecca."[81] A little later Mithqal invited Seabrook to recite out loud the Islamic testimony, or *shahada*, "There is no God but Allah and Muhammad is his Prophet," in order to become a Muslim and enter Paradise; Seabrook immediately agreed. Mithqal was very pleased and made him repeat the formula for the rest of the evening whenever a new guest entered the tent. The next morning Mithqal presented his guest with a silver amulet containing a miniature copy of the Quran. But when his slave pushed the matter too far by insisting on teaching Seabrook the prayers, Mithqal abruptly shut him up.[82]

Two testimonies regarding Mithqal's later life corroborate the impression that he had deep religious feelings. Perhaps his faith grew stronger with age or as a result of his more intense contact with urban life. His daughter testifies that he was very religious and prayed often. He was also intolerant to Muslims who did not pray or did not fast during the month of Ramadan.[83] A man who knew Mithqal well in 1941 described him as a devout and faithful Muslim.[84]

.   .   .

During the first decade after the creation of the modern state of Transjordan, Mithqal reached the height of his power. He enjoyed wealth, influence, and fame well beyond the borders of the country. He created an elevated position of power within his tribal confederacy and the wider emirate of Transjordan for himself. He enjoyed personal autonomy and could do almost anything he wished, limited only by the social norms his tribal society cherished. He exercised leadership in a very confident and reassuring way. In fact, Mithqal's lifestyle, status, and material prosperity were similar to those of his father and his shaykhly forebears. At this early stage, the modern Jordanian nation-state had a similar influence on tribal society as that of the Ottoman Empire in its closing decades.

But from the end of the 1920s on, especially in the early 1930s, times were irreversibly and rapidly changing. Nomadic society experienced a deep and prolonged crisis, which brought about fundamental changes in its structure, culture, and economy. In order to secure what he had so laboriously achieved, to maintain his position, and to bequeath it to the next generation, Mithqal had to adapt quickly. His growing predicament demanded a very creative problem-solving strategy.

5 TIMES OF CRISIS

ONE DAY AT THE BEGINNING OF 1930, Mithqal was riding his mare in the desert accompanied by only one man. It was during the winter season, and the Bani Sakhr had migrated east towards Wadi Sirhan. Suddenly, Mithqal and his escort were surprised by an ambush set by members of an enemy tribe. A bullet grazed the side of Mithqal's head, almost killing him, and he was hit in the shoulder. Mithqal and his escort fired back and managed to drive off their attackers, but Mithqal was badly wounded. His escort tied a piece of cloth around his bleeding shoulder, pulled him over his mare, and rode on quickly to seek aid. They arrived in the nearby camp of a Bani Sakhr tribesman and asked for his help in fetching a car to take Mithqal to a hospital. He sent one of his men by camel to the encampment of Shaykh Haditha al-Khuraysha, who in turn sent a messenger to Amman. A car finally arrived, but in the meantime, Mithqal was suffering from loss of blood and in great pain. Mithqal spent twenty days in an Amman hospital. He survived, but the damage was irreversible. For the rest of his life, he could hardly use that arm, which dangled nearly lifeless from his shoulder.[1]

The decade that began with this life-threatening incident also proved crippling in another way. The conditions prevailing during the first decade of the emirate's existence, which had greatly benefited Mithqal and his tribal confederacy, soon changed drastically. Beginning in the early 1930s, like other nomadic tribes in Transjordan and other parts of the Fertile Crescent, the Bani Sakhr were faced with a severe crisis. Mithqal was now confronted with the greatest challenge of his long career.

THE NOMADS' CRISIS IN THE 1930s

Over the course of the summer of 1930, the Transjordanian authorities' enormous efforts to stop tribal raids on the Transjordan-Najd border collapsed. Massive raids against the Huwaytat tribal confederacy resulted in heavy casualties and the loss of thousands of camels and sheep. They had to flee from the desert and move westward into the settled area, losing still more animals during this flight. To compensate for their losses they raided local tribes.[2] Pressed by London to pacify the frontier, British officials in Amman adopted increasingly repressive measures. They deployed military units in the desert, and the RAF carried out reconnaissance flights along the border. In April 1930, it prevented the tribes from grazing near the border, threatening to fire at any party found in the area. The ban lasted a few months and resulted in overgrazing and a water shortage and thus in the loss of even more animals. All the while, the Najdi tribes continued to raid, slipping past the Transjordanian defenses time and again.

The failure to stop the raiding, and a growing sense among officials in Amman and Jerusalem that, in the words of Resident Henry Cox, the British measures against the raids were the "gravest injustice" to the nomads, brought about a change in British policy.[3] The high commissioner for Palestine and Transjordan called for imposing direct British rule in the desert and secured the Colonial Office's approval of this, as well as the necessary funds. To execute the plan, the Transjordanian government enlisted the services of Captain John Glubb, a British officer who had made a name for himself in Iraq as an expert on desert tribes.[4]

Glubb arrived in Amman in November 1930 and quickly familiarized himself with the emergency situation, which by the time of his arrival had only got worse. After being briefed by the local officials and examining the relevant files at the disposal of the Arab Legion, he proceeded to assess the facts on the ground. He went out into the desert to visit the Huwaytat, who by then had suffered the most. Remarkably, he traveled in the desert without an escort. It was important to him to dissociate himself from the Arab Legion and cultivate friendly relations with the tribesmen.

Upon returning to Amman, Glubb sat down to write a long memorandum in which he detailed the situation on the frontier. His report corroborated the position expressed by the Transjordanian authorities over the previous two years, who put the blame for the crisis along the border on Ibn Saud and his tribes. He gathered incriminating evidence of Ibn Saud's encouragement of raiding parties and his deliberate seduction of Transjordanian tribes to cross over and swear allegiance to him. Glubb also demonstrated the impoverishment of the Huwaytat. It was this destitution, Glubb explained, that motivated their continued raiding in the hope of retrieving some of their losses. Glubb forcefully showed how Britain had failed to protect subjects living under its mandate.[5]

After establishing the severity of the situation, Glubb spent the winter of 1930–31 in the various camps of the Huwaytat and Bani Sakhr. Within weeks, he had managed to overcome the nomads' hostility to a government that had previously tried to prevent them from raiding in Najd and, from the nomads' perspective, persecuted them. Glubb persuaded them to stop raiding and organized their defense against raiders from Najd. In doing so, he was able to put his good Arabic and exceptional knowledge of nomadic life to work. He also distributed money to shaykhs and ordinary tribesmen, relieving their material misery. The arrival from Iraq of four of his former Arab desert policemen, and their recounting of his activities in Iraq against the Ikhwan, enhanced his reputation. He later reported that it was his reputation, more than anything else, that helped him gain the cooperation of the Huwaytat.[6]

In February 1931, after securing the cooperation of shaykhs and tribesmen, Glubb formed the nucleus of the "Desert Patrol," as an integral part of the Arab Legion, with twenty salaried recruits. Enlisting in a regular army was something of a revolution for the nomads. Still, within several months, Glubb had succeeded in recruiting ninety men, the full personnel quota designated for the new unit. Soon those demanding to join outnumbered the available posts. Glubb was able to create a somewhat aristocratic force, giving priority to the sons of shaykhs. The new unit was a small but effective police force, staffed solely by nomads who volunteered. It was deployed at several desert forts and was highly mobile, equipped with cars, camels, and radios. The RAF provided aerial reinforcement upon request. By the middle of 1931, Glubb's unit was a force to be reckoned with.

By 1931, cross-border raids had already been reduced to a minimum. The majority of tribesmen abstained from raiding; attacks from Najd ceased altogether. This was partly thanks to cooperation between Glubb and his Saudi counterpart, the inspector of the northern frontier, which was further reinforced by British diplomatic pressure on King Ibn Saud. The last raid occurred in July 1932; apart from rare exceptions, peace has prevailed in the desert ever since.

Not only did Glubb and his men manage to halt the raids, but they also succeeded within a few years in forcing the nomadic tribes to submit to the rule of the central government. In doing so, they enabled the administration to expand its reach into the desert. By recruiting their best warriors into his force and by sharing administrative power with their shaykhs, Glubb was able to limit both the nomads' ability and motivation to resist him. Under his command, the Desert Patrol became the prime instrument of control in the desert. It collected taxes, regulated grazing areas, solved disputes among tribesmen, and, from 1937 on, executed the decisions of tribal courts formed by Glubb.

Glubb and the Desert Patrol also provided the nomads with many government services, including formal education and modern health care. They distributed welfare in the form of clothes, food, and relief work in government construction projects. Glubb also encouraged tribesmen to diversify their sources of income by cultivating their land, which was a revolutionary transformation of the desert. For that purpose, he and the government provided agricultural training and free seed and assisted in the development of water infrastructure in desert areas.

Glubb's remarkable success owed as much to the tribes' predicament as to his exceptional skills. By the early 1930s, in addition to fear of and heavy losses to the Najdi tribes, Transjordan's nomads were suffering a severe economic crisis.[7] This was the primary motivation for tribal cooperation with Glubb and his policies. Under famine conditions, they accepted government initiatives to ease their situation, even at the cost of their autonomy.

Some of the economic difficulties the nomads faced were not new, and many aspects of the nomadic pastoral economy had been in decline since the end of World War I. By the mid-1920s, the establishment of law and order in the settled areas west of the Hijazi railway prevented nomads from raiding farming communities and collecting the *khawa* payment from villages and towns; intertribal raiding in the desert was much reduced as well. New international boundaries cut across tribal domains and limited the access to winter grazing grounds. The loss of Wadi Sirhan to Ibn Saud in 1925 was particularly harmful, because the Bani Sakhr and other tribes were forced to pay taxes when they entered their traditional grazing grounds. Then, upon returning in the spring, they were taxed again by the Transjordanian government. Most important, trains, cars, and airplanes gradually replaced the camels and horses that had been the region's means of transport and the nomads' main livelihood for centuries.

Exceptional climatic conditions exacerbated these already challenging circumstances. Between 1929 and 1936, Transjordan was badly affected by severe, persistent drought. Two heavy locust attacks in 1930 and 1932 further reduced the vegetation in the desert and stripped cultivated fields. The growing difficulty of migrating across the new borders limited the nomads' ability to find alternative grazing areas. Shaykhs like Mithqal whose cultivated land was their main source of wealth could not assist the members of their tribes as they had done before.

The nomads were also affected by the global economic crisis of the 1930s, which greatly reduced the viability of their camel-based economy. Camels, as opposed to horses, were still valuable to the nomads, who could sell them in Egypt, where camel meat was eaten. The Great Depression hit the Egyptian economy hard, however; camel prices fell drastically, from £16–20 for a camel in the late 1920s to a mere £3–5 in 1932–33.[8] In order to maintain a basic level of income, nomads had to sell more camels, and their herds were quickly depleted.

Combined, these factors had devastating effects on the nomadic population. Many tribes were much reduced in numbers; the poorest died and many others migrated to Palestine as casual laborers or beggars.[9] The magnitude of the crisis was revealed by statistics gathered by the colonial authorities: 84 percent of the Sirhan, Huwaytat, and Bani Sakhr suffered from malnutrition, while nomadic holdings in livestock fell by 70 percent between the years 1932 and 1936.[10]

The crisis affected ordinary tribespeople and shaykhs alike. Indeed, several tribal leaders were reduced to abject poverty. Shaykh Haditha al-Khuraysha, second only to Mithqal among the Bani Sakhr, and his large family had to survive on the kind of cheap barley used to feed cattle. By 1934, Muhammad abu Taya of the Huwaytat, the son of the famous 'Awda abu Taya of the Arab Revolt, had only four camels in his possession and was sustained only by economic assistance received from Glubb.[11] Mithqal himself was not reduced to poverty, but he nevertheless faced growing economic problems.

At the beginning of the 1930s, Mithqal was still one of the richest individuals in Transjordan. His main assets were the two villages of Umm al-'Amad and Jiza. The villages' land was cultivated by sharecroppers, and depending on the different arrangements between them, Mithqal received from one- to four-fifths of the agricultural yield. He also possessed large livestock holdings. In return for helping the government to enumerate his tribes' animals, he was able to cut commissions from the taxes due on them.[12] Furthermore, his position within the administration proved to be lucrative: as a member of the Legislative Council (1929–31 and again in 1934–37), he was paid a handsome salary of £200 per year,[13] and his participation in meetings of the Tribal Control Board was also remunerative. Mithqal also accepted many gifts from the Bani Sakhr and from other tribes, and apparently also from Abdullah. Furthermore, Mithqal could count on the assistance of his in-laws, the wealthy Khayr family of Amman. Mithqal's brother-in-law Hashim, who emerged as a prominent politician in the latter part of the 1920s, largely because of his family connection with Mithqal, was closely involved in the management of Mithqal's financial affairs.[14]

But Mithqal's economic condition was nonetheless precarious: during the better part of the 1930s, his expenses exceeded his earnings. He was in permanent need of cash, which he found difficult to raise. When it was cultivated at all, farming his land depended on rain, and during drought years, grain crops were poor. Even before the big drought, much of the land in Jiza was left fallow.[15] Cultivated or not, the owner of land had to pay tax, however lightly assessed. Even if the land bore good crops, moreover, landowners suffered from the sharp decrease in the price of grain and the lack of export markets. As one agricultural expert noted, "the characteristic feature of agriculture [was] extreme poverty."[16] Furthermore, Mithqal could not liquidate his real-estate holdings by selling them for cash, since land had no commercial value in contemporary Transjordan.

Mithqal's rapidly diminishing income posed a problem, because he could no longer meet the high expenses incumbent upon a shaykh of his stature. Vast resources were required in order to continue to provide constant and generous hospitality, to cultivate and reinforce political alliances, and to support the needy. The demands on the shaykh to assist his kinsmen were dramatically increased during times of great difficulties. On the personal level, Mithqal needed great sums of money to maintain his large, dependent household, which included four wives, many children, and a retinue of guards, slaves, and other workers.

The tension between the way Mithqal performed his shaykhly duties and the new economic reality reverberated through a gathering at the house of Mithqal's brother-in-law, Hashim Khayr, that took place in August 1932. The participants lamented the economic difficulties caused by the poor harvest everywhere in the country. They also complained about the government's pressure on them to pay the taxes regardless of the situation. During the course of the conversation, Mithqal asked Hashim how much money he was expected to pay the government in taxes. Hashim said that he was required to pay £1,200 and teased Mithqal for continuing to host huge feasts, with hundreds of guests, regardless of the severe economic strains. Mithqal responded that "only God has the solution, we humans follow our tradition and must respect it."[17] Clearly, he insisted on performing his role as shaykh of shaykhs as usual.

The increasing pressure on Mithqal's dwindling cash reserves quickly drove him into debt. By 1928, he was already reported to have mortgaged a large portion of his property. This soon led to legal troubles as well when he failed to make his payments on time. Further defaults on loans led to more extensive legal action. In 1929, a merchant to whom Mithqal owed money sued him in court. In February of that year, Mithqal's overdue debts led the government to put three tracts of his Jiza landholdings, totaling 850 dunam, up for sale. Fortunately for him, by August no buyer had come forward; no one dared to make an offer that might potentially provoke the formidable Mithqal's wrath.[18] The situation was only exacerbated in 1930, when the government demanded that he pay the difference between the tax on the actual extent of the land he owned in Jiza and on the incorrect and possibly fraudulent early assessment made upon his receipt of it from Abdullah nearly ten years prior.[19] Mithqal's exact debt is difficult to assess, but it amounted to several thousand pounds, certainly a hefty sum at that time.[20]

Indebtedness was not particular to Mithqal or a result of especially poor financial mismanagement; it was a general phenomenon among landowners in Transjordan during that time, many of whom faced government auction of their properties.[21] One member of the Legislative Council declared with confidence that "there is not a single person in Transjordan who is not indebted, even the ministers are."[22] Though the legislator was exaggerating slightly, his statement was not very far from the truth: investigations conducted by the government clearly showed the farmers' dire situation.[23]

Personal financial difficulties aside, Mithqal was facing increasing pressure from other quarters as well. As shaykh of shaykhs and representative in the Legislative Council when the crisis broke out, Mithqal was expected to ease the difficulties faced by his tribes, and it can be safely assumed that he was pressed by the other tribal shaykhs of the confederacy to act. Mithqal was also affected by Glubb's increasing control over the desert. Although Glubb's assistance to the nomads during their crisis was necessary and well taken, his work ultimately had to come at the expense of tribal autonomy and the influence of their leaders.

New laws that were meant to help Glubb in limiting cross-border raids, further threatened tribal autonomy and the shaykhs' well-being. By adopting the legal concept of collective responsibility, these laws allowed the government to send a shaykh to prison if the culprit from his tribe was unknown or managed to flee. When the government submitted one such draft law for the Legislative Council's approval, members protested the exceedingly difficult situation in which shaykhs found themselves. Haditha al-Khuraysha, who replaced Mithqal in late 1931, asked rhetorically, "Would the entire tribe be held responsible if one member of the tribe committed a crime and fled the country? Is it the shaykh's fault and would he face prison as a result?" To justify his opposition, he reminded the members that "the shaykhs do not receive salaries and they don't enjoy the authority they once possessed any more."[24] Another member of the council highlighted Glubb's role in undermining the shaykhs' leadership and complained that "the shaykhs no longer have the authority they once had, especially since the establishment of the Desert Patrol, the construction of the check posts along the emirate's eastern borders, and the signing of the agreements with the neighboring government to extradite criminals." He further recommended rejecting the clause providing for shaykhs to be arrested, so that "they would be able to maintain what is left of their dignity."[25]

Glubb's influence in the desert increased at the expense, not only of the tribal shaykhs, but also of Abdullah and his cousin Shakir. After a short but decisive power struggle with the former and the death of the latter in 1934, Glubb was able to consolidate his power. Although Abdullah continued to be involved in tribal matters and still wielded much influence, the final word gradually became Glubb's. By the mid-1930s, he had become the undisputed authority in the desert. The diminishment of Abdullah's power was bad news for Mithqal, because one of his greatest assets was the patronage he received from the emir.

Mithqal had no choice but to find a modus operandi with the British officer. His support of the new British policy in the desert and his early cooperation with Glubb are suggested by the fact that the Bani Sakhr were the second-largest tribal group among the Desert Patrol's first recruits, and that Mithqal's support was essential in enabling Glubb to complete his mission among the Bani Sakhr. Mithqal likely supported Glubb because he recognized the threat Najdi raiders posed to his tribes. Ultimately, as Abdullah's ally, he could not go against the emir's policy. Abdullah was busy pacifying the desert, and he supported Glubb's mission before he realized the cost to his own authority.[26]

Despite his cooperation, Mithqal resented Glubb's growing influence, and their relations grew strained. Though he could not directly resist him, Mithqal pushed back in other ways. He was among the Legislative Council members who refused to approve the 1931 state budget because a large part of it was allocated to the Desert Patrol. So fierce and unrelenting was their objection that Emir Abdullah had to use his constitutional prerogative to dissolve the council and call for new elections.[27] The enmity between Mithqal and Glubb was mutual, and it lasted throughout Glubb's long tenure in Jordan. Whereas Glubb had been able to establish a rapport with many shaykhs, which even approached friendship, his relations with Mithqal remained at a working level only. Glubb's official reports reveal his dislike of Mithqal. In one, Glubb described Mithqal as "more unscrupulous and shameless than the rest [of the chiefs]," and compared him unfavorably to Shaykh Haditha, "a man of sincere religion and a high standard of honour."[28] It is obvious that Mithqal constituted a great challenge to the British administrators; his power, influence, and aggressive, bullying behavior made him a tough, and consequently unpopular, rival.

LOOKING FOR REMEDY

Faced with such mounting pressures, Mithqal recognized the need to realign himself. No more could he sit idly in his big tent, sipping coffee and chatting days on end with his guests. Such indolence soon gave way to a busier, even hectic, way of life. While he didn't neglect his traditional role as shaykh of shaykhs and maintained close relations with the different segments of his confederacy, most of his time came to be spent in Amman and on frequent travel abroad. He could no longer rely on his special position at Abdullah's court and was looking for new patrons to strengthen his political and economic standing. He cast his net wide.

Under the new circumstances, Mithqal could not afford any bad blood between himself and Abdullah, the government, or the British. Their goodwill was necessary to ensure that his mounting debts remained on paper and were not collected. He also needed the government's help protecting his tribes. Mithqal abandoned his oppositional stance from the time of the ratification of the Anglo-Transjordanian treaty in 1929 and began to mend his relations with Abdullah. He also supported Abdullah's attempts to co-opt the opposition and unite the country's tribal leaders and notables around him. Such attempts reached fruition in November 1930, when Mithqal hosted a hundred notables, representing two rival parties.[29]

Mithqal also cultivated good relations with the British officials and tried not to step out of line. By the early 1930s, he had managed to win the sympathy of some British officials for his growing difficulties. Apart from Glubb, he was in touch with Resident Cox, Lieutenant Colonel Peake, and the high commissioner, Arthur Wauchope. When the latter visited an archeological site in Madaba around the end of 1932, Mithqal pitched a tent on the way. Ambushed in this way, Wauchope came in and drank coffee. Mithqal reportedly told him that this would not do, because an Arab (meaning a Bedouin) concludes an alliance, not by drinking coffee, but by sharing a meal. Wauchope promised to take up the invitation at a later date. This happened a year later when the high commissioner and his large entourage came to Mithqal's estate in Umm al-'Amad. Twenty sheep were slaughtered for the sumptuous feast, attended also by scores of tribesmen. Mithqal went to great lengths in trying to impress Wauchope.[30]

Beyond such niceties, Mithqal tried to capitalize on his status as "one of the most influential men in Transjordanian politics"[31] in order to lobby Abdullah, the British officials, and the government. He was the first to introduce the issue of the economic crisis in the Legislative Council's meetings. As early as November 1930, Mithqal protested the difficult economic situation in the country and the refusal of the government to exempt the citizens from paying taxes, thus setting the agenda for the other members of the council. This was done with the understanding and full support of Abdullah, according to the shaykh's own testimony.[32]

Some weeks after Mithqal raised the issue, other members picked up on what would become recurrent themes in the discussions of the council throughout the first half of the 1930s, as well as a bone of contention between council members and the government. A tribal shaykh representing Karak referred the government's attention to the dire situation in the south of the country and called for tax exemption. The representative of the northern district followed suit. Mithqal interrupted the northern representative's speech, saying that "the people [are so poor that they] took off their clothes and sold them."[33] Naturally, the records of the meetings constitute only a literal transcription of what was said in the council. Nevertheless, in reading them, one can almost hear the rage and frustration in Mithqal's voice.

The Legislative Council provided Mithqal with an important platform for cementing his relationship with the local Transjordanian elite. The council was composed of city notables and merchants as well as tribal shaykhs. Like Mithqal, many of the members were major landowners, with many shared interests; these included the development of their estates with government help, the reduction of taxes on their land, and the appointment of locals to government positions, rather than non-Transjordanian Arabs, who made up the majority of the bureaucracy. In essence, they lobbied for such interests. On occasion, they were able to block or mitigate government initiatives that harmed their economic interests and personal autonomy.[34]

Mithqal usually sat silently at the Legislative Council's meetings, allowing his colleagues to take the lead in the battle against the government. The illiterate shaykh probably felt unqualified to deal with the ministers on their own terms, contesting the nuances and legal jargon that appeared in the draft laws that the council was asked to ratify. But on rare occasions, Mithqal was provoked to protest. His typically short interventions reveal his fierce objection to the government's attempts to limit tribal autonomy, contempt for its conduct, and frustration at the council's limited ability to check it. In one instance, Mithqal reminded the ministers that they were "those who wear [the] tarbush [fez]." In other words, that the country was populated largely by nomads and peasants rather than by city dwellers like them. Saying that "a house without pillars is bound to collapse," he criticized them for imposing European laws on the Arabs. Referring specifically to the law that stipulated the establishment of a special Transjordanian-Syrian court to judge cross-border raids, he said, "And now you [have] introduced a law to establish a court whose members are English and French and you want to enforce their laws on us. You have no fear of God. You have given up the Arabs and their cause." He then asked the council members to reject the law, arguing that "each time we object to something in the law we are told that the council has already approved it."[35] During a discussion on the amendment of the state budget, Mithqal said, "it is all about budgets and expenses of the government, but there is no mention of the poor people and nothing of this goes to them. They are starving themselves and their children in order to pay the government expenses and the salaries of its officials."[36]

Mithqal's criticism was justified. Despite some token successes, such efforts by the council's members to demand that the government improve the economy were largely unproductive, because both the government and the emir had very limited resources. The British government in London was very slow in responding to the persistent requests—coming from its representatives both in Amman and Jerusalem, as well as from Abdullah and local notables—to invest more in Transjordan and ease the suffering of its population. Ultimately, Mithqal and his tribes got no assistance beyond that given by Glubb.

The most serious offer to relieve Mithqal's financial problems came only in 1934. Following a meeting between Mithqal and Resident Cox, the latter offered Mithqal a loan equivalent to £1,000. This would have allowed him to develop his agricultural estate and work to alleviate some of his other woes. According to the terms of the proposed loan, Mithqal's land would have been placed under the management of a professional agriculturist appointed by the director of agriculture.[37]

This unusual British offer—no other person in the country received such attention—indicates that, several years into the crisis, Mithqal was still seen by the Mandate authorities as a powerful, even dangerous shaykh, whose goodwill had to be secured. Justifying the additional expenditure, the acting high commissioner wrote the Colonial Office that the loan and the development scheme "will probably set Mithqal Pasha on his feet, and will tide this important Bedoui[n] chieftain over the difficult period of transition from the nomadic to the settled life." He added that the loan would serve the double purpose of restoring Mithqal's position and of encouraging the Bani Sakhr to adopt better methods of agriculture by following Mithqal's example.[38] To strengthen this appeal, the high commissioner sent his own letter less than a fortnight later. Wauchope was especially concerned about the shaykh's potential for obstructing the important land reform project, which was the most ambitious program the British introduced in Transjordan.[39] Wauchope understandably wanted to ensure its success: "I attach great importance to the urgent issue of this assistance to prevent complete insolvency of this large and influential landowner which would result not only in default of payment of land taxation but would have other unfortunate political reactions in view of his ability to obstruct land reform."[40]

Although the Colonial Office had approved the loan, after securing the consent of the British Treasury, Mithqal turned it down. He rejected the condition that he submit his property to the tight control of the Transjordanian government.[41] Put differently, Mithqal refused to give up his autonomy. By that time, he could rely on financial support from outside the country.

Mithqal realized quickly that a remedy to his financial difficulties would not come from within Transjordan, and so decided to explore other options. Already by 1929, he had become known as an Arab national leader who defied British colonialism and who visibly supported the Arabs in Palestine. Now he tried to turn such nationalist credentials into financial gains. He decided to offer some of his land for sale.

Building on this reputation, and despite being illiterate, Mithqal recognized the value of the press in promoting himself beyond his immediate tribal surroundings. He also recognized that the press could be used to publicize certain messages that were important to him. When he was looking for a potential buyer for his land, he did so also through an interview with the newspaper *Filastin*'s Amman correspondent. A few days later, he visited its offices in Jaffa in order to give a briefing about the dire economic situation in Transjordan. The result was a headline story, which appeared the following day.[42]

The time and effort Mithqal spent in what would be called today a public relations campaign did not go to waste. It is likely that he paid several journalists and editors for their services, as this was a common practice in the Arabic press at the time.[43] Through the reports about him in the Arab and Jewish press, and the interviews he gave, Mithqal soon became a household name in Palestine. *Filastin* went so far as to feature his visit to Palestine and Egypt in 1931 on its front page, printing his picture and describing him as "the great Arab leader" and "one of the heroes of Arabism."[44] Mithqal was very active in briefing journalists about his activities, giving interviews or denying certain reports.[45]

While courting public opinion in Palestine, Mithqal also cultivated the Palestinian national leadership. At least since 1928, he had been in touch with the Grand Mufti of Jerusalem, Hajj Amin al-Husseini, and sometimes added his name to petitions or letters in support of the Palestinian cause. According to one report, Mithqal was especially close to the other prominent leader of the Palestinian national movement, Musa Kadhim al-Husseini.[46] In the summer of 1931, Mithqal went to Jerusalem to meet with the Mufti, but came away empty-handed. From Jerusalem, he proceeded to Jaffa, where he met other Palestinian activists, but with no better results.[47]

Undeterred by his failure in Palestine, Mithqal proceeded from Jaffa to Egypt to explore another option. He was distantly related to Shaykh Hamad al-Basil, a wealthy and prominent tribal leader and the deputy chairman of the Egyptian national Wafd party, and he decided to exploit such genealogical connections. Al-Basil sent Mithqal an invitation and prepared a state visit.

In September 1931, Mithqal and his entourage, among them prominent merchants from Amman, spent over two weeks in Egypt, where they were welcomed with the honors typically reserved for national heroes. On the day of his arrival, Mithqal's photo appeared on the front page of *al-Ahram*, the most important and widely circulated Egyptian newspaper at that time. Mithqal spent a few days at al-Basil's estate in Fayum (an oasis southwest of Cairo), and from there he traveled to Alexandria to meet Mustafa Nahhas, the leader of the Wafd and a former and a future Egyptian prime minister. In the meeting, Mithqal and Nahhas each praised the other's national movement. In Alexandria, Mithqal also attended a reception for his old acquaintance King Faysal of Iraq. Upon his departure from Egypt he was bid farewell at the train station by (among others) al-Basil and Dr. ʿAbd al-Rahman al-Shahbandar, the famous Syrian national leader, who happened to be in Egypt. On arrival in Palestine, he was invited for lunch with Hajj Amin; perhaps the Mufti was impressed with Mithqal's reception in Egypt and wanted to mollify him.[48] Mithqal's trip was heavily laden with political symbolism: for a brief moment, he had stood side by side with nearly all the great national leaders of the Arab Middle East in the 1930s.

Despite all the honors bestowed upon him and the impressive media coverage, both in Palestine and in Egypt, Mithqal returned home disappointed, having achieved very few tangible results. He had entertained high hopes that Hamad would be able to assist him, perhaps by giving him a loan. Reportedly, all he got from Hamad was a piece of land and a manor house in Fayum. Mithqal's expectations can also be seen in the special gifts he brought with him for his host—two thoroughbred racing horses, whose lineage was said to go back seven hundred years, and a gold sword worth £400. Returning to Transjordan empty-handed, all Mithqal could do was send Emir Abdullah a petition signed by the Bani Sakhr shaykhs, urging him to order the government to provide the confederacy with urgent assistance. Mithqal was careful to send a copy of the petition to *Filastin*, which endorsed it and published some excerpts.[49]

COURTING THE ZIONIST MOVEMENT IN PALESTINE

While trying to find relief among Arab circles, Mithqal tried another, seemingly contradictory tack—cultivating the favor of the Zionist movement in Palestine. Mithqal's relations with the Zionists were one of his main preoccupations during the early 1930s; indeed, they constituted his main strategy to cope with his growing leadership difficulties. In the Zionists, he found willing new patrons.[50]

Since its inception in the last quarter of the nineteenth century, the Zionist movement had reserved a prominent place in its imagination for Transjordan. The Zionist leaders viewed the Land of Israel (Eretz Israel) as stretching across both banks of the Jordan River, including the fertile areas, west of the pilgrimage route to Mecca (later the Hijazi railway). In the late nineteenth century, there had already been attempts to purchase land east of the river and settle it, though without much success. Following the 1917 Balfour Declaration on the creation of a Jewish national home in Palestine and the establishment of a British mandate there, the British government's 1922 White Paper excluding Transjordan from the Jewish national homeland and forbidding Jewish settlement east of the Jordan River was a blow to rising Zionist hopes. The Zionist movement was determined to reverse this ban. In the early 1930s, the conditions were ripe for a more assertive Zionist policy towards Transjordan. Following the 1929 Wailing Wall disturbances, the Jewish Agency (the body that represented the Jewish community in Palestine vis-à-vis the Mandate authorities, which was closely attached to the World Zionist Organization) decided to counter Palestinian opposition by cultivating better relations with the neighboring Arab countries. The Zionists also feared a British ban on land purchase inside Palestine because of growing Arab opposition and explored the option of buying land east of the river.

The economic crisis in Transjordan made this move seem realistic, as many landowners were looking to sell their land. It played into the hands of the Jewish Agency, who had long argued that Transjordan was in need of foreign capital and skilled labor, and that only Jewish settlement could bring about its economic development. Emir Abdullah, who aspired to annex Palestine to his domain, welcomed closer relations with the Zionist movement and already in the 1920s encouraged Jewish involvement in the development of his country. Abdullah also developed a personal stake in the matter. He had just become a landowner himself. The British had granted him a large estate in the Jordan valley, but he lacked the means to develop it. The emir was always short of money, owing to strict British supervision of the emirate's budget and the modest civil list allocated to him by the British Exchequer. In the circumstances, the Zionist connection made sound financial sense.[51]

Mithqal was the first landowner to identify the new business opportunities that derived from a growing Zionist interest in the affairs of Transjordan. In December 1930, through an intermediary, he approached Nahum Paper, a Zionist official from the Palestine Land and Development Company. At the time, Paper was conducting the first thorough agrarian survey of Transjordan on behalf of the Jewish Agency. Mithqal proposed to sell his village of Jiza, the land (30,000–35,000 dunams) for which the government held him indebted and that it threatened to confiscate. He demanded the exorbitant price of £1 per dunam, ten times the price he had paid. He also expected an advance of £2,500, explaining that he could not sell the land until he had paid his debt to the government.[52]

Paper recommended exploring the shaykh's proposal seriously. He emphasized Mithqal's influential position in Transjordan, his personal friendship with Abdullah, and his ability to face any opposition to the idea of Jewish entrance into Transjordan. Paper predicted that a favorable response to Mithqal would encourage other landowners to sell their land. He concluded his recommendation by saying that "if we take proper advantage of the friendship offered us by him, we have an opportunity of opening a new era in the history of our relations with Transjordan."[53]

The offer was discussed at the highest levels of the Zionist movement. From a Zionist point of view, a close relationship with Mithqal seemed attractive. He was the biggest landowner in Transjordan and was actively seeking to sell part of his holdings. He enjoyed political influence in Abdullah's court, as well as among the circles of notables who formed the country's elite. In addition, and here the Zionist understanding was greatly exaggerated and certainly influenced by the traumatic events of 1929, Mithqal possessed what was seen as great, independent military power, namely, leadership of the Bani Sakhr, who enjoyed the reputation of being skilled, courageous warriors. The fact that Mithqal had almost led his people to attack the Jewish population in Jerusalem only a year prior increased the importance of pulling him over to the Zionist camp. Despite the many potential benefits inherent in Mithqal's offer, the Agency could not ultimately accept it. The reason was financial, rather than ideological: Chaim Weizmann, president of the World Zionist Organization and an ardent supporter of the Transjordanian option, failed to secure the required funds.[54]

Mithqal was not dissuaded and renewed his proposal in the autumn and summer of 1931. He did so immediately after his meeting with the Mufti, during which he raised the same offer. Thus, the shaykh exploited the rivalry between Jews and Arabs in Palestine, in order to exert pressure on the Jewish Agency to accept his offer. This trick worked and the Jewish Agency was prompt to act. Through an Arab intermediary, the Agency persuaded Mithqal that he had little to gain from the Mufti and recommended the establishment of direct contact with the Jewish Agency instead. Mithqal accepted the invitation, met with the director of the Arab Bureau of the Zionist Executive (the predecessor of the Jewish Agency), and raised his offer to 100,000 dunams of land. A fortnight later, he sent a message in which he repeated his offer and promised to defend the Jewish colonies that would be established on his land. He demanded an immediate response to his proposal.[55]

Mithqal's initiative correlated with the appointment of Haim Arlosoroff as the new head of the Jewish Agency's Political Department. Arlosoroff aimed to exploit the economic difficulties in Transjordan in order to facilitate Jewish colonization and promote political bonds with the local leadership.[56] He favored a positive response to Mithqal's offer, but despite the early enthusiasm of both parties, the negotiations dragged on. The Zionist officials hesitated because they lacked the necessary funds and had failed to secure British approval for their plans in Transjordan. At the same time, they cherished their relationship with Mithqal and tried not to alienate him.

While Mithqal was waiting to hear from Arlosoroff, the Zionist official also maintained contact with Emir Abdullah, who received him in his palace in Amman in March 1932 on an official public visit, angering Arab public opinion. In response to the visit, the umbrella opposition body Transjordanian Arab Congress convened in Amman to discuss "the Zionist enterprises in Transjordan," among other things. During the conference, a dispute erupted between the nationalists and several shaykhs, among them Mithqal, who ultimately withdrew from the meeting.[57] Arab nationalists in the country were a small group, but nevertheless influential. Thanks to their education, many of them served in senior administrative positions or worked in the private sector, and they were also represented in the Legislative Council.

Mithqal was not deterred by this stormy atmosphere and continued his efforts to get the Jewish Agency to accept his proposal, using all his political skills to achieve this goal. In the summer of 1932, following another drought year, he stepped up his efforts, pursuing a few parallel channels. Though Mithqal understood why the Zionists were reluctant to conclude a large land purchase and settlement deal, at least for the time being, he nevertheless demanded immediate assistance on a smaller scale to relieve him of his debts. He proposed to mortgage some of his land in return for a loan to pay his debt to the Transjordanian treasury. Mithqal continued his visits to Jerusalem to talk with Jewish Agency officials, stressing his economic difficulties each time. He argued that by talking with government officials and tribal shaykhs, he had prepared the way for Jewish penetration of Transjordan.[58] He also put pressure on the Agency by employing two private Jewish and Arab land dealers, who in turn conveyed the shaykh's new offers to the Agency and pressed for their acceptance.[59] In addition, Mithqal hosted Avraham Shapira, a prominent Zionist known for his close relations with Palestinian Arabs, who was simultaneously cultivating the shaykhs of Karak, in his house.[60]

Mithqal also maintained his contacts with the Palestinian national leadership, still hoping that an Arab buyer of his land might present himself, or at least for a loan to placate his creditors. More important, these contacts were another tactical means to achieve rapprochement with the Zionists, by now

Mithqal's principal political strategy. A report received by the Jewish Agency in May 1932 clearly reveals these tactics. During a meal hosted by the Mufti, and in response to his criticism of Mithqal's contacts with the Zionists, Mithqal was reported to have replied bluntly, "Stop giving us orders, as though we were soldiers and you were our commander. The days of the Turkish army are over, praise Allah. We had best think about our own advantage. So far not all of your advice to us has proved right."[61] If this was indeed said and not concocted by the Jewish Agency's principal Arab secret agent in Transjordan, who reported it, it was probably meant, first and foremost, for Jewish ears. In the summer of 1932, Mithqal himself gave Jewish interlocutors a detailed account of his extensive talks with several Palestinian leaders, which had come to naught.[62] Mithqal walked a fine line between proving his friendship to the Jews and maintaining a position of strength over the course of the negotiations. In so doing, he successfully played off one political movement against the other to increase his own leverage and independence of action, once again displaying an astute assessment of the political realities.

Parallel to his frequent visits to Jerusalem and perhaps as a result of them, the Palestinian press exposed Mithqal's contacts with the Zionist movement, of which it was consistently critical.[63] These contacts were particularly painful to Arab public opinion, because the same press had hailed Mithqal as an Arab national leader in 1929–31. Moreover, the exposure of Mithqal's Jewish contacts only a few months after the Zionist leader Haim Arlosorrof's visit to Emir Abdullah, together with news of Shapira's visit to Mithqal and other shaykhs, inflamed the atmosphere. Mithqal was able to weather the storm, but he also needed to be cautious.

At this point, before anything was signed and sealed with the Jewish Agency, Mithqal tried to conceal his relations with the Zionists. During a newspaper interview in August 1932, Mithqal denied that he had sold his land to the Jews and undertook not to do so in future.[64] In November, he was more ambiguous. He complained to the editor of an Arabic newspaper about the false rumors of him selling land to the Jews. But when asked if he was negotiating with them on the potential sale of his land, Mithqal equivocated by saying, "I will conduct negotiations even with monkeys, because we want to feed the hungry and save our land."[65] In mentioning monkeys, Mithqal may very well have been alluding to the Quranic story of Allah transforming some Jews who had violated the Sabbath into apes.[66] Reports and rumors of Mithqal's dealings with the Jews only served to prompt other landowners to put forward similar offers. During

1932 and 1933, some of the most prominent tribal shaykhs and landowners approached the Jewish Agency.[67]

The local British authorities soon noticed the increased contacts between the Jews and the Transjordanian notables. While London was slow in forming its policy vis-à-vis the question of Jewish enterprise in Transjordan, its men on the ground, Cox, Peake, and Glubb, firmly opposed and tried to frustrate such initiatives. According to information gathered by the Jewish Agency, Cox summoned Mithqal and other shaykhs who were involved in the project in the summer of 1932 and criticized them for this. Several months later, it was reported that Cox and Peake had warned the heads of the tribes not to sell their land to the Jews.[68]

Mithqal's resilience, patience, and intensive activity eventually bore fruit; by the end of 1932, the Jewish Agency was ready for a deal. Arlosoroff reported to the members of the Agency's executive that, on top of his original offer, Mithqal proposed to bring in other Bani Sakhr shaykhs, which would make a total offer of a half million dunams. According to another ambitious plan, he would buy another half million dunams himself in order to sell them later to the Agency. Mithqal clearly had an exaggerated impression of the financial capabilities of the Jewish Agency. Arlosoroff explained that those offers could not be taken up in the near future, but he stressed the need to continue and to nurture personal relations with the Transjordanian notables, assuming that they might become the internal power that could persuade both the British and the local governments to open up the country to Jewish capital and labor. Arlosoroff therefore accepted Mithqal's less ambitious offer of a mortgage on his land in the village of Barazayn in return for a loan (see map 4, p. 86).[69] Henceforth the Zionists would seek to secure what they saw as Mithqal's friendship for the sake of building a political alliance, rather than concluding a deal over purchasing his land.

In this hopeful atmosphere, Mithqal was invited to Jerusalem in November 1932 to meet the senior Zionist leader, Nahum Sokolow, who had replaced Weizmann as president of the Zionist Organization the previous year. Mithqal's speech in the presence of Sokolow and Arlosoroff was full of rhetoric that was very pleasing to Jewish ears, but it also reveals something of his attitude regarding his contacts with the Jewish Agency.[70] He saw them in terms of tribal politics, which are typically characterized by political alliances based on personal trust. Mithqal described his relations with Arlosoroff as an alliance that would last forever, to be preserved in perpetuity by his successors. He assured Sokolow of his loyalty, saying he was famous for it, and recalled his alliance with the Ottomans, to which he had remained true until the very last moment. Mithqal went on to describe his relations with the Jews as a covenant based on mutual benefit. He was convinced that Jewish emigration to Transjordan would be a blessing to the country, and that it was the only hope for relief from its economic plight. For Mithqal, the huge difference between the prosperous economy of Palestine and that of Transjordan was clear justification for this belief. Once, before World War I, Palestinian peasants had come to work the harvest in Transjordan; now the situation was reversed.

Mithqal had no particular ideological compunction about allowing Jews into Transjordan. For him, this made perfect sense; it was pure business, and based on practical considerations. When referring to his own property, he presented his traditional concept of tilling the land: vast tracts lay uncultivated, and Bani Sakhr land could accommodate thousands of new settlers; and, finally, the Bani Sakhr did not till the earth themselves, but were pastoral nomads, whose land was cultivated by tenants. Some of these tenants were permanent, while others continually changed over the years.[71] Mithqal saw no difference whatsoever between potential Jewish cultivators and the Bani Sakhr shaykhs' Egyptian or Palestinian tenants, who had worked their land since the late nineteenth century.

Mithqal's attitude towards the Jews was possible because his thinking was devoid of any nationalist ideology. This should not come as a surprise. In a tribal and largely nomadic society, such as Transjordan was in the 1930s, nationalist feeling was slow in developing. Studies have clearly established that literacy and urban life, as well as the erosion of primordial forms of loyalty, are preconditions for the emergence of nationalism.[72] Transjordan was a small society, numbering between 200,000 and 300,000 people, with no major cities. In 1930, its capital, Amman, had just over 10,000 residents, and Salt, the largest town, was only slightly bigger.[73] It was a rural, mostly illiterate society. Moreover, Transjordanian tribal groups were cohesive, kin-based entities, and identification with the small and familiar society of the tribe postponed the imagining of a large and somehow abstract national community of the kind prevailing in a modernized, industrial, and urban society.[74] Contacts with the Jews were thus not problematic for Mithqal ideologically.

But it is also quite clear that what the Zionists interpreted as Mithqal's friendship was also far from reality. Mithqal was willing to give them as much sympathy and friendship as they wanted as long as he saw practical benefits from doing so. It was a game he played very well. This is not to say that he deceived them all along, although that was how Resident Cox interpreted the entire affair in 1936, when he wrote: "Mithqal has always said quite frankly that if he sold his land to the Jews he would destroy them later on and thus get his property back again."[75]

While Mithqal and other shaykhs were negotiating with the Jews, Emir Abdullah was also expanding his contacts with them. On January 3, 1933, Abdullah granted the Jewish Agency a leasehold option on 60,000 dunams of his newly acquired land in the Jordan Valley, known as the Ghawr al-Kibd, for £500 (see map 4, p. 86). The transaction was contingent, and the Agency didn't get much for its money. If Abdullah decided to activate the option within six months, the Jewish Agency would lease the land and cultivate it for a period of thirty-three years, paying Abdullah rent and a small share of the profit. Despite the efforts of both parties to keep the deal under wraps, the Arab and Palestinian press soon uncovered it. The huge row that erupted alarmed the British authorities, who advised Abdullah against such a deal. The combined pressure of Arab nationalists and the British compelled Abdullah to deny the existence of the transaction, but he surreptitiously extended the option three more times, in return for large sums of money on each occasion. The lease option provided both parties with a somewhat respectable veneer for what was basically a gift to Abdullah in order to maintain his friendship.[76]

In light of his special relationship with both Abdullah and the Jewish Agency, Mithqal was perfectly placed to play an intermediary role in the Ghawr al-Kibd affair. During the course of negotiations, he briefed the Jewish Agency on the emir's position. Later, in 1934, Abdullah dispatched him to the Jordan River bridge to greet and facilitate the entry into the country of Aharon Haim Cohen, secretary of the Arab Bureau of the Jewish Agency's Political Department, who had come to pay the emir for extending the land-lease option.[77]

Just before Abdullah signed the option, negotiations between Mithqal and the Zionists had been close to conclusion. But achieving this took another visit by Mithqal to Jerusalem in December, when he insisted on seeing Arlosoroff even though he had no appointment. Mithqal was now angry at the long delay and demanded that the deal be sealed. He accused Arlosoroff and his aides of not appreciating what he had done for them, claiming that his open, public position on the sale of land to Jews and their admission to Transjordan had brought a change in public opinion in favor of the project and facilitated Abdullah's negotiations with the Jewish Agency. He laid out his financial difficulties and demanded immediate assistance. On top of trying to enlist the sympathy of his interlocuters, Mithqal added: "Perhaps you think that you will do better through your negotiations with the emir. I swear to you that against my will no Jew would enter Transjordan."[78] The combination of his emotional appeal and the threat had its effect. Three weeks later, he was in Jerusalem again to conclude the deal. In that meeting, he succeeded in squeezing even more money out of the Zionists, persuading them to pay him another £200, bringing the total to £675.[79]

The actual registration of the mortgage had to be postponed, however, because Arlosoroff got cold feet after the eruption of the Ghawr al-Kibd controversy. He requested Mithqal's understanding and patience, lest the Arab nationalists get more ammunition for their anti-Zionist campaign. Mithqal was upset about the delay, but received £200 in advance. In April 1933, Arlosoroff's deputy Moshe Shertok and another Jewish Agency's official went to Transjordan and registered a mortgage on 400 dunams. Subsequently, they paid Mithqal the remainder of the loan, which was never to be returned. The fact that the director of the office where the mortgage was officially registered was a relative of Mithqal's probably facilitated the transaction.[80] Although the Jewish Agency negotiated with many landowners, the Barazayn and Ghawr al-Kibd deals with Mithqal and Abdullah respectively were the only ones concluded, and despite what is popularly believed in Jordan today, even these did not involve full transfer of ownership.

LEADING A POLITICAL CAMPAIGN

Parallel to the last negotiations on the mortgage, and more so after their conclusion, Mithqal moved on to attempt an ambitious plan of cooperation with the Zionists. By now, he was out in the open in his support of the Zionist enterprise in Transjordan; he had chosen the Zionists as his new patrons. This was a risky gamble, but a calculated one. Should the Zionist project ultimately prove successful—and this did not seem such a fanciful notion at the time as it may from today's perspective—Mithqal would be the main beneficiary. Even if not, in the meantime, he would be able to extract money from the Jewish Agency that would relieve him of his growing financial difficulties.

Mithqal presented his idea of organizing the landowning shaykhs and notables and putting pressure on the government and the British authorities to allow Jewish settlement in Transjordan to the Agency in January 1933. He suggested convening a conference of landowners who wished to sell land to the Jews. An informal meeting in his house led to an impressive formal gathering in February in preparation for a conference that resulted in telegrams protesting the economic crisis to the emir and the high commissioner. The participants also demanded that the government stop seeking to extract uncollected old taxes and facilitate additional sources of capital, empowering the emir to "save the country through any means and development project that he sees fit."[81] The text's wording was a clear reference to Jewish money, but it was vague enough to allow many local leaders to attach their signatures. Before the meeting at Mithqal's house, a delegation of shaykhs and notables went to Abdullah to encourage and support him, counterbalancing the opposition the emir faced in the aftermath of the Ghawr al-Kibd affair.[82]

At this point Mithqal had remarkable political status in Transjordan. He was the focal point of the Transjordanian local elite of shaykhs and notables and enjoyed close cooperation with the most important tribal leaders in the country. Some leaders supported his leadership because of his close connections with the Jewish Agency. For others, his power derived from his close relations with Abdullah, which continued to grow in importance and intensity.

Abdullah needed Mithqal's support against his nationalist opponents. During January and February, the Jewish Agency learned of Mithqal's frequent visits to the palace and his consultations with Abdullah. He also escorted Abdullah during his visit to Jerusalem.[83] Mithqal's increased leverage vis-à-vis Abdullah was illustrated by an incident in which a man named Hamdi Anis killed two persons who had "damaged" his tribal honor. The fact that one of the victims was a policeman only made the crime more severe from the legal perspective of the state. The murderer fled to Mithqal, who extended him his customary protection. Later, the fugitive was smuggled to the Hijaz, and a civil court sentenced him to death in absentia. Mithqal brought Hamdi back at Abdullah's request, but only after his sentence had been commuted to fifteen years' hard labor. Mithqal asked the emir to release him, but this was repeatedly refused until February 1933, when he finally persuaded Abdullah to pardon Hamdi. Celebrating this at his house in Amman, dozens of guests came to congratulate Mithqal, whose insistence on giving tribal custom precedence over state law enhanced his shaykhly reputation, as did the demonstration of his influence.[84]

By early 1933, the joint efforts of Mithqal and the Jewish Agency had borne fruit. A distinguished group of landowning tribal shaykhs and notables who wished to see the opening of Transjordan to Jewish immigration and settlement had emerged. Under his leadership, this operated as an interest group seeking to change the official policy on the Zionist enterprise. The members of this group met frequently, mainly at Mithqal's houses or at the palace, coordinated their actions, and held consultations with Jewish officials. Some members were, like Mithqal, on the payroll of the Agency and received small "loans" from it.[85] Part of this group operated openly and was not afraid to confront criticism. Mithqal went so far as to form a political party, the Jordanian Solidarity Party, which, according to the British Resident, was "openly in favor of Jewish immigration."[86] The paper *Filastin* called this the "Arab Zionist party."[87] Most landowners did not join the party; instead, they waited for more practical results and expressed their sympathy only privately.

Whether out in the open or in secret, the group led by Mithqal backing Jewish immigration was significant in the number and identities of its members and the size of their landholdings. In May, a Jewish Agency secret agent assessed that it was composed of around a hundred big merchants and landowners, who together possessed almost ten million dunams. Though this was likely an exaggeration, British Intelligence reports paint a very similar picture.[88]

In April 1933, building on this success, Mithqal and the Jewish Agency stepped up their public campaign to persuade the British to allow Zionist colonization in Transjordan. Since it was important for the Zionists to prove that there was Arab support for the idea, they organized a public reception in honor of Mithqal and his associates at the King David Hotel in Jerusalem. The shaykhs met Weizmann and other senior Zionist officials, and they lunched together. In his opening speech, Arlosoroff highlighted Mithqal's pioneering role in establishing friendship and cooperation. For his part, Mithqal described Weizmann as "a friend to the Arabs and in particular a sympathizer with those of Transjordan." He expressed hope for future cooperation between the Zionist leadership in Palestine and Emir Abdullah that would "bring about a true alliance that will stand forever."[89]

But however successful the King David Hotel party was as Zionist propaganda, it was a Pyrrhic victory, which resulted in a fierce attack on Mithqal and his associates and the rapid disintegration of the group of landowners willing to sell. Open criticism came now, not only from the Palestinians and small circles of nationalists in Transjordan, but also from tribal leaders, including shaykhs of the Bani Sakhr. Several shaykhs from Karak went so far as to send an open letter condemning Mithqal's contacts with the Zionists and accusing him of treason.[90] Going to Jerusalem to embrace the Zionist leadership publicly was too much even for those who were not ardent nationalists to stomach.

While many landowners who had initially expressed interest in selling land to the Jews withdrew their offers, Mithqal still allowed himself to ignore the wrath of public opinion, which was increasing in its intensity. Indeed, the participants at a meeting of the Palestinian leadership following the King David Hotel party acknowledged that Mithqal was a "tough nut." One speaker said that the Bani Sakhr tribes backed Mithqal and would do everything for him. He advised avoiding direct action against Mithqal, since it might incite the Bani Sakhr and other tribes against them.[91] In the meantime, Mithqal insisted on convening the economic conference, which only gave his opponents more ammunition against him and made them ever more determined to frustrate his plan. The publication of the letter of condolence that Mithqal sent to Arlosoroff's widow after the Zionist leader's mysterious murder on the beach at Tel Aviv had a similar effect.[92]

Mithqal went too far. He exaggerated his own power and influence and played down the effect of Arab nationalism, which increasingly limited his room for maneuver. In the following weeks, he experienced several embarrassing failures that served further to undermine his position. After several delays, the economic conference that Mithqal organized with the financial help of the Jewish Agency convened at his house in Amman on June 30, 1933. The idea behind the conference was to promote cooperation with the Jews for the development of the local economy. Despite much effort and money spent by Mithqal and the Agency—Filastin reported that on the eve of the conference, Aharon Cohen had come to Amman and given Mithqal £200[93]—attendance was poor and the conference was a failure. According to reports in the Arab press, the participants could not agree among themselves, and Mithqal threw out two men who demanded that Zionism be condemned. Its only outcome—apart from the money Mithqal received—was a proclamation to the Arab world describing the poverty, famine, and despair prevailing in Transjordan and calling for mercy and assistance. It was a far cry from the conference's original ambitious goal.[94]

Only one day before the conference, the government released a statement that exposed Mithqal's financial situation in an attempt to embarrass him and tarnish his reputation. In his statement, the director of the Agricultural Bank claimed that Mithqal's pretext of being obliged to mortgage his land to the Jews was invalid, since he owed the bank only £200 and there was no intention to take over his land. The statement went on to reveal a detailed account of Mithqal's taxes in the previous three years, indicating that the taxes he paid on his large estates were actually very low.[95] A month later Mithqal suffered another blow. The leading shaykhs of the country refused him membership in a new body they formed around Abdullah, which they named the Jordanian People's Congress. Instead, the Bani Sakhr were represented by Haditha al-Khuraysha and Dahir Dhiyab al-Fayiz. The latter's participation was especially significant, since he was Mithqal's main rival for leadership of the Fayiz tribe.[96] With this, Mithqal was now isolated from his most natural milieu.

By now, even mighty Mithqal was affected and was forced to offer some concessions to his opponents. Perhaps, too, he had become a liability for Abdullah, on whose patronage he still relied. In August, he sent the emir a long letter, which the palace then released to the press. In it, Mithqal reiterated his loyalty to Abdullah and explained that his dealings with the Jews were devoid of any political goal and only meant to relieve his and his people's plight. *Filastin* was quick to celebrate this letter as a great national triumph. Although it is difficult to see a clear reference to that in the text, the newspaper commented that it was a sign of Mithqal's repentance and that he had renounced his contacts with the Jews.[97] This is also the interpretation of Muhammad 'Abd al-Qadir Khrisat, the only Jordanian historian writing in Arabic who has explicitly reported on Mithqal's relations with the Zionists, which at the time of this writing is still a very sensitive topic in Jordan.[98]

Either way, Mithqal continued his relations with the Zionist movement and did not shy away from public scrutiny. He had no other alternative at the time. He was deeply identified with the Zionists and could not switch to another patron. So a few days after he sent the letter to Abdullah, Mithqal was again in Jerusalem to complain of the slow pace taken by the Agency and the insufficient financial assistance delivered to him. Mithqal urged the Zionists to take more decisive and vigorous action. In December, he asked for £500–700 for a propaganda scheme to pave the way for Jewish entrance into Transjordan and another £1,000 to secure the election of sympathetic candidates to the new Legislative Council.[99] He also met with the Transjordanian prime minister and asked him whether the government would give permission to register his land in Jiza in the name of Jewish buyers. When asked to make a formal application, Mithqal declined to do so. Perhaps he knew that the Zionists would not pay and wanted to prevent another embarrassment.[100]

At any rate, by that time relations with Mithqal had lost much of their value for the Jewish Agency. In May 1933, the British government finally articulated its policy towards Jewish settlement in Transjordan during a meeting in London between the colonial secretary, the high commissioner, and a high-level Zionist delegation. The British officials expressed their sympathy with the idea of Jewish settlement in Transjordan as far as the future was concerned but insisted that it was unrealistic at the moment.[101] Consequently, the intensity of Zionist contacts with Mithqal decreased over the course of 1934–35, and so too did some of their intimacy. Still, it was important for the Agency to keep his friendship. This was done by maintaining contact with him and giving him small sums of money and presents from time to time. In April 1934, Moshe Shertok, who succeeded the late Arlosoroff as head of the Political Department, visited Mithqal in Amman. In his report, he mentioned that he noticed new furniture, purchased from the £50 recently given to the shaykh, and that coffee was served in a silver-and-glass set that he had brought Mithqal from Prague. A few months later, Mithqal received the financial assistance from the Agency that he had asked for in order to secure his election to the Legislative Council.[102]

Mithqal himself continued to ingratiate himself to his Jewish counterparts. When a group of scouts from Haifa stumbled on his encampment in the Jordan Valley in February 1934, he lavished his famous hospitality on them and reiterated his willingness to allow Jewish settlement on his land. He told his guests that he was a friend of the Jews; because of his support for the idea of Jewish immigration to Transjordan, he was in a state of *qawm*, a tribal term for a conflict or war, with the entire country. Three days later, he went to Haifa at the invitation of the scouts and was given a tour of the city's educational institutions and industry, which were a showcase of the Zionist enterprise. Accounts of both events were published in the Hebrew press.[103]

A close relationship had developed between Mithqal and Aharon Cohen and his family. One night around midnight, Cohen returned home accompanied by Mithqal, who had come to stay with him. He woke up his wife and asked her to prepare food for the hungry shaykh. Mrs. Cohen tried to argue but Cohen insisted, saying that Mithqal had asked specifically for bean soup. The next morning, Cohen and his family were astonished to discover that Mithqal had left a £5 note—almost the equivalent of Cohen's monthly salary. A few days later, moreover, a sack full of beans arrived from Transjordan. The family saw the money as thanks for their hospitality and the beans as a friendly hint that bean soup should be made with black beans, not red ones.[104] Alternatively, these gestures may well have been subtle criticisms of his hosts. Mithqal might have been suggesting to the Cohens that they had made him feel like a client, rather than a welcome guest, and that the soup was some-how inadequate, perhaps because of the reluctant spirit in which it had been prepared.[105] Either way, Mithqal's gestures and charisma went a long way to charming his Jewish interlocutors and making them feel obliged to respond to his requests.[106]

It is difficult to establish the exact monetary value of the Jewish Agency's support of Mithqal; many reports only mention that assistance was given, but do not specify the exact sums. An accurate account is further complicated by the fact that private or semi-official land dealers also supported him. Yehushua Hankin of the Palestine Land and Development Company was involved in the deal over Barazayn and in late 1933 gave Mithqal a "large loan."[107] In a letter to the Jewish Agency in 1943, a private dealer who had worked with Mithqal in the early 1930s claimed that the Agency had never reimbursed him for his great expenses. He mentioned two instances, in which he had given Mithqal £80 and £35 respectively in order to appease him after unsatisfactory meetings with Agency officials.[108] Also, in a letter sent to Mithqal in December 1935, a promi-nent Jerusalem merchant offered to provide him with a piece of agricultural machinery, as well as to ask the Agency to give him a "limited sum" in order to relieve him of his difficulties.[109] But even without exact accounting, there is little doubt that both the official and personal relationships that Mithqal estab-lished with the Zionists, and the accompanying financial benefits, helped him to endure the most difficult years of the 1930s.

But Mithqal's relationship with the Zionists entailed important political ad-vantages as well. His connection to the Zionist movement at least temporar-ily offset the growing interference of the Transjordanian government in tribal affairs and the undermining of the role of the shaykhs. It increased his po-litical importance in Transjordan, helping him to maintain leverage vis-à-vis the government and the British. It also improved his relations with Abdullah, who was looking for local approval of, and support for, his own contacts with the Zionists. And, most important, in securing a source of income indepen-dent of the state for himself, Mithqal succeeded in safeguarding his autonomy. Ultimately, the financial assistance Mithqal received from the Jewish Agency allowed him to reject the British offer of a loan of £1,000 in 1934 and thus to save himself from government intervention in the affairs of his estate.[110] Judg-ing from Mithqal's point of view and personal interests, it is possible to assert that he was successful in choosing the Zionist option and in fact dutifully ful-filling his role as shaykh of shaykhs.

THE 1936 ARAB REVOLT

By the beginning of 1936, Mithqal was ready to change his strategy again. By that time, his relations with the Jewish Agency had grown strained, with a Zionist report alluding to a "known misunderstanding."[111] This was probably a reference to Shertok's refusal at the beginning of 1936 of Mithqal's request for a Jewish Agency "loan" of £100. On top of the rejection, and to add insult to injury, Shertok instructed Cohen to inform Mithqal that because of the lack of political progress, the Agency's executive had decided to stop all expenses on matters regarding Transjordan.[112] This was particularly bad news for Mithqal, since it came after another disappointing winter. His relations with the Zionists had reached a dead end.

On top of losing the financial patronage of the Jewish Agency, Mithqal was increasingly concerned about the undermining of his tribal and personal autonomy. His activity in the Legislative Council indicates his state of mind at the time. Abandoning his typical silence, he became very active in the council's discussions and expressed his fierce objection to any government attempt to limit tribal autonomy, especially that of the nomadic tribes. During a discussion of a draft law regulating hunting, a frustrated Mithqal cried: "You don't leave anything [untouched]. Now you are preventing people from hunting."[113] Mithqal's anger did not end with words. In January 1936, he led the successful opposition to the government's attempt to legislate immunity for Arab Legion officers from legal claims. In what became a self-fulfilling prophecy, he warned that this move, if accepted, would "provoke revolt in the country."[114] And indeed a revolt there was. But it erupted first west of the Jordan River rather than on its eastern bank.

Tensions between Jews and Arabs in Palestine had risen high for several months when on April 15 an attack on a convoy that resulted in two Jewish drivers being killed led to a revenge attack the following day, with two Arab dead. Riots now broke out in Jaffa and Tel Aviv, with casualties on both sides. These riots quickly spread throughout Palestine and soon escalated into a general uprising directed against both the British government and the Jews. The Arab leadership called a general strike that lasted until October. Frustration with the inability to stop the Zionist project in Palestine, especially after several years of dramatically increasing Jewish immigration following the Nazi rise to power in Germany, was one of the main causes of what is known as the Arab Revolt, one of the most momentous developments in the history of Palestine.[115]

East of the Jordan, the turmoil in Palestine soon provoked opposition to the British, the government, and sometimes even to Emir Abdullah personally. Attacks on telegraph and telephone lines became commonplace. So did sabotage of the pipeline connecting the oil fields in Iraq with the port of Haifa, financial support for the rebels, arms smuggling, and demonstrations and conferences in support of the Palestinian cause. Some Transjordanians protected Palestinian guerrilla bands; others even fought alongside them. Several tribal leaders offered active support to the Palestinians, risking direct conflict with the government. Even nomadic tribes, hitherto thought to be immune to national politics and ideology, showed increasing signs of sympathy with the Palestinians, which caused much alarm among British officials, the Transjordanian government, and the Jewish Agency. Glubb reported that, "propaganda and incitement gradually penetrated during the month of June [1936] to the furthest tribal areas. Even the Huwaitat camped in the far desert were intensely excited."[116] The Zionists, too, were alarmed by what one report called "the stormy atmosphere against us in Transjordan."[117] They hurried to respond to Abdullah's request for financial assistance and provided him with £500 in order to help him restrain the population. The Jewish Agency would do this several times during the revolt.[118] The support for the Arab Revolt in Transjordan and defiance of central authority it sparked were the result of sympathy for the Palestinian struggle and growing national consciousness among educated circles. Many Transjordanians also took advantage of a government seen to be in a precarious position. The prolonged years of economic crisis and growing frustration with the government's interference in tribal affairs had taken their toll, fomenting anti-colonial hostility and alienation, as well as increased tribal receptivity to the Palestinians' appeals to join them.

Mithqal seized the new opportunity presented by the Arab Revolt with both hands. To the surprise and dismay of the Jewish Agency, he "crossed the lines" and joined forces with the leaders of the Arab movement in Palestine. In supporting the Arab Revolt, he defied Abdullah, the British, and the Zionists. He was fortunate in being able to find a new patron shortly after the previous Zionist one became irrelevant to him. In good shaykhly manner, he did not shy away from changing patrons and playing them off against each other.

In June 1936, Mithqal issued invitations to "almost every tribal leader in Transjordan," in the words of Glubb, to attend a meeting in his village of Umm al-'Amad in order to consider intervention in the affairs of Palestine. For that purpose, Mithqal reportedly received £150 from the Arab Higher Committee, the body that Mufti Hajj Amin al-Husseini formed and chaired to lead the revolt.[119] Glubb was alarmed at this new development, to the point of mild panic. The news of the conference, Glubb reported, provoked excited rumors; there was a danger that such a gathering might lead to "violence which could have dragged the whole country into rebellion."[120]

Fortunately for the British, this did not materialize; the conference did not lead to united action by the tribes, as the British had originally feared. Due to Abdullah's timely intervention, most important tribal leaders did not attend. Glubb claimed that "tribally, the affair was a fiasco." He went on to assert that the end result was the strengthening of government power in tribal areas. Yet Glubb admitted that the conference had a great effect on ordinary tribesmen, which was reflected in their daily behavior. The belief that the government was experiencing difficulties gave rise to acts of defiance "in many small ways; a truculence of manner, a loudness of voice and a generally swashbuckling manner."[121]

If the British panic over the potential dangers of the conference was exaggerated, their celebration of Mithqal's "failure" was as well. This was partly caused by a systemic misreading of the shaykh's objectives. Mithqal's support of the revolt did not in fact represent a change of heart and a new adherence to national ideology, any more than his dealings with the Jewish Agency reflected sympathy with Zionism. Moreover, it is doubtful that Mithqal wanted to rock the boat and stir up a rebellion, because that might result in the severance of his relations with Abdullah and would risk all-out conflict with the British authorities. Simply put, Mithqal had too much to lose. Rather, positioning himself as the head of the opposition to the British and as a great friend of the Palestinians entailed many practical benefits for Mithqal. It allowed him to repair his public image in the Arab world after years of being under suspicion of sympathy with the Zionists. The new political alliance also had its financial benefits as well; he received money from the Palestinian leadership and perhaps viewed it as another pressure tactic to influence the Zionists to resume their payments to him. More important yet, this strategy served Mithqal as a way to aggrandize his political position in Transjordan. He was now able to demonstrate his autonomy to the government and tribesmen alike and to remind the authorities that his good behavior could not be taken for granted.

In point of fact, Mithqal's speech at the conference was quite moderate; it did not go much beyond declaring sympathy with the Palestinian national struggle, criticizing British policy, and expressing an unspecific willingness to come to the rescue of the Palestinians. His most practical suggestion was to send telegrams to Abdullah and to the Colonial Office; indeed, the conference produced just such a telegram to the British government. It is also interesting to note that Mithqal's nationalist rhetoric was blended with tribal concepts. Mithqal warned against the persistence of the provocation against the Palestinians and demanded that they obtain their rights, as promised by Britain during World War I. Failing this, "the leaders of the Arab lands will be compelled to rescue their brothers without hesitation. This is what the Arab customs, first and foremost chivalry [*nakhwa*] and the duty to come to [their] rescue [*najda*], demand." He went on to ask rhetorically, "If the Arab is willing to sacrifice his life for the stranger"—referring to the customary duty to offer hospitality and protection to anyone who sought them—"how would he not do so for his own family [*ahl*] and the sons of his own people [*qawm*]?"[122]

After the meeting in his village, Mithqal continued his deep involvement in Palestinian politics. He traveled to Syria and Palestine to mobilize the Arab public against the Jews, sent protests to the high commissioner and the emir, held frequent meetings with the Arab Higher Committee and especially with the Mufti, gave anti-Jewish statements to Arab newspapers in Palestine and Syria, and organized protest rallies.[123] In November 1936, the rebels' supreme commander, Fawzi Qawuqji, slipped away from Palestine and crossed the Jordan on his way to Iraq with the help of the British. Mithqal, accompanied by Shaykh Haditha, escorted him through the desert to ensure his safe journey.[124] Mithqal continued his involvement in Palestinian politics in the first months of 1937. Glubb attributed what he saw as restlessness and insubordination among the Bani Sakhr to their leader's activity.[125]

Mithqal's involvement in the Arab Revolt was characteristically impressive. In the words of Glubb, Mithqal "made himself the principal instrument of the agitators advocating violence in Transjordan," becoming "almost the only sheikh in Transjordan who tried to raise disturbances in 1936 in sympathy with the Palestine rebels."[126] In his relations with the Palestinians, Mithqal demonstrated the same characteristics that he had once shown in dealing with the Zionists—leadership, shrewdness, resourcefulness, flexibility, courage, and willingness to take risks and to gamble, the traits that had been the basic qualifications for the role of shaykh for generations.

Mithqal's strategy proved successful. He once more enjoyed a positive reputation among Arabs both within and outside Transjordan. More important, he created the image of an independent leader who posed a threat to the government and who dared to defy the British. After years of increased government interference in tribal affairs, and the consequent undermining of the shaykhs' standing, it was a clever political move. Mithqal employed a defiant attitude but managed to avoid falling out with the emir. Indeed, on the contrary, his actions only increased his leverage with Abdullah. When the emir distributed subsidies to the shaykhs as part of a new policy to improve security that was supported by both the British and the Zionists, Mithqal received the generous sum of £200. Similarly, Muhammad al-Unsi, the head of the Palace Bureau and the liaison between Abdullah and the Jewish Agency, conveyed Abdullah's complaints about the Jewish Agency's strained relations with Mithqal to Cohen, suggesting that the Zionists amend their relations with him.[127]

Mithqal himself tried to bring about reconciliation with the Jewish Agency and was careful to keep all options open. In October 1936, immediately after the Palestinian leadership called off the general strike and thus brought a temporary halt to the revolt, Mithqal rented a hotel room in Jerusalem, where a meeting would take place in hope of mending his relations with the Zionists. He might have feared that in time of peace he would no longer be an asset to the Palestinian leadership. He did not offer his guests a drink, and instead followed the tribal custom that when adversaries met, they did not drink or eat together until they had reached an agreement. In the event, no such agreement was forthcoming. Jewish Agency officials viewed his past conduct as a betrayal and were not impressed now by his conciliatory attitude. Mithqal repeated his overtures directly or through mediators, but the Agency demanded a written apology, which Mithqal was not willing to give.[128] It was now Jewish nationalism that limited Mithqal's room to maneuver. He got burned whenever he went too decidedly against nationalist sentiment, Jewish or Arab. He was not equipped to take either seriously enough and failed to read the situation correctly.[129]

Mithqal's worries about peace in Palestine were unfounded. In July 1937, the Peel Commission of Inquiry appointed by the British government to investigate the causes of the revolt and suggest a new policy published its report. It recommended the partition of Palestine into Jewish and Arab states, the latter to be linked with Transjordan. This solution fell short of Palestinian aspirations for full independence throughout the Mandate, and violence soon resumed. What was known as the second phase of the revolt was mostly a peasant-led violent rebellion against the British, but it soon also developed into an internal Arab civil war. The British police and army used increasingly brutal means to suppress the revolt, which they did in the summer of 1939.

Mithqal, too, resumed his activities and became immersed in the politics of the revolt, perhaps also because he had failed to win over the Zionists. Shortly after the publication of the Peel report, he met the Arab Higher Committee in Jerusalem and upon his return, sent his nephew to Palestine.[130] According to local oral history, he also defied Abdullah's orders and harbored fugitive Palestinian fighters in his camp. This is corroborated by the written testimony of a Jewish mechanic who worked on Mithqal's farm for several months in 1941, who suspected that several members of Mithqal's household were veterans of the revolt who had found refuge with the shaykh.[131]

Not surprisingly, Mithqal's support for the Palestinians carried with it financial gains. In 1937, he owned a combine harvester, perhaps the first to be employed in Transjordan and a valuable asset on a huge farm like Mithqal's. Rumor had it that this was a gift from the Palestinian national leadership in return for Mithqal's support during the revolt. Either that or it was purchased with the help of 'Abd al-Hamid Shuman, the founder and director of the Arab Bank. Already in 1934, Shuman had granted Mithqal a £1,000 loan at low interest. In his memoirs, Shuman explained that while living in the United States, he had been impressed by the story of Mithqal's arrest of Peake in 1920 and his audacity in defying colonial rule. When he returned to the Middle East, he met Mithqal and developed a sympathy with him. The cordial relationship became an important factor in Mithqal's and his family's prosperity. Subsequently, Mithqal would be able to borrow from the Arab Bank when he needed to.[132]

Perhaps Mithqal's renewed involvement in the Arab Revolt was intended to enhance his tribal position. Just before the resumption of violence in Palestine, Mithqal faced the greatest threat thus far to his strong-handed leadership of the Bani Sakhr when the shaykhs of the Zaban tribe challenged it. They gathered in what a British report described as a demonstration against Mithqal with their men fully armed. The issue at stake was a long-standing dispute over ownership of a piece of land. What provoked the Zaban was Mithqal's decision to involve the civil governor in a case that should have been settled by tribal custom. A clash was only averted by the timely mediation of a reinforced contingent of the Desert Patrol.[133]

If Mithqal's activities in Palestine boosted his leadership, they also carried a price: towards the end of 1937, Mithqal and Abdullah fell out. The ultimate cause of the dispute was the intensification of Mithqal's involvement in Palestine and his close association with Abdullah's rival, the Mufti. This was the first serious quarrel between these two close old allies. At a tribal party in the palace, the emir publicly rebuked Mithqal and forbade him to visit the palace. Mithqal reacted by commencing negotiations with the Saudi government on moving into its territory. The result was what some reports describe as a "mutual boycott."[134] There was nothing more troubling for Abdullah than seeing his old protégé flirting with his arch-rival Ibn Saud. Perhaps it was a time for a new patron for Mithqal. Once again, he was playing off different patrons against each other.

The deterioration of the relationship between Mithqal and Abdullah alarmed the British. Cox reported that there was "an element of danger in the situation." He viewed the cause as not necessarily related to Mithqal's involvement in Palestine, but rather his attempts to arrange for candidates unacceptable to the emir to be elected to the Council.[135] Regardless of the exact reason, Cox's concern over the tense relations between Mithqal and Abdullah, as well as Glubb's anxiety over the unruly behavior of the Bani Sakhr, clearly indicate the magnitude of the challenge Mithqal posed to the British. Despite the success of the Arab Legion in controlling the tribes, such control was precarious, and Glubb feared that in times of crisis, the government might lose its grip altogether. Glubb and the government had not yet achieved full control over Mithqal in particular and the tribes in general. This is why the British saw Abdullah's moderate influence over him as essential.

For his part, Mithqal did not seek conflict with Abdullah and much preferred to amend his relationship with the emir. An account by the Jewish Agency reported on a visit by Abdullah's elder son, Prince Talal, to Mithqal's tent, asking that he make peace with his father. Cox, too, met Mithqal and urged him to make peace. Such mediation was successful, and a reconciliation was achieved. Seeking to take advantage of his positive response to Cox, Mithqal asked for a £1,000 loan. When this was refused, he suggested that he be paid the salary he had received during Ottoman times, but again without luck.[136]

One of the concessions Mithqal was forced to offer as a price of reconciliation with Abdullah was to promise to limit his own involvement in Palestine. He seems to have been genuine; there are no indications of such activities during 1938–39, apart from a quite halfhearted attempt to mediate between rival parties in the Hebron area at the Mufti's request.[137] Abdullah himself took precautions. When, in late summer 1938, there were growing signs of Palestinian guerrilla activity in Transjordan, Abdullah went on another tour in the desert and successfully induced the tribes to resist the incursions from Palestine. His powers of persuasion were undoubtedly enhanced by his powers of the purse; it is likely that he brought some money for the shaykhs with him. During this tour, he camped with Mithqal and brokered a peace between him and his rival for the leadership of the Fayiz tribe, Dahir Dhiyab. Al-Unsi explained that it was done to prevent them from cooperating with the Mufti.[138] A few years later, boasting of his own activities in Palestine, 'Akif al-Fayiz recounted that he had stopped this involvement only after the emir "begged" him and his father to do so.[139]

Mithqal's disengagement from the affairs of Palestine was a small concession to Abdullah. In any case, it cost Mithqal little; by that time, he had already reaped the fruits of his support for the Arab Revolt, both financially and politically. His constant juggling between different, often rival, allies over the course of the decade proved successful. Probably more than any other shaykh in Transjordan, Mithqal was successful in finding new ways and resources to maintain his leadership and privileged position. Despite the growing pressure on him from the government, he managed to keep it at arm's length, and, in so doing, to preserve much of his own autonomy. Although he was unable to stop the process of state formation, and the concomitant increase in government power and encroachment on tribal affairs, he did manage to mitigate the process and postpone it—at least for a few more years.

6 DISGRUNTLED ACCOMMODATION

BY 1937, the prolonged drought was over. One could almost hear a sigh of relief all over Transjordan. Nomads now benefited from rainfall levels typical of the country or even above average. Not only did the better climate improve the pastoral economy but the Transjordanian authorities made an effort to support it. A financial contribution from the British government enabled John Glubb and the Desert Patrol to develop water resources in the desert, which they did with the active participation of the nomads themselves, the Bani Sakhr in particular. During 1937–39, they dug wells, cleaned old Roman cisterns, and drilled two wells equipped with water pumps. Nomads were soon able to find better grazing and water in the desert for their animals, and with Glubb's help and guidance, more and more of them even took up cultivation. Peasants, too, felt the change, since they enjoyed good crops, helping them to pay down their debts. There was a bumper harvest in 1937. Government officials who feared that economic difficulties would encourage people to join the Arab Revolt in Palestine or rebel in Transjordan were also pleased. This was not merely a temporary respite but a turning of the corner, the beginning of a period of relative prosperity in Transjordan that allowed its struggling inhabitants to recover.[1]

As the largest landowner in the country, Mithqal was one of the main beneficiaries of the improving economic climate. His extensive landholdings represented his main source of income and provided the financial basis to support his influence and leadership. At least for a while, he was able to scale back the political machinations that had characterized his activity in earlier years. Instead, he invested his remarkable energy in cultivating and developing his farms. He once more enjoyed a stable, secure leadership position among the

Bani Sakhr. But he soon had to deal with new challenges, which were all about another climate, the political one.

CONSOLIDATION OF POWER

From the late 1930s, Mithqal's large estates once again became a profitable source of wealth enabling him to reinforce his leadership position. On top of the improvement in agricultural production thanks to the end of the drought, Mithqal was also a beneficiary of the rise in cereal prices resulting from the prolonged instability in Palestine caused by the Arab Revolt. Prices remained high following the outbreak of World War II in the fall of 1939.[2] Mithqal actively exploited these opportunities to increase his profits. He was the first landowner in Transjordan to mechanize his operations to take advantage of the improved situation. By the end of the 1930s, he began accumulating a fleet of motorized plows and combines so large and so heavily used that he had to hire a professional mechanic from Palestine to maintain it.[3] The mechanization of agriculture allowed Mithqal to cultivate tracts hitherto left fallow. It also allowed him to reduce the number of tenants working on the land and thereby increase his share of the yield. Some of the permanent sharecroppers of Jiza whose ancestors had been brought from Egypt by Mithqal's father also left the village after they realized that they would never become landowners. In 1938, during land settlement in the village, these peasants failed to claim the land as their own, and Mithqal registered it as his private property.[4]

Mithqal put his new wealth to use in expanding his already large holdings of about 70,000 dunams. He purchased as much land as possible south of Amman, also acquiring large tracts that had previously belonged to members of his tribe and family.[5] These burgeoning holdings did not go unnoticed; in the summer of 1938, Lieutenant Colonel Frederick Peake, commander of the Arab Legion, reported that Mithqal was profiting nicely from agriculture, describing him as someone who "has now become a power in the land."[6] A British agricultural expert's later description of Mithqal's estate after a year of bountiful, widespread rain further illustrates the considerable benefits it yielded: "Here, and for some miles approaching Madaba, the countryside presents the appearance of a vast sea of wheat. So great is the area that one looks in vain for fallow land for next year's crop and it appears as though wheat may follow wheat annually on the land."[7]

Another lucrative source of income was the mediation of disputes, a role that also brought the convenient benefit of enhancing Mithqal's prestige and political influence. Following years of conflict with the authorities in Amman, especially during his involvement in the Arab Revolt in Palestine, Mithqal was careful to maintain good relations with the British and the government. He took advantage of his improved standing with the government to settle cases in favor of "Arab litigants" who paid him for the service.[8]

More important was the resumption of the alliance between Mithqal and Emir Abdullah, upon which much of the former's influence and prosperity depended. Abdullah's patronage and the close cooperation between the two men resembled their relationship before the outbreak of the Arab Revolt and even during the early years of the emirate. Mithqal enjoyed free access to the emir and is even said to have mediated in spats between Abdullah and his son Talal.[9] John Glubb, who succeeded Peake as the commander of the Arab Legion in 1939, attributed Mithqal's success as a mediator and his subsequent wealth to Abdullah's favor. Annoyed by Mithqal's steady elevation, he lamented what he perceived as his deliberate manipulation of the emir. Glubb believed that Abdullah granted Mithqal favors, not out of genuine affection, but because he regarded him as a man of great influence. According to Glubb, however, Mithqal's influence in fact derived primarily from his receipt of such favors.[10]

Mithqal's relations outside Transjordan relied on his reputation as Abdullah's ally, which he parlayed into an independent network extending all over the Middle East. In 1938, the British consul in Damascus reported that Mithqal planned to give a large reception in Amman for Syrian notables. High on Abdullah's political agenda at that time was his "Greater Syria plan," the unification of Transjordan with Syria and Palestine under his monarchy. His British patrons actively discouraged the idea, so Abdullah enlisted the connections of his ally Mithqal. Indeed, a year later, British intelligence learned that Mithqal was in Syria and had twice met the French deputy high commissioner in connection with the plan to unite Syria and Transjordan under Abdullah.[11]

Although Mithqal enjoyed a prominent position in Transjordan, he was conscious of the risk of putting all his eggs in one basket. Whether promoting Abdullah's interests or his own, he was typically busy cultivating relationships with influential personalities across the region. In May 1939 he spent a few days in Damascus on his way to Baghdad to attend the ceremony marking forty days since the death of King Ghazi, the son and successor of King Faysal. He maintained his contacts in Egypt and, in 1939, he hosted the tribal leader and Wafd party politician Shaykh Hamad al-Basil, his relative. When the latter died a few months later, Mithqal traveled to Egypt to attend the funeral.[12]

Mithqal also maintained intermittent connections with the Jewish Agency. In 1938, he asked the Agency to help him arrange an appointment with a famous specialist to treat an eye disease he had suffered from for most of his life, and that seems to have worsened as he grew older. Perhaps, however, this was a pretext to resume contact with the Zionists. Moshe Shertok, head of the Political Department, had not forgiven Mithqal his anti-Zionist activity during the Arab Revolt and refused to help. But a year later, an old acquaintance, Aharon Cohen, escorted Mithqal to Tel Aviv to see another Jewish doctor who was visiting Palestine. Cohen's daughter recalled how Mithqal's tribal robes and sword had attracted attention in the streets of Tel Aviv.[13]

Mithqal's most interesting and certainly most sensitive external contact during this period was with Ibn Saud, Abdullah's archrival since the days of the Hashemite Arab Revolt. Mithqal maintained close relations with the king through his cousin Dahham al-Fayiz, whose half-sister had married Ibn Saud around 1936. Shortly thereafter, the bride had invited the young Dahham to keep her company at the king's court in Riyadh. In March 1940, the Transjordanian authorities discovered a coded correspondence between Mithqal and Ibn Saud, undertaken via Dahham and 'Akif al-Fayiz. It was believed that the latter had been sent by his father to meet with the king. The authorities also found Saudi propaganda material in 'Akif's possession defaming Abdullah and his government.[14] Once revealed, the correspondence between Mithqal and Ibn Saud upset Abdullah and affected the intimacy of their relationship.

Glubb could not ascertain why Mithqal would connect with Ibn Saud, but suspected that it was done to impress Abdullah.[15] This may well have been the case, but another possible motivation is that the Saudis represented an insurance policy against the possibility of a future conflict with the Transjordanian government. Mithqal had already used the "Saudi option" as a negotiation ploy during his previous fallout with Abdullah in 1937, and he reportedly considered the possibility of moving permanently to Saudi territory at subsequent times of crisis.

The establishment of secret contacts with Ibn Saud represented an abandonment of the cautious line Mithqal had taken since 1937–38. His willingness to run such risks reflected the extent to which growing state power threatened to encroach on his traditional autonomy. By 1939, the emirate of Transjordan had already acquired many traits of a modern state. First and foremost was a government monopoly on coercive power. At the beginning of 1939, the Desert Patrol numbered three hundred men, triple its original complement.

Later that same year, the British established a reserve force numbering several hundred men, all from nomadic tribes. After the outbreak of war in Europe, the British continued to sign up new recruits, bringing the overall strength of the Arab Legion to about four thousand men by 1942.[16] The Legion's growing numbers, together with the improvement of the road network, enabled it to carry out large-scale operations throughout the country and made it easier to contain occasional acts of tribal resistance. The Legion also achieved an impressive degree of control over the country's borders, as demonstrated by the arrest of Mithqal's son. At the same time, the expansion of the civil administration apparatus greatly expanded the government's ability to intervene in the daily lives of ordinary people. In 1939, the British government amended the Anglo-Transjordanian Treaty to allow the local government more autonomy. Subsequently, the prime minister initiated a structural reorganization of the government, which was followed by rapid expansion of administrative personnel. The tendency of state agencies to regulate society and interfere in tribal matters, which had begun around 1930, had considerably increased a decade later.

Mithqal and other shaykhs were increasingly concerned by these growing threats to their autonomy, and the outbreak of World War II permitted them to hope that Britain's predicament in Europe would undermine its grip on its Middle Eastern possessions. Shortly after the arrival of news from Europe, several tribal shaykhs approached the British Resident and asked to be paid subsidies in return for guaranteeing the peace. By that time, the British authorities were so confident of the Arab Legion's ability to deal with malcontents that the Resident dismissed the offer out of hand.[17] Nevertheless, Mithqal was tempted to test the limits of the government, a strategy he had honed since his early days as a tribal leader. Perhaps his growing wealth and influence also gave him an inflated sense of power, and his attitude towards Abdullah, the government, and the British authorities became increasingly bold.

But the British were losing patience. They were already outraged by Mithqal's secret correspondence with Ibn Saud, and barely a month had passed before they were obliged to confront him on a different matter altogether. Prompted by revelations in the Syrian press that the government there subsidized its shaykhs, Transjordanian notables demanded to be treated similarly. Unlike the others, Mithqal did not limit himself to verbal appeals, but "showed signs of becoming troublesome."[18] The dispatch of a detachment of the Desert Patrol to the vicinity of the Bani Sakhr was deemed necessary to deter any possible trouble.

Reporting on the incident, the new British Resident Alec Kirkbride, said, "it is probable that sooner or later an example will have to be made of a tribal leader who goes too far in his endeavours to extort blackmail from the government."[19]

Mithqal was not deterred. On the contrary, he resumed his political machinations, believing that wartime conditions played into his hands and that he could make himself useful to the British. In September, the Palestine government enlisted Mithqal's services as a mediator, his guarantee of good behavior allowing a Palestinian activist to return to his village after being deported. Mindful of the severity of the Arab Revolt, the British made special efforts during the war to improve their relations with the Palestinians.[20] The war seemed to have presented another opportunity for Mithqal to find a new patron. In November 1940, he traveled to Syria for two weeks, the pretext being an invitation he had received from his sister, who lived in Lebanon. According to the British Resident, Mithqal went to Syria following rumors about money being distributed to Syrian tribal leaders by the Italian Armistice Commission, which oversaw French colonies following the Italian and German victory over France. Mithqal returned empty-handed and disgruntled.[21]

Upon his return from Syria, Mithqal tried to mend his relationship with Abdullah. A serendipitous opportunity presented itself when Abdullah had to sell ninety of his best she-camels to a Saudi merchant to pay for the wedding of his son Nayif. When Mithqal bumped into the caravan on its way to Najd, he immediately recognized his friend's camels, bought them for £750 and returned them to Abdullah, saying that it was not proper for the emir to sell his camels in order to wed his son.[22] Later, when Nayif married, Mithqal brought an expensive present for the young prince. Such gift-giving was a two-way street: Abdullah gave expensive clothes and "a truck full of various exquisite presents" to Mithqal's eldest sons, Nawwash and 'Akif, when they married.[23]

His sons' joint wedding in 1940 provided Mithqal with the perfect occasion to demonstrate his power and wealth. It was hailed in the press as the biggest party ever held in the country, and Mithqal's generosity was commended with superlatives in newspapers. "Anyone who saw the lambs on the table might have thought at first glance that it was an entire flock sleeping in the meadow," the Amman paper al-Urdunn declared.[24] Generosity, hospitality, and the exchange of gifts constituted important cultural markers in tribal societies and remained symbols of shaykhly legitimacy and power. Indeed, shaykhs were all but expected to perform these duties. But the projection of power through hospitality became even more important as actual shaykhly power began to dwindle. In the face of an increasingly powerful government, it was crucial for shaykhs to maintain at least the appearance of strength. Those few who could afford to lavish hospitality on a personage as exalted as Abdullah earned even more respect. During the 1940s, Mithqal's displays of hospitality and generosity became ever more extravagant.

True to the pattern of their relationship, however, Mithqal failed to maintain Abdullah's support for long, and a couple of months later they had another falling out. A young kibbutznik employed as a mechanic on Mithqal's farm, Yitzhak Avira, reported in March 1941 that Mithqal hadn't visited Abdullah in nearly a month, compared to nearly daily meetings earlier. When Abdullah phoned him to arrange a meeting, Mithqal rebuffed him by saying that he was preoccupied with work and could not come.[25]

At the time, Mithqal was at loggerheads with the government over the granting of a visa to his Jewish mechanic, who had been working for him illegally. His passport was taken by the police, and attempts by 'Akif and Mithqal to collect it were refused. Avira was threatened with two months' imprisonment or a fine of £16. Avira's impression was that Mithqal was too proud to let the government win by completing the steps to legalize his trusted mechanic's stay in the country. This would have compromised his personal autonomy. Mithqal could have solved the problem easily by asking Abdullah to intervene, but he was probably unwilling to make such a request while relations were so tense. In the meantime, Avira was obliged to remain in Mithqal's immediate presence, which ensured him complete immunity. Ultimately, a compromise was reached. Mithqal paid a fine of £3.5 and in an effort at reconciliation, invited several senior officers of the Arab Legion to his house for a meal. As was customary, all the guests stood in his honor upon his entrance to the dining area, save for two officers. Mithqal said nothing, but was unable to conceal his obvious displeasure. Unwilling to make further concessions, Mithqal never applied for a visa.[26]

Avira's enforced stay over three months left him well placed to offer detailed and colorful reports of Mithqal and his household. He wrote them secretly and sent them to his friends in the kibbutz. They soon reached the files of the Jewish Agency's Political Department in Jerusalem and were probably read with great interest. The reports to a large degree resemble those in which Mithqal's guests ten years earlier reported on him. Yet they are also revealing in their description of the many changes that the intervening years had wrought, both in Mithqal's lifestyle and in his role as a tribal leader.[27]

By this time, Mithqal had left his original two-story house in Amman, which he rented out to the government for use as an orphanage, and economized by renting a smaller, less expensive flat. It is possible this exchange was an austerity measure during the years of economic troubles. Yet for all its apparent modesty, the new home was still spacious enough to enable Mithqal to fulfill his public duties. He resided there fulltime during the winter, and occasionally during the summer. This was in sharp contrast to his practice ten years earlier, when he would spend the winter months among his tribesmen in the desert or in the Jordan Valley during seasons of bad grazing.

The apartment was a mixture of tribal, Arab urban, and European styles, as befitted the varied identity of the guests entertained within its walls. It centered on a large, six-meter-square parlor, or *diwan*, with handsome Damascene furnishings that projected wealth and worldliness, including a radio, a rarity in Transjordan during the early 1940s.

The *diwan* was directly accessible via a stairwell leading one floor down to the ground level. This internal organization of the flat allowed male guests to enter, without exposing female residents to their gaze, which might offend their modesty and honor. In that respect, the house functioned exactly as the tent once did.[28] In fact, the *diwan* resembled the *shigg* of the traditional Bedouin tent. Regardless of the presence of chairs, Mithqal and his guests, who sat opposite him, usually sat on a carpet of large goatskins spread out on the floor. In between, there was an iron stove, on which coffee was brewed.

The style of hospitality corresponded to the identity of the guests. When they were Arab, lunch was served in the room opposite the *diwan*. Tradition was slightly modified to suit the conditions of the apartment, and the requirements of the new era. A carpet would be laid on the floor, with white ceramic plates, silverware, and a white napkin for each guest arranged around it. Big china bowls with the food would be placed in the middle; each guest was welcome to help himself to rice, roast meat with tomatoes, green broad beans (*ful*), milk, and slices of thick pita bread. After the meal, the party would adjourn to the *diwan* to drink coffee and to smoke the water pipe . When the guests were senior army officers and government officials, the meal was served in a European or urban fashion. A dining table was laid on the big balcony and the guests sat at the table on chairs. Avira observed that Mithqal did not like this eating arrangement.

Mithqal had many and varied guests, both rich and poor. The traffic in the house was nonstop. Many came with a specific purpose in mind. Mithqal was consequently busy with many different matters, which included the selling of grain and sheep, the leasing of land, efforts to obtain pardons in criminal cases, the resolution of interpersonal conflicts, and women's affairs, as well as tending to needy people who came asking for charity. Even when walking in the streets of Amman, many people would stop him and ask for his help. Sometimes he grew so tired of dealing with people that he retired to Umm al-'Amad for some rest. But after a few hours, he inevitably returned to make himself available to the public. His role as a mediator and judge depended on his accessibility.

As a stranger who was not supposed to be in contact with the women of the Amman house, Avira's interactions were predominantly with Mithqal's sons and slaves. His description shows that slaves continued to play an important role in Mithqal's large operation. One of the slaves was Mithqal's driver. Another, a tall black man named Shushan, was described by Avira as Mithqal's "blue-eyed boy." Shushan and his family lived in another apartment at Mithqal's expense, but he spent most of his time at his shaykh's side. Avira had the impression that the talkative, outgoing Shushan expressed the thinking of his cautious, reserved boss.

After solving the bureaucratic hurdle over his visa, Avira moved to Umm al-'Amad, where he spent most of his time working and observing the running of the estate. Mithqal and family resided there most of the summer. During the winter, the house was kept locked and watched over by a family of caretakers. In 1941, Mithqal and his urban wife 'Adul lived in quarters built above the barns and stables. 'Adul, who previously spent all her time in Amman, was responsible for the women's quarters of Umm al-'Amad. Mithqal's two other wives each resided in her own tent. One was Sat'a; the other, Mithqal's youngest wife at the time, bore him Mashhur and Nashmi, then aged twelve and eight respectively.[29] In the big tent formerly used by Mithqal the newlywed Nawwash and his wife Nada now resided.

The high level of education attained by the children of the illiterate shaykh impressed Avira. During most of the year, they were enrolled in one of Amman's primary schools. The children spent the summer break in Umm al-'Amad, where they studied for four to five hours a day in a tent. The teacher Mithqal hired for that purpose had been born in Palestine and studied in Cairo at the highest institution for Islamic and Arabic studies, al-Azhar University. He was also responsible for leading the prayers outside the tents. Another al-Azhar graduate taught the children of Umm al-'Amad's residents. Mithqal gave him and his family a house and paid him a small fee for his role as the muezzin of the village's makeshift mosque.

The children of all ages showed respect and deference to their father. When a child met him, he would clasp Mithqal's hands, kiss them, and press them against his forehead. This acknowledgement of authority was the custom of everybody who met the shaykh. But it would not have been appropriate for Avira, as a stranger, to do the same. Instead, they shook hands, and Mithqal held Avira's for a few seconds. When Mithqal met people he was not happy to see, he offered his hands but withdrew them before the person had the chance to kiss them. In the course of a conversation, Mithqal did not shout, even when angry. When he was, he raised his voice a little, expressed understated displeasure, but maintained a dignified bearing.

In addition to his hectic life in Amman, Mithqal was also busily involved in managing every aspect of his farm. He woke up early in the morning and headed to the barn during the harvest season. He dealt with everything personally, doctoring injured horses, selling grain, purchasing camels, inspecting work done, examining the fields and warehouse, and looking after the domestic requirements of the house. His commercial transactions with Arab merchants from Palestine ran into the hundreds of pounds, a considerable sum at the time. When spare parts were needed for one of the tractors, Mithqal, accompanied by Avira, the tractor's driver, and his indispensable advisor, the scribe Abu Khalid, traveled to Tel Aviv to purchase them. Side by side with his farm chores, Mithqal continued with his public duties of mediation, philanthropy, and hospitality.

Despite Mithqal's personal involvement in the affairs of the farm, the sheer size and complexity of the estate necessitated the hiring of a professional manager, rather than a slave or a relative, as in the past. This was Sa'id Qaryuti, a merchant and owner of a tract of land in Umm al-'Amad, which Mithqal had either bestowed on him as a gift or given to him in return for an unpaid debt. The intelligent, well-educated Qaryuti was one of Mithqal's right-hand men. As such, he enjoyed much influence both within the household and among the inhabitants of Umm al-'Amad. In addition, Mithqal's eldest son Nawwash was also closely involved in the farmwork. At the time of Avira's arrival in Amman, Nawwash took Mithqal's herd of camels to Palestine, where grazing was available. By that time, the camel trade had been revived due to the shortage of spare parts for motor vehicles during the war.[30]

One day Mithqal took Avira to ride in his vast fields. Mithqal told him of his wish to bring Jews, who would settle the land and develop it as they did in Palestine. Knowing his words would be reported back to Jerusalem, he also declared that he would respect all the undertakings and promises he had given the late Haim Arlosoroff, former head of the Jewish Agency's Political Department. Perhaps this was the reason he had chosen to employ a Jewish mechanic in the first place.[31] His decision paid off as far as Avira's reports were concerned. Avira formed a positive impression of Mithqal, stressing his exceptional personality: "For the first time I meet a Bedouin shaykh with a human conscience. He regrets his sins and the mistakes he had made. He is assertive, forceful, and ambitious but [a man] with a good and generous heart who chooses the right path. One can influence him easily if succeeding in evoking his sense of integrity and mercy."[32]

Avira's concluding report gives a further assessment of Mithqal: "A good-hearted, scrupulous Bedouin, but also fickle and indecisive, often making his decisions based on a temporary mood. He is a devout, faithful Muslim, self-respecting, and ambitious. He loves his people, sympathizes with them in his soul, agonizes over their sufferings, and wants to promote their cause."[33]

SHOWDOWN

The British occupation of Syria in the summer of 1941 and the subsequent handover of the territory to the Free French government-in-exile headed by General Charles de Gaulle opened up new opportunities for Mithqal. One of them was a chance to reconcile with Emir Abdullah. Shortly after the occupation, Mithqal traveled to Syria in hopes of promoting Abdullah's Greater Syria plan by engaging in propaganda among the tribes and speaking with politicians, clerics, and British officials. Likely prompted by Abdullah, he also joined other Transjordanian notables in sending telegrams to General de Gaulle and the British ambassador in Cairo calling for the unification of Transjordan and Syria. Mithqal was particularly useful to Abdullah here because his sister was married to Nuri al-Sha'lan, shaykh of shaykhs of the Ruwala, the largest tribal confederacy in Syria, whose leaders were influential actors in Syrian politics.[34]

Mithqal's involvement in Syrian affairs served as a pretext for his reconciliation with the Jewish Agency. After his return from Damascus, Mithqal went to Jerusalem and met with Eliyahu Sasson, the new head of the Jewish Agency's Arab Bureau. He urged the Agency to support Abdullah's unification plan and gave a detailed account of the situation in Syria. He also brought an oral invitation to Shertok to meet Abdullah.[35] With the resumption of his contacts in Jerusalem, Mithqal sought to position himself as a mediator between conflicting parties who could open "doors in high places." The hope was that such a reputation would make him someone worth cultivating. He wanted to prove himself useful to Abdullah by helping to persuade the Zionists to support the emir's greatest ambition. By the same token, he wished to impress the Zionists with his close ties to the emir, and his extensive regional contacts. To cement the impression, he sent one of his relatives, a young Ruwala shaykh, to Jerusalem, who offered the Agency his friendship, assistance in Syria and Saudi Arabia, and even to sell his land.[36]

But after Syrian tribal shaykhs called on Abdullah, the Allied occupation of Syria also negatively affected Mithqal, who badly miscalculated the new political climate in Transjordan. In September 1941, he barged into the prime minister's office in Amman, slapping the soldier at the door, and complained of the neglect of local shaykhs and the government's demand for taxes, contrasting this with the subsidies being given to shaykhs in Iraq and Syria. To his astonishment, after consultation between Prime Minister Tawfiq Abu al-Huda, Glubb, and British Resident Kirkbride, and with Abdullah's reluctant consent, Mithqal was summarily arrested and imprisoned.

Mithqal immediately went on a hunger strike, while his immediate relatives began to rally in the vicinity of Umm al-ʿAmad. As a precaution, a unit of the Desert Patrol was deployed to deter any further conflict. The British reported, with some satisfaction, that with the exception of Mithqal's immediate kinsmen, the Bani Sakhr took no action over the affair. Mithqal, for his part, claimed that it was he who had ordered his people to restrain themselves.[37] In any event, Mithqal was released three days later, but not before enduring a further bitter blow to his pride. He was forced to apologize to the prime minister and to pay all his taxes for that year, which amounted to £500. He also had to promise, supported by the guarantee of several notables, to behave himself from then on.

According to a contemporaneous report by Kirkbride, Mithqal's behavior stemmed from two recent developments in tribal politics. The first was the falling out between Abdullah and Shaykh Haditha al-Khuraysha, the other senior shaykh of the Bani Sakhr, in the summer of 1941 and the latter's temporary refuge at Ibn Saud's court. This left Mithqal as the only important leader of the Bani Sakhr and therefore worthy of Abdullah's cultivation, which may have contributed to an inflated sense of self-importance and increasingly recalcitrant attitude on Mithqal's part. The second was the news of generous subsidies to Syrian shaykhs by the Transjordanian authorities. Mithqal had enviously demanded similar largesse from the emir, the British Resident, and Glubb. Refused by all three, he had then approached British Army Headquarters in

Jerusalem and then, finally, the prime minister's office.[38] In so doing, Mithqal not only eroded Abdullah's patronage of him but played into the hands of his adversaries, who were already entertaining the idea of checking his power.

It was abundantly clear that Mithqal had failed to grasp the full meaning of the changes now under way. After his release, he returned to his village and declared a moratorium against the government, refusing to come to Amman unless it resigned in its entirety. Since Abdullah rejected this demand, speculation mounted inside his house and across the country that Mithqal might depart for Saudi Arabia. Mithqal encouraged this speculation in order to put pressure on Abdullah.[39] He did not cross the border to Saudi Arabia, though he boasted that King Ibn Saud had personally invited him.[40] Ultimately, his stake in Transjordan was too high. His most important property and source of income was cultivated land, and its immovability was alone enough to make him swallow his pride.

Through intermediaries, he finally made his peace with the government, and with Abdullah. Mithqal thus once again recovered his former position of influence, both with the emir and among the tribes. On Mithqal's behalf, Abdullah continued to interfere in the running of the government, even appointing Mithqal's brother-in-law to the senior position of head of the palace office in 1942. The undermining of government authority in Mithqal's favor nearly brought about the resignation of the prime minister. When the new shaykh of shaykhs of the Ruwala visited Amman in 1943, he chose Mithqal as his host. Even Glubb, never a great admirer of Mithqal, attended the large party held at the shaykh's house.[41] Yet this recovery in his fortunes was temporary, and merely delayed Mithqal's final subjugation to the state's central authority.

In the summer of 1943, events came full circle. What the British called "unruly behavior" on the part of the Bani Sakhr prompted a military operation in order to "correct the sense of proportion."[42] The First Mechanized Regiment of the Arab Legion, a formidable force of 600 men,[43] occupied several villages (apparently Umm al-'Amad and others of the Fayiz tribe) for more than two weeks. While there, they first arrested so-called "absconded offenders" and "wanted" individuals. Their next move was to enforce the collection of back taxes owed to the government. Ultimately, they raised £12,000, £2,500 of it from Mithqal. More significantly, Mithqal paid his debt of £2,000 for the land of Jiza, which dated back to 1930–31.[44] Concurrently, Abdullah himself confronted Mithqal. Without permission, the shaykh had sown land belonging to the late Emir Shakir that lay adjacent to his own. When harvest time came, Abdullah, on behalf of Shakir's widow, demanded the customary one-fifth of the crop. Mithqal refused, and the emir sent his men to harvest the fields under the protection of the Arab Legion.[45] Beset on all sides, Mithqal reportedly followed through with his threat to move to Saudi Arabia, until the political maelstrom passed. Though circumstantial in nature, evidence exists to support such a claim.[46] Fleeing to Saudi Arabia in the face of political trouble had been the practice among the Bani Sakhr for several decades.

THE LAST TWENTY YEARS

Upon his return, Mithqal reconciled himself to the new situation. He limited his political activity, focused on developing his farm and was careful to toe the line. This new disposition was the price he had to pay in order to maintain his influence, as his power increasingly derived from the central government's recognition of his status and his role as a representative of the tribes in official matters. To sustain this position, maintaining good relations with the government was an imperative.

The evidence for Mithqal's newly subdued disposition is reflected in the relative silence of the archives during this period. From 1943 on, the references to Mithqal in state documents are far and few between, suggesting that he stopped presenting a problem for the government to deal with. Mithqal's entry in the first British "personalities report" for independent Transjordan, from 1946, clearly supports that conclusion. Although Mithqal was "a source of much trouble during the early years of the Amirate of Transjordan, owing to a greedy and turbulent nature," he had "matured and quietened by age. From being a raider of renown in his youth, Mithqal is now a landowner with a residence at Amman."[47]

Still, despite this change in Mithqal's status, his position of shaykh of shaykhs remained significant. Mithqal acted as a judge, solved conflicts, lavished hospitality, and helped his people in many ways. Far from losing its relevance amid the march of modernity, the role of the shaykh as an intermediary between the tribes and the central government had acquired new meaning. As the government expanded its administrative apparatus, the need for mediation and its volume only grew, because the country's citizens, many of whom were illiterate, needed help to cope with the spreading bureaucracy. For their part, government officials encouraged the shaykhs' involvement because it made their task easier and cheaper. The modernization of the Transjordanian state thus brought about the inception of the modern shaykh.

Such was Mithqal's important role in the settlement of Bani Sakhr land. Land reform was one of the most impressive and intrusive British initiatives in mandatory Transjordan. The preparation of a cadastral survey and the registration of title deeds often reignited latent disputes over land. Officials were only too happy to be assisted by shaykhs to resolve some of these conflicts.[48] As early as 1939, Mithqal was called upon to judge a conflict over a well between two leading shaykhs of the Bani Sakhr, each of whom had complained to the Arab Legion about the other's transgression.[49]

Mithqal's contribution to an agreement between all the shaykhs of the Bani Sakhr following the settlement of the confederacy's land in 1945 was more significant. Mithqal seems to have been very cooperative, a fact that undoubtedly made the process smoother. The agreement was reached under the auspices of Glubb and marked a deeper involvement of the government in tribal life, establishing it as the final arbiter of land use. It also formalized a trend that was many years in the making: the growing importance of individual tribes at the expense of the confederacy as a whole. This shift affected the position of Mithqal as shaykh of shaykhs and further eroded his authority. At the same time, the agreement institutionalized the role of shaykhs in administering the affairs of their tribes, so long as it was done with government approval.

The Bani Sakhr shaykhs resolved in the agreement[50] to partition the land east of the settled zone on the fringe of the desert among themselves. Previously, this land had been part of the general *dira*, or tribal domain, of the confederacy, but the expansion of cultivation into this area required regulation of its ownership and the marking of the boundaries between each tribe. The area further east was declared to be communal grazing land for the entire Bani Sakhr confederacy, and tilling it was forbidden without government approval. Additionally, every member of the Bani Sakhr continued to enjoy free access to any uncultivated land within the areas now owned by each tribe.

Another article in the agreement affected the relationship between the shaykh and some of his men and defined his role as far as landownership was concerned. Shaykhs who had been sole landowners among their tribes now had to allocate some parcels from the tribe's territory to those who did not own it. This allocation of land was to be done "under the supervision of the government and by the shaykhs."[51] In 1953, Mithqal reported that he had granted land from his domain to a landless tribesman. Mithqal explained that he was required under the terms of the agreement to give land to such people.[52]

Apart from land matters, Mithqal was engaged, thanks to his improved standing with the government, in solving many other bureaucratic and tribal problems.[53] In later years, he mediated with the help of his son, 'Akif, who rose to political prominence and enjoyed much influence in his own right. For example, a member of the Bani Sakhr recalled that when he wanted to sit the matriculation exam as a young boy, the Ministry of Education had required him to provide proof of identity. Since he did not possess any, he applied for a passport but again was required to provide an official document. By chance, the boy's father encountered Mithqal, who agreed to resolve this kafkaesque bureaucratic complication. Mithqal asked 'Akif, who was then a member of Parliament, to help. A simple note from 'Akif to the director of the Passport Department did the trick.[54]

Sometimes the mere mention of Mithqal's name and a claim of some association with him were sufficient to open doors. The famous Palestinian scholar Ibrahim Abu-Lughod recalled being arrested along with his brother and scores of refugees in a police station in Amman following their flight from Jaffa in 1948. He asked an officer for permission to call "Mithqal Pasha." When questioned as to how he knew Mithqal, Ibrahim replied, truthfully, that his uncle had taught Mithqal's children. That was enough to obtain the release of Ibrahim and his brother.[55]

On the national level, Mithqal continued to be involved in public activity and politics and to enjoy high status. He was, alongside other tribal leaders and notables, an important member of the state elite that revolved around Abdullah and, after the latter's assassination in July 1951, around his son Talal and grandson Hussein. In May 1947, Mithqal was one of the founding members of the new Arab Renaissance Party, composed of shaykhs and notables loyal to Abdullah, led by Hashim Khayr, which won the majority of parliamentary seats in the election of that year. One of the seats was won by 'Akif.[56] In 1954, Mithqal's interest in political intrigue revived, and he supported former Prime Minister Samir Rifa'i, with the help of Syrian political circles. During the same year, he also considered running for Parliament after 'Akif was banned from doing so by the government.[57] This was exceptional, since several years earlier, Mithqal had already handed over most of his political functions to his son.

Mithqal was still involved in the affairs of Palestine, against the background of the ever-escalating conflict between Arabs and Jews. Nevertheless, he confined his activity to what was acceptable to both the government and Abdullah. In February 1944, he hosted a delegation of Jewish experts who came to examine whether his land would be suitable for the resettlement of Palestinians.[57] Unaware of the new and short-lived Zionist transfer design, he suggested beginning by settling Jews on his land, thus creating facts on the ground until they were permitted to own land themselves. The Zionists quickly lost interest in Mithqal's land owing to the lack of water there, but his efforts were not completely in vain; he received £300 for arranging the experts' licenses to enter Transjordan.[58] A few months later, Mithqal attended a meeting of leading shaykhs in support of the Palestinians. His participation was probably intended primarily as a show of support for Abdullah, under whose auspices the meeting was held. Still, in early 1947, Hajj Amin al-Husseini, the leader of the Palestinian national movement, tried to make use of Mithqal's influence and sent him a telegram asking for his assistance.[59]

Al-Husseini was not wrong in perceiving that Mithqal continued to enjoy Abdullah's favor. Following Transjordan's independence and his enthronement as king in 1946, Abdullah awarded Mithqal an honorary title and subsequently visited him when he fell ill in 1949. Both the visit and Mithqal's recovery a few weeks later were reported in the local newspaper.[60] It is most likely that Mithqal continued to frequent the palace, and that from time to time Abdullah paid him visits as well. On such occasions, Mithqal organized horse and camel races, celebrating what remained of the nomadic desert culture.[61]

But the relationship between the two men was not merely symbolic; it was a continuation of their long-standing political alliance. On the eve of the 1948 Palestine War, Mithqal organized a tribal gathering, following which an estimated 1,200 tribal volunteers joined the Arab Legion. As the entire Legion numbered only 4,500 fighting men, this contingent made a significant contribution to the Jordanian war effort.[62] Abdullah succeeded in occupying and later annexing what would become the West Bank, thus partly fulfilling his old ambition to expand his rule beyond Transjordan.

As time progressed, the alliance between Mithqal and Abdullah was increasingly maintained through the former's sons. In 1947, Nawwash served as intermediary between Abdullah and the famous Druze leader Sultan al-Atrash, Mithqal's old friend, who had returned to Syria a decade earlier after his long exile.[63] Another son, 'Ali, briefly served in the Arab Legion when there was an effort to recruit the sons of prominent shaykhs and notables.[64] 'Akif was the son who played the most important role in maintaining the alliance with the Hashemite family, however. Abdullah recognized his value, and in 1946, he appointed him head of protocol for tribes, a new court position.[65] With that, the alliance moved into the next generation.

SUCCESSION

As time went on, and as 'Akif's position in independent Jordan grew stronger, Mithqal gradually began to hand over more and more of his political responsibilities to him. Beginning in the mid-1950s, 'Akif became the main representative of the Bani Sakhr in the Jordanian political establishment, allowing his aging father to tend to the internal affairs of his tribes.

Originally, Mithqal had designated two of 'Akif's elder half-brothers to succeed him, but these died in 1930 and 1934 respectively. Although 'Akif, who had been born in Amman and had grown up there with his mother, the mayor's daughter, rather than in a tent in the desert, seemed an unlikely candidate for the role of shaykh of shaykhs, he was chosen because his father felt special affection for him and thought highly of his leadership qualities.[66] Other factors probably included the unsuitability of his other brothers or their young age. Most likely, the choice was made because Mithqal correctly read the changing times and preferred the educated son who had proved himself to be a skilled political operator to a camel herder or a tribal judge. As it turned out, the choice would stand the test of time.

Mithqal began grooming 'Akif for a leadership role from an early age, probably even before he chose him to be his successor. As part of the process, Mithqal took 'Akif to meet Emir Abdullah on two occasions, when the boy was only eleven years old. The second meeting proved remarkable for both father and son: the emir, seeking to entertain his guests, had prepared an envelope and declared that the first person to enter the room would receive it as a present. It was young 'Akif's good fortune to be that visitor. When they left the palace, his father opened the envelope and discovered it to contain £240. The then hard-pressed shaykh gave his son £0.5 and kept the rest.[67]

Young 'Akif often joined his father in visiting other shaykhs and participating in tribal gatherings. Mithqal wanted his son to observe and experience how he dealt with a variety of issues, both to prepare him for taking responsibility and to build his character. 'Akif learned from his father how to treat people and help them, as well as how to articulate his thoughts and make decisions, skills that would help him later in his own career. Thanks to this training, he acquired self-confidence at an early age.[68] Furthermore, Mithqal made the calculated and expensive decision to send 'Akif to Lebanon for secondary schooling, which included agricultural training.

By 1940, Mithqal had begun to involve 'Akif in his activities, both inside Transjordan and regionally. 'Akif acted as Mithqal's liaison to the Saudi court;

in the aftermath of Mithqal's 1941 arrest and his voluntary confinement to his farm, 'Akif maintained the lines of communication with Amman. 'Akif also took over the task of maintaining Mithqal's relationship with the prominent Basil family of Egypt, especially with his contemporary, 'Abd al-Sattar al-Basil, after the latter's father Hamad died.[69] In 1944, 'Akif came to Jerusalem to escort the Jewish agricultural experts who inspected Mithqal's land.[70]

Initially, 'Akif attempted to emulate Mithqal's example of forty years earlier by nurturing a tribal base of support built on a foundation of military success. He had once boasted that, during the last year of the Arab Revolt in Palestine, he had rallied the youths of the Bani Sakhr; allegedly, only Emir Abdullah's pleas had prevented their attacking Jewish targets. During World War II, perhaps inspired by his father's initiative during World War I, 'Akif offered the services of five hundred mounted tribesmen to the British Military Recruiting Office in Jerusalem. Times had changed, however, and the young shaykh was politely turned down.[71]

Having failed to become a military leader, 'Akif chose the role of politician and was successful at it, partly owing to his father's support. In 1947, he resigned his post in the palace in order to run for a seat in Parliament. According to him, he won because his father was able to persuade all but one of the Bani Sakhr shaykhs to endorse his election to Emir Abdullah.[72] 'Akif was nevertheless no sycophant. As a member of the first post-independence Parliament, 'Akif often criticized the government. This had consequences: 'Akif's attempts to return to the legislature in 1951 and 1954 failed, likely because of government interference. However, 'Akif won a seat in the 1956 elections, widely considered to have been some of the freest ever held in Jordan,[73] even though they took place in the context of an unprecedented challenge to the rule of the inexperienced young King Hussein.

The 1950s marked the rise of Egyptian President Gamal Abdel Nasser and the Arab nationalist movement. For Arab nationalists, Jordan and its monarchy were illegitimate expressions of Western colonialism in the Middle East and thus had no right to exist. This ideology struck a chord with Palestinian citizens who had been incorporated into Jordan following the annexation of the West Bank in 1950, and who now constituted two-thirds of the country's population. Abdel Nasser and his ideas also became popular among educated Transjordanians, including senior army officers. To respond to the nationalist challenge, Hussein sacked John Glubb, the British commander of the Arab Legion, in March 1956 and ordered new free elections. The new Jordanian government, headed by Sulayman al-Nabulsi, was inspired by the changing regional zeitgeist. Al-Nabulsi questioned the validity of the old political order, challenging the king's authority to rule. Matters came to a head in April 1957, when Hussein's dismissal of the government was followed by an attempted coup d'état.[74]

'Akif stood firmly by the monarchy throughout these unsettled times. At first, he attempted to mediate between al-Nabulsi and the king. When this failed, it was 'Akif who alerted the king to hostile preparations being made in the military, after he learned about them from two Bani Sakhr officers. When the king faced down the conspirators, two thousand Bani Sakhr tribesmen answered 'Akif's call, gathering in Amman to support Hussein.[75] In the aftermath of the failed coup, 'Akif joined what were popularly known as "the King's men," a small circle of veteran politicians who stood by the young King Hussein during his first few years on the throne. These men, who had previously served Abdullah, helped Hussein guide the country through the turmoil of the 1950s and early 1960s. Grateful for this support, in 1957 Hussein appointed 'Akif to be the minister for agriculture, construction, and development, making him the first member of a Bedouin tribe to serve in government. Ultimately, 'Akif became one of the most important, powerful politicians of the era, serving in most governments or as the speaker of Parliament.[76]

Initially, 'Akif's reputation and popular support were derived from Mithqal's. By the early 1960s, however, 'Akif had become a senior politician in his own right: Mithqal was now described as the father of 'Akif in the local newspapers, not the other way around.[77] 'Akif's clout, like his father's, resulted from his tribal base of support and his close relationship with the Hashemite monarch. This relationship increased his influence among the Bani Sakhr even further, as did his ministerial and parliamentary positions. As minister of agriculture, he financed projects in the desert that benefited the nomads, many of them Bani Sakhr. In 1957, his ministry allocated 60,000 dinars (= £60,000) for the digging of new wells and the repair of old ones to help the nomads water their herds.[78] According to U.S. diplomatic reports, 'Akif transferred resources from the American aid program to his family farm and ordered the employment of Bani Sakhr on the project. When he served as minister of defense, 'Akif used his base of support in the army, namely, senior officers from the Bani Sakhr, to strengthen his status and that of his tribes against the powerful Majali tribe from Karak. This near conflict between two tribal groups in the army forced Hussein to remove 'Akif from office.[79] But no more than two years passed before 'Akif returned to the government.

As 'Akif's star was rising in the political sphere, Mithqal remained active as a tribal leader and landowner. He closely followed political events in Jordan and beyond. His daughter-in-law visited him every day and read the newspapers to him.[80] He acted as a judge until shortly before his death; a photograph taken in 1964 or 1965 shows him dictating a verdict.[81] First and foremost, he continued to manage the business of his farm, which he did with the same vigor that characterized him in his youth. Sometime in 1957 or 1958, the U.S. Embassy in Amman was apparently informed that Mithqal had appropriated a tractor belonging to a U.S. development project, kept it for ten days, stopping all work on the project, and returned it in disrepair.[82] Although the embassy staff could not verify this, the story serves to illustrate Mithqal's sense of entitlement. On a somewhat similar note, in 1963, he asked the prime minister for credit to buy seeds in order to sow 18,000 dunam of his land.[83]

Sometimes, though, Mithqal's bold behavior necessitated the intervention of 'Akif to prevent embarrassment. Mithqal features in an oral tradition that circulated in the small Gypsy community of the old city in Jerusalem. In the mid-1960s, Kurdi, a Gypsy from Gaza, and his loved one, the beautiful Amina, wandered through Jordan earning a living as a musician and dancer. One day, they arrived in Mithqal's camp, where Amina danced for the old shaykh. Mithqal took a liking to the girl and decided that he wanted to have her. Kurdi pleaded with the shaykh in vain and was finally chased away. Meanwhile, Mithqal wooed Amina with gifts until she was persuaded to stay with him. Kurdi did not give up; he went to the police station, but the police feared the shaykh too much to help him. Kurdi was then taken by another Gypsy to seek the help of Shaykh Turki al-Zaban, Mithqal's rival in the Bani Sakhr. When Turki heard the story, he became angry and demanded the return of Amina to her beloved. 'Akif, already speaker of Parliament, intervened. He persuaded Mithqal to send Amina away and brokered a peace between his father and Shaykh Turki. Kurdi and Amina were reconciled and, the story goes, lived happily ever after, as in all fairy tales.[84]

Mithqal's ill temper also doubtless had something to do with his health. This began deteriorating soon after the death in 1962 of his favorite wife 'Adul, 'Akif's mother, which was a severe blow to Mithqal. In the last five years of his life, he suffered from progressively declining health.[85] Though he was fortunate enough to receive superb medical treatment in Cairo, Beirut, and Europe, diabetes and other age-related illnesses brought about his death in his late eighties in April 1967.[86]

Mithqal's passing attracted much attention among both Jordanians and foreign observers. Despite the fact that he died one day prior to a general election, the local newspapers devoted prominent space to his death and the king's condolence call on 'Akif. One daily also published an obituary.[87] In its weekly report of events, the U.S. Embassy informed Washington that "Mithgal al-Fayez, paramount sheikh of the Beni Sakhr tribe and father of the speaker of Jordan's last Parliament, died on April 14 at the age of 90 years."[88] A few days later, Eliyaho Epstein, now Eilat, published a comprehensive article about Mithqal in a popular Hebrew daily, which told of his visit to the shaykh's camp in 1931.[89]

Even in death Mithqal played a fateful role in Jordanian politics. In 1967, an election was held following the dissolution of Parliament, which, under 'Akif's leadership, was hostile to the government of Wasfi al-Tall, Jordan's most celebrated prime minister. Wasfi was determined to bring about the downfall of his bitter enemy 'Akif by supporting another candidate for the Bani Sakhr seat. But in order to prevent this further blow to the bereaved family, King Hussein intervened personally and secured 'Akif's election.[90] Thus, in dying, as it turned out, Mithqal had secured a prominent position for his son for many years to come. Two months later, Jordan lost the West Bank to Israel in the Six-Day War, and since its Parliament was elected by voters on both banks of the Jordan River, no general elections could take place until the country's political disengagement from the West Bank. This did not occur until 1988, and in the interim, 'Akif was able to keep his seat, holding it for the next twenty-one years and even serving as speaker of Parliament again between 1984 and 1988.

EPILOGUE:
JORDAN AFTER MITHQAL

DUST SETTLED OVER UMM AL-'AMAD. The mourning period was over and the dignitaries and ordinary people left Mithqal's house. The bereaved family was left to deal with the huge void created by Mithqal's demise. It was undisputed that the elder son, 'Akif, would become the head of the family and the main bearer of his father's legacy. But he was not recognized as shaykh of shaykhs. Perhaps Mithqal was too large a personality to be replaced by anyone else. Besides, times were changing, and King Hussein's drive to modernize the country suggested that such institutions were anachronistic. Whatever his reasons, the king had a perfect excuse. Owing to his urban roots and his focus on ministerial and parliamentary work, 'Akif lacked the necessary qualifications to be a shaykh in the full sense of the word. For many years, the office remained vacant.

One of the first things the family did was to gather to distribute Mithqal's huge landholdings. By the time of his death, Mithqal had accumulated at least 120,000 dunams (30,000 acres). By his instructions, two grandchildren, the sons of his eldest son Sultan, whom he raised as his own after their father's premature death, enjoyed equal shares of the inheritance.[1] Several years later, the family sold a large portion of that land to the Jordanian government. Today, Amman International Airport stands on what used to be Mithqal's fields and the pastures in which his camels and sheep grazed.[2]

With the passing of his father, 'Akif became the most senior member of the Bani Sakhr in Jordan and their principal representative to the king and the political establishment. Immediately after being reelected to Parliament in April 1967, ʿAkif returned to the government, serving in several ministerial positions. In 1968 King Hussein offered him the position of prime minister. With the country reeling from its defeat in the 1967 Six-Day War, he hesitated to take the role, and it was offered to someone else.[3] A year later, he was deputy prime minister. In 1970, he served in government for the last time.

That year was a momentous one for Jordan. After the Six-Day War, the most important organizations of the Palestinian national movement, the PLO and Fatah, turned Jordan into their base of operation, threatening the sovereignty of the king and the country's government. Refugee camps, urban neighborhoods, and large stretches of the Jordan Valley fell under control of Palestinian militias. In September 1970, matters got out of hand, and after he nearly lost his life in a confrontation with Palestinian fighters, King Hussein ordered the army to restore law and order. The civil war of 1970–71, commonly known as Black September, was a major national, regional, and international crisis. It resulted in heavy casualties and the expulsion of Palestinian militias from Jordan to Lebanon.

But the civil war also fundamentally altered the character of the Jordanian state. Following the war, the regime abandoned the policy, in place since 1948, of integrating the Palestinians into Jordanian life. In its place, it made a determined effort to reestablish its traditional support base among the Transjordanian sectors of society. The tribes in particular constituted the backbone of the Jordanian Arab Army, and proved loyal to the regime during its most difficult crisis. Ever since, the regime has leaned heavily on that segment of society. The army, police, internal security organization, and much of the state bureaucracy are staffed by these "original" Jordanians.

With the initiation of this new policy, King Hussein made a conspicuous effort to cultivate the support of the tribes and show respect for tribal values. Reviving his grandfather's long habit of camping among tribes, King Hussein conducted long tours of the country (known as *ziyaras*) to visit different tribal communities. During these visits, he allowed every tribesman or woman to approach him and raise complaints, pleas for assistance, or just enjoy the opportunity to meet him in person.[4] In addition, the government gave priority to development projects in tribal communities and university scholarships for young tribesmen and women.

In this new political climate, ʿAkif's position was greatly enhanced. With or without an official position, he continued to enjoy considerable influence. He was the main authority to whom his tribesmen turned when they needed intercession with the state bureaucracy, including lowering tax assessments, allocating licenses and commercial concessions, and securing jobs or places at university. A phone call from 'Akif to a senior government official solved many problems swiftly.

The regime's near exclusive reliance on East Bankers was accompanied by a concerted effort to nurture Jordanian nationalism and paint it in tribal colors. The regime sought to rally East Bankers to counterbalance the Palestinian segment of society. Consequently, tribal values and Bedouin heritage were hailed as the core values of the nation. The regime emphasized the historical role tribes had played in the establishment of Jordan. To this day, the founding myth of Jordan and the origin of the monarchy's legitimacy is the Arab Revolt, the alliance of tribes led by the Hashemites in 1916. Tribal culture was appropriated by the regime, which actively promoted it.[5] For example, tribal practices of conflict resolution continued to operate alongside the formal law. Although the government abolished the Mandate-era tribal courts law in 1976, state officials, from the king down, not only allowed but actively encouraged this trend of informal dispute resolution, and sometimes acted as mediators in conflicts resolved by tribal custom. Tribal customary law remained an integral part of the Jordanian legal system, and continues to operate to this day.[6] When liberal intellectuals criticized the prominent role of tribalism in Jordanian politics in the mid-1980s, the king defended the tribes and made clear he did not side with their critics.[7] In the last two decades of Hussein's reign, tribalism became an important part of the Jordanian public discourse. Ever since, tribes have been seen as building blocks of the nation and society.

In this new political and social environment, Mithqal's memory was repurposed and assumed an entirely new importance. Jordanian nationalism hails Mithqal as one of the small but distinguished group of founding fathers who surrounded King Abdullah I during Jordan's beginnings. In particular, he is seen as a fierce opponent of British colonialism. The arrest of the British officer Frederick Peake in 1920 is the best-known story about Mithqal in Jordanian collective memory. It is easy to understand why a tribal leader's act of defiance against British rule has such appeal. Jordanian nationalists cannot boast of major instances of dramatic resistance like the anti-colonial revolts in Palestine, Syria, Iraq, or Egypt. Mithqal's confrontation with Peake is one of the few episodes to have captured the national imagination.[8]

Mithqal is also hailed as an Arab nationalist in view of his support for the Syrian and Palestinian revolutions in the 1920s and 1930s and his contribution to the war effort in 1948. Jordanian intellectuals invoke Mithqal's memory to denote a bygone era in which heroic, autonomous leaders led their tribal communities. In this way, Mithqal has become a totem for a new generation. History books, newspaper articles, and web sites testify to this phenomenon. In 2012, two Jordanian authors published the first biography of Mithqal, based on interviews with family members and contemporaries.[9]

Mithqal's family made its own contribution to keeping his memory alive. 'Akif built a large, attractive mosque next to his father's palace in Umm al-'Amad, with Mithqal's grave in its center. When the Amman municipality began to designate street names three decades ago, it named one of the quietest, most elegant streets of Amman after him. A few years ago, the Fayiz family built a huge assembly hall for the Bani Sakhr opposite Mithqal's old palace and named it the Diwan Mithqal al-Fayiz after him.

'Akif al-Fayiz died in 1998, several months before the passing of King Hussein. The respect he received was similar to his father thirty years earlier. When 'Akif was on his deathbed, King Hussein visited him in hospital. After 'Akif's death, the king and the rest of the royal family came to the Fayiz family home to offer their condolences. A few days after the funeral, the Fayiz family paid for huge announcements in the newspapers thanking the Hashemites for their condolences. For many days the news of 'Akif's death, details of his large funeral, and the condolence visits of prominent Jordanians dominated the headlines. The newspapers published obituaries, eulogies, farewell articles, and poems praising 'Akif as a Jordanian and Arab patriot, a tribal leader, and a loyal supporter of the Hashemites. Many private citizens, organizations and communities published death notices, which together numbered in the hundreds.[10] The way the Jordanian media presented the close relations between the Hashemite and Fayiz families was a clear testimony to the central position of tribes in Jordan and to the Fayiz family in particular.

After 'Akif's death, King Hussein appointed Mithqal's son ('Akif's half-brother) Sami as shaykh of shaykhs of the Bani Sakhr. The revival of the office was another indication of the prominent role of tribes in Jordan. Sami had grown up in the desert rather than the city and was intimately familiar with nomadic culture. He was appointed a tribal judge by King Hussein in 1958 and was the main Fayiz shaykh to deal with tribal affairs after the passing of Mithqal. Sami embodied tribal life and nomadic culture in his lifestyle and conduct, which to a large degree resembled Mithqal's. Until his death in November 2012, Sami served as judge and mediator, lavished hospitality on his many guests and traveled around the Bani Sakhr villages, honoring his hosts with his company. He always wore the traditional robe and headgear, married many wives, and had many children. He even kept a large herd of sheep and went out with it to the desert in spring.[11]

The current representative of the Bani Sakhr in the palace and government is 'Akif's son, Faysal al-Fayiz. Born in 1952 and schooled in Amman, Faysal studied at British and American universities. He began his career as a diplomat, serving as the Jordanian consul in Brussels, and then moved to the palace. Since Abdullah II's assumption of power in 1999, Faysal has moved up the ladder with remarkable speed. Shortly after assuming power, King Abdullah appointed Faysal as chief of the royal protocol of the Royal Hashemite Court, an office similar to the one his father held some fifty years earlier. In March 2003, Abdullah made him minister of the Royal Hashemite Court, the closest position to the king. In October, Faysal was appointed prime minister, and remained in office for a year and a half. In 2010–11, he served as the speaker of Parliament. He is now president of the Jordanian Senate.[12]

The next generation of the family is already assuming a prominent place in the life of the nation. Faysal's cousin, Hind al-Fayiz, Mithqal's great-granddaughter, represents the fourth generation of Mithqal's descendants in the Jordanian political scene. Young, energetic, and articulate, Hind won a seat in the 2013 parliamentary elections and quickly became a prominent MP, attracting much media attention. She is not afraid to stand up to the government or her colleagues. Several of Mithqal's great-grandsons work in the royal palace or serve the king in other state institutions. As a myth, a symbol, and the founder of a political dynasty, Mithqal left a legacy that survives him.

REFERENCE MATTER

NOTES

ABBREVIATIONS

CMS   Church Missionary Society Archives, Birmingham, England
CO   Colonial Office (UK)
CZA   Central Zionist Archives, Jerusalem
FO   Foreign Office (UK)
Glubb's report   John Glubb, "A Monthly Report on Events in the Deserts of Transjordan," MEC, Glubb Papers
HA   Hagana Archives, Tel Aviv
ISA   Israel State Archives, Jerusalem
IWM   Imperial War Museum, London
Al-Jarida al-Rasmiyya   Al-Jarida al-Rasmiyya li-Hukumat Sharq al-Urdunn [Transjordanian Government Official Gazette]
Al-Majlis al-Tashri'i   Mudhakkirat al-Majlis al-Tashri'i [Minutes of the Legislative Council] (Jordan)
MEC   Middle East Centre, St Antony's College, Oxford, England
UKNA   United Kingdom National Archives, London
USNA   United States National Archives, College Park, Maryland

INTRODUCTION

1. Assaf David, *Jordan Update: October 2012* (Tel Aviv: Economic Cooperation Foundation, 2012). On the eve of the rally, October 3, 2012, an editorial in the government-owned English-language Amman daily *Jordan Times* titled "Decisive Day" spoke of "volatile times."

2. The text of King Abdullah's speech can be found at http://kingabdullah.jo/index.php/en_US/speeches/view/id/507/videoDisplay/0.html, and it can be viewed at https://www.youtube.com/watch?v=e17kBQTs1Zk (both accessed October 28, 2015).

3. Assaf David, *Jordan Update: November 2012* (Tel Aviv: Economic Cooperation Foundation, 2012).

4. Miflih al-Nimr al-Fayiz, *'Asha'ir Bani Sakhr: Ta'rikh wa-mawaqif hata sanat 1950* (Amman: Matabi' al-Quwwat al-Musallaha, 1995), 166; "Tribesmen Split over Political-Reforms amid 'Transformation' of Tribe's Social Role," *Jordan Times* (Amman), March 2, 2011.

5. For video of the gathering on November 17, 2012, see www.youtube.com/watch ?v=lLCukiEN_Z8 (accessed October 28, 2015). On Faysal al-Fayiz's support of the king, see Yoav Alon, "From Abdullah (I) to Abdullah (II): The Monarchy, the Tribes and the Shaykhly Families in Jordan, 1920–2012," in *Tribes and States in a Changing Middle East*, ed. Uzi Rabi (London: Hurst, forthcoming). For more recent examples, see "Al-Fayiz: Al-'Arsh al-Hashimi wal-wahda al-wataniyya khatt ahmar," March 4, 2014, http://hoqook. wordpress.com/2014/03/05, and "Tasa'ulat la budda min muwajahatiha," January 14, 2014, *Al-Ra'y* (Amman), www.alrai.com/article/626672.html (both accessed October 28, 2015).

6. Several pioneering works inspired the writing of this book, and it is worth noting my intellectual debt to them. This study constitutes what sociologists term a "social biography," namely, the particular case study of an individual whose detailed analysis enables us to learn about the general phenomenon. Mithqal al-Fayiz was a historical protagonist in his own right, but his life represents the wider phenomenon of tribal leadership in modern times. Clifford Geertz's *The Social History of an Indonesian Town* (Cambridge: Cambridge University Press, 1965) was perhaps the first social biography to appear. See his definition on pages 153–53. The method was implemented and further developed by Dale Eickelman in his *Knowledge and Power in Morocco: The Education of a Twentieth-Century Notable* (Princeton, NJ: Princeton University Press, 1985). Two important previous attempts to analyze the office of the tribal shaykh and highlight the ways in which such men reached power, struggled to maintain it, and exercised their leadership were based on the Yemeni experience: Paul Dresch, "The Position of Shaykhs among the Northern Tribes of Yemen," *Man* 19, no. 1 (March 1984): 31–49, and Andrew Shryock, "The Rise of Nasir Al-Nims: A Tribal Commentary on Being and Becoming a Shaykh," *Journal of Anthropological Research* 46 (1990): 153–76.

7. The Iraqi case is particularly illuminating: see Hanna Batatu, *The Old Social Classes and the Revolutionary Movements of Iraq* (Princeton, NJ: Princeton University Press, 1978); Phebe Marr, *The Modern History of Iraq* (Boulder, CO: Westview Press, 1985); Yitzhak Nakash, *The Shi'is of Iraq* (Princeton, NJ: Princeton University Press, 1994); Amatzia Baram, "Neo-Tribalism in Iraq: Saddam Hussein's Tribal Policies, 1991–96," *International Journal of Middle East Studies* 29, no. 1 (1997): 1–31; Charles Tripp, *The History of Iraq* (Cambridge: Cambridge University Press, 2002); Toby Dodge, *Inventing Iraq: The Failure of Nation-Building and a History Denied* (New York: Columbia University Press, 2003); Falah Jabar, "Sheikhs and Ideologues: Deconstruction and Reconstruction of Tribes under Patrimonial Totalitarianism in Iraq, 1968–1998," in *Tribes and Power: Nationalism and Ethnicity in the Middle East*, ed. Falah Jabar and Hosham Dawod, 69–109 (London: Saqi, 2003); Peter Sluglett, *Britain in Iraq: Contriving King and Country, 1914–1932* (New York: Columbia University Press, 2007); Michael Eisenstadt, "Iraq: Tribal Engagement Lessons Learned," *Military Review*, September–October 2007, 16–31; Noga Efrati, *Women in Iraq: Past Meets Present* (New York: Columbia University Press, 2012). On Syria, see Haian Dukhan," Tribes and Tribalism in the Syrian Revolution," *Open Democracy*, December 19, 2012, www.opendemocracy.net/haian-dukhan/tribes-and -tribalism-in-syrian-revolution; "Syrian Tribes Unite in İstanbul as Border Conflicts Test Cease-fire," *Today's Zaman*, April 16, 2012, www.todayszaman.com/news-277672-syrian-tribes-unite-in-istanbul-as

-border-conflicts-test-cease-fire.html; Rana Abouzeid, "Who Will the Tribes Back in Syria's Civil War?" *Time*, October 10, 2012, http://world.time .com/2012/10/10/who-will-the-tribes-back-in-syrias-civil-war; "Islamic State Executed 700 People from Syrian Tribe: Monitoring Group," *Reuters*, August 16, 2014, www.reuters .com/article/2014/08/16/us-syria-crisis-execution-idUSKBN0GG0H120140816, and Lauren Williams, "Tribes of Syria and Iraq Drawn into Uprising—Feature," *Daily Star* (Beirut), November 15, 2012, http://www.dailystar.com.lb/News/Middle-East/2012/Nov-15/195112-tribes-of-syria-and-iraq-drawn-into-uprising.ashx (all accessed November 12, 2015); On Libya, see Mohammed El-Katiri, *State-Building Challenges in a Post-Revolution Libya* (Carlisle, PA: Strategic Studies Institute, U.S. Army War College, 2012). On Yemen and the Gulf, see Paul Dresch, *Tribes, Government, and History in Yemen* (Oxford: Oxford University Press, 1989); Farea al-Muslimi, "Tribes Still Rule in Yemen," *Al-Monitor*, October 10, 2013, www.al-monitor. com/pulse/originals/2013/10/yemen-tribes -revolution-politics-saleh.html (accessed November 12, 2015); Nazih N. Ayubi, *Over-stating the Arab State: Politics and Society in the Middle East* (London: I. B. Tauris, 1995), 132–33, 231, 242–43.

CHAPTER 1: BORN A SHAYKH

1. Eugene L. Rogan, *Frontiers of the State in the Late Ottoman Empire: Transjordan, 1850–1921* (Cambridge: Cambridge University Press, 1999), 7; Norman Lewis, *Nomads and Settlers in Syria and Jordan, 1800–1980* (Cambridge: Cambridge University Press, 1987), 3, 124; Nawfan Raja al-Hamud al-Sawariyya, *'Amman wa-jiwaruha khilal al-fatra 1864–1921* (Amman: Bank al-A'mal, 1996), 149.

2. Philip S. Khoury and Joseph Kostiner, "Introduction: Tribes and the Complexities of State Formation in the Middle East," in *Tribes and State Formation in the Middle East,* ed. id. (1990; London: I. B. Tauris, 1991), 8–11; Nazih N. Ayubi, *Over-stating the Arab State: Politics and Society in the Middle East* (London: I. B. Tauris, 1995), 52–53; Emanuel Marx, "The Tribe as a Unit of Subsistence: Nomadic Pastoralism in the Middle East," *American Anthropologist* 79 (1977): 348; id., "The Political Economy of Middle Eastern and North African Pastoral Nomads," in *Nomadic Societies in the Middle East and North Africa: Entering the 21st Century,* ed. Dawn Chatty (Leiden: Brill, 2006), 89; Rogan, *Frontiers of the State,* 7; Hanna Batatu, *The Old Social Classes and the Revolutionary Movements of Iraq* (Princeton, NJ: Princeton University Press, 1978), 67; Antonin Jaussen, *Coutumes des arabes au pays de Moab* (1907; facs. ed., Paris: Librairie d'Amerique et d'Orient, 1948), 114–15. My analysis of the Bani Sakhr is neatly consistent with Emanuel Marx's definition of a "tribe" ("Tribe as a Unit of Subsistence," 344). It follows that his formulation better suits the level of tribal confederacy, such as the Bani Sakhr, rather than a tribe, such as al-Fayiz. As for tribe, I would suggest the following definition: a tribe is a local group of people distinguished from other groups by notions of shared descent, whether real or imagined.

3. F. G. Peake, *Ta'rikh Sharqi al-Urdunn wa-qaba'iliha* (Jerusalem: Matba'at Dar al-Aytam al-Islamiyya, 1935), 214; Miflih al-Nimr al-Fayiz, *'Asha'ir Bani Sakhr: Ta'rikh wa-mawaqif hata sanat 1950* (Amman: Matabi' al-Quwwat al-Musallaha, 1995), 30; 'Abd al-Ra'uf al-Rawabda, *Mu'jam al-'asha'ir al-Urdunniyya* (Amman: Matabi' al-Mu'assasa

al-Suhufiyya al-Urdunniyya, 2010), 113–14; Max Adrian Simon Oppenheim, *Die Bedu-inen*, vol. 2 (Leipzig: O. Harrassowitz, 1943), 232.

4. Abi al-ʿAbbas Ahmad b. ʿAli al-Qalqashandi, *Qalaʾid al-juman fil-taʿrif bi-qabaʾil ʿArab al-zaman*, ed. Ibrahim al-Abyari (2nd ed., Cairo: Dar al-Kutub al-Islamiyya, 1982), 66, 68, 80; W. D. Hütteroth and K. Abdulfattah, *Historical Geography of Palestine, Trans-jordan and Southern Syria in the Late 16th Century* (Erlangen: Frankische Geographische Gesellschaft, 1977), 169–70.

5. Lewis, *Nomads and Settlers*, 3, 8, 11, 124. On oral history in Jordan, see Andrew Shryock, *Nationalism and the Genealogical Imagination: Oral History and Textual Au-thority in Tribal Jordan* (Berkeley: University of California Press, 1997).

6. Rogan, *Frontiers of the State*, 7; Lewis, *Nomads and Settlers*, 124; al-Sawariyya, *ʾAmman wa-jiwaruha*, 149.

7. Lewis, *Nomads and Settlers*, 124; Enno Littmann, "Eine amtliche Liste der Bedu-inenstämme des Ostjordanlandes," *Zeitschrift des Deutschen Palästina-Vereins* 24 (1901): 28; Carlo Guarmani, *Northern Najd: A Journey from Jerusalem to Anaiza in Qasim* (1866; London: Argonaut Press, 1938), 68.

8. Littmann, "Eine amtliche Liste," 28; Guarmani, *Northern Najd*, 68.

9. H. B. Tristram, *The Land of Israel: A Journal of Travels in Palestine* (London: So-ciety for Promoting Christian Knowledge, 1865), 489.

10. Ibid.

11. Rogan, *Frontiers of the State*: 28; Tristram, *Land of Israel*, 555; Claude R. Conder, *Heth and Moab: Explorations in Syria in 1881 and 1882* (3rd ed., London: Watt, 1892), 316; H. B. Tristram, *The Land of Moab: Travels and Discoveries on the East Side of the Dead Sea and the Jordan* (London: John Murray, 1873), 109; Jaussen, *Coutumes des arabes*, 128, 163; Guarmani, *Northern Najd*, 17, 109, which specifies the annual payment of each fam-ily in Tafila to the Bani Sakhr.

12. Charles Leonard Irby and James Mangles, *Travels in Egypt and Nubia, Syria and Asia Minor during the Years 1817 & 1818* (2nd ed., London: John Murray, 1845), 146 (em-phasis in original).

13. Suraiya Faroqhi, *Pilgrims and Sultans: The Hajj under the Ottomans, 1517–1683* (London: I. B. Tauris, 1994), 57; Lewis, *Nomads and Settlers*, 124; Gray Hill, "A Journey to Petra—1896," *Palestine Exploration Fund Quarterly Statement* 29 (1897): 38; Jacob M. Landau, *The Hejaz Railway and the Muslim Pilgrimage* (Detroit: Wayne State University Press, 1971), 58–59.

14. William Lancaster, *The Rwala Bedouin Today* (Cambridge: Cambridge Univer-sity Press, 1981), 141–42; Lewis, *Nomads and Settlers*, 28, 35, 125, 210; Raouf Saʿd Abujaber, *Pioneers over Jordan: The Frontier of Settlement in Transjordan, 1850–1914* (London: I. B. Tauris, 1989), 184; Mary S. Lovell, *A Scandalous Life: The Biography of Jane Digby* (1995; paperback ed., London: Fourth Estate, 2010), 256.

15. This holds true even if there was a gap between ideology and practice and some families enjoyed more respect and privileges than others. See Dale F. Eickelman, *The Middle East and Central Asia: An Anthropological Approach* (1981; 4th ed., Upper Saddle River, NJ: Prentice-Hall, 2002), 80–82; Ayubi, *Over-stating the Arab State*, 54.

16. Lancaster, *Rwala Bedouin*, 77, 84–5, 87, 92; Marx, "Tribe as a Unit of Subsistence," 355–56; id., "Political Economy," 89–90; Philip Carl Salzman, "Hierarchical Image and Reality: The Construction of a Tribal Chiefship," *Comparative Studies in Society and History* 42 (2000): 49–66.

17. Paul Dresch, *Tribes, Government, and History in Yemen* (Oxford: Clarendon Press, 1989), 231–32, 373; Andrew Shryock, "The Rise of Nasir Al-Nims: A Tribal Commentary on Being and Becoming a Shaykh," *Journal of Anthropological Research* 46 (1990): 164– 65; Khoury and Kostiner, "Introduction," 9.

18. Ayubi, *Over-stating the Arab State*, 54; Batatu, *Old Social Classes*, 67; al-Fayiz, *'Asha'ir Bani Sakhr*, 189.

19. Ahmad al-Budayri al-Hallaq, *Hawadith Dimashq al-yawmiyya, 1154–1175h / 1741–1762m* (Cairo: Al-Jam'iyya al-Misriyya lil-Dirasat al-Ta'rikhiyya, 1959), 22. On Dahir al-'Umar, see Amnon Cohen, *Palestine in the 18th Century* (Jerusalem: Magnes Press, 1973).

20. Abdul-Karim Rafeq, *The Province of Damascus, 1723–1783* (Beirut: Khayats, 1966), 113–15; F. E. Peters, *The Hajj: The Muslim Pilgrimage to Mecca and the Holy Places* (Princeton, NJ: Princeton University Press, 1994), 161.

21. Al-Hallaq, *Hawadith Dimashq*, 203–4.

22. Guarmani, *Northern Najd*, 68; Oppenheim, *Beduinen*, 239.

23. CMS, Frederick Klein, "Tour in the Trans-Jordanic Country (Jebl Ajloon & the Belka) Aug 1868," CMS/B/OMS/C M O41/279–280.

24. Rogan, *Frontiers of the State*, 9–12; Resat Kasaba, *A Moveable Empire: Ottoman Nomads, Migrants and Refugees* (Seattle: University of Washington Press, 2009), 86–93; Mostafa Minawi, *The Ottoman Scramble for Africa* (Stanford: Stanford University Press, 2016).

25. Rogan, *Frontiers of the State*, 45.

26. Lewis, *Nomads and Settlers*, 29–30.

27. Ibid., 30, 35, 225; Daha Shati, "Tawassu' al-badu fi bilad al-Sham wa-inhisaruhum," in *Al-Mu'tamar al-duwali al-thani lil-ta'rikh bilad al-Sham*, vol. 1 (Damascus: Jami'at Dimashq, 1978), 409, cited in al-Sawariyya, *'Amman wa-jiwaruha*, 123.

28. Unless indicated otherwise, the following paragraphs are based on Rogan, *Frontiers of the State*, chaps. 2–3, in particular, and id., "Bringing the State Back: The Limits of Ottoman Rule in Jordan, 1840–1910," in *Village, Steppe and State: The Social Origins of Modern Jordan*, ed. Eugene Rogan and Tariq Tell (London: British Academic Press, 1994), 32–57. See also Lewis, *Nomads and Settlers*, 124–25.

29. *Kitab min wali Suriya Muhammad Rashid Basha ila jinab al-maqam al-'ali*, October 12, 1867, 1/15//1/3, Salih 'abd al-Karim Fayiz Abu 'Urabi 'Adwan's documents, on the web site of the Jordanian National Library, www.nl.gov.jo/ar/Pages/default.aspx (accessed October 28, 2015). The document was reproduced and probably translated from the Ottoman original; in order to retrieve it, a search for the Arabic term *shaykh al-mashayikh* in the category of government documents is required.

30. Rogan, *Frontiers of the State*, chap. 4.

31. Abujaber, *Pioneers over Jordan*, 85.

32. Klein cited n. 23 above.

33. Rogan, *Frontiers of the State*, 48–52; Lewis, *Nomads and Settlers*, 125–26; oral testimony of 'Awad bin Sattam al-Fayiz, Fandi's grandson, in 1985, cited in Abujaber, *Pioneers over Jordan*, 177.

34. Lewis, *Nomads and Settlers*, 126.

35. Peake, *Ta'rikh Sharqi al-Urdunn*, 219; Jaussen, *Coutumes des arabes*, 114.

36. Anne Blunt, *A Pilgrimage to Nejd* (2nd ed., London: John Murray, 1881), 1: 42, 72.

37. "Bayan asma' 'asha'ir al-'urban al-mutawattina fil-Balqa' wa-jihatay al-sharq wal-qibl wa-'adad hamilina al-silah minhum bi-wajh al-takhmin," reproduced in Littmann, "Eine amtliche Liste," 28. Littmann dates this to the mid-1870s (26), but an Arab Ottoman official probably wrote it some years later, after Fandi had delegated leadership of the Bani Sakhr to his son Sattam.

38. Al-Fayiz, *'Asha'ir Bani Sakhr*, 189; Conder, *Heth and Moab*, 317–18; Alois Musil, *Arabia Deserta: A Topographical Itinerary* (New York: American Geographical Society, 1927), 2: 2.

39. Al-Fayiz, *'Asha'ir Bani Sakhr*, 189; Conder, *Heth and Moab*, 317–18.

40. Tristram, *Land of Moab*, 106, 167–68.

41. Ibid., 180, 356.

42. Conder, *Heth and Moab*, 116; Charles Warren, "Expedition to East of Jordan, July and August 1867," *Palestine Exploration Fund Quarterly Statement* 1–2 (March 31 to June 30, 1870), 293; Frederick Klein, "The Original Discovery of the Moabite Stone," ibid., 281.

43. Tristram, *Land of Moab*, 294.

44. See, e.g., Conder, *Heth and Moab*, 115–16; Warren, "Expedition to East of Jordan," 284; A. E. Northey, "Expedition to the East of Jordan," *Palestine Exploration Fund Quarterly Statement* 4 (1872): 58–59, 62; Gray Hill, "A Journey East of the Jordan and the Dead Sea, 1895," ibid. 28 (1896): 25; id., *With the Beduins* (London: Fisher, 1891), 259, 261; Mark Sykes, "Narrative of a Journey East of Jebel Ed-Druse," *Palestine Exploration Fund Quarterly Statement* 31 (1899): 47, 50. On 'Adwani shaykhs and their interaction with European travelers, see Shryock, *Nationalism and the Genealogical Imagination*, esp. chap. 5.

45. Conder, *Heth and Moab*, 322; Warren, "Expedition to East," 297–98; Gray Hill, "Journey East," 25, 40–42. Doughty says that while he stayed briefly at Fandi's camp in 1876, the shaykh demanded ransom and threatened him, thus perhaps violating the rules of hospitality (Charles Montagu Doughty, *Travels in Arabia Deserta* [1888; London: Cape, 1926], 55).

46. Kathryn Tidrick, *Heart-Beguiling Araby* (Cambridge: Cambridge University Press, 1981); Yoav Alon, "'Heart-Beguiling Araby' on the Frontier of Empire: Early Anglo-Arab Relations in Transjordan," *British Journal of Middle Eastern Studies* 36, no. 1 (2009): 55–72.

47. Rogan, *Frontiers of the State*, 188; Lewis, *Nomads and Settlers*, 126; Abujaber, *Pioneers over Jordan*, 113, 185–86; al-Sawariyya, *'Amman wa-jiwaruha*, 97.

48. Abujaber, *Pioneers over Jordan*, 185, 192; Conder, *Heth and Moab*, 118, 120, 317–18.

49. Mithqal al-Fayiz's testimony cited in Yusuf Salim al-Shuwayhat al-'Uzayzat, *Al-'Uzayzat fi Madaba* (no further details), 72.

50. Blunt, *Pilgrimage to Nejd*, 26; Abujaber, *Pioneers over Jordan*, 180–81. The ʿAdwani version is different, claiming that the land was a wedding gift. See Shryock, *Nationalism and the Genealogical Imagination*, 193–94.

51. Abujaber, *Pioneers over Jordan*, 180–81; Mustafa Hamarneh, "Social and Economic Transformation of Trans-Jordan, 1921–1946" (PhD diss., Georgetown University, 1985), 57–59; Lewis, *Nomads and Settlers*, 129; Bashar Muhammad Abu Nusayr al-Masarwa, *ʿAshaʾir Masarwa al-Jiza min 1864–1958* (Madaba, Jordan: n.p., 2000), 40, 58. On the presence of Egyptians in Gaza, see Johann Büssow, *Hamidian Palestine: Politics and Society in the District of Jerusalem, 1872–1908* (Leiden: Brill, 2011), 259.

52. Marion Farouk-Sluglett and Peter Sluglett, "The Transformation of Land Tenure and Rural Social Structure in Central and Southern Iraq c. 1870–1958," *International Journal of Middle East Studies* 15, no. 4 (1983): 493–95; Michael Fischbach, *State, Society and Land in Jordan* (Leiden: Brill, 2000), 22–29.

53. Eugene Rogan, "Asiret Mektebi: Abdülhamid II's School for Tribes (1892–1907)," *International Journal of Middle East Studies* 28, no. 1 (1996): 85; Philip S. Khoury, "The Tribal Shaykh, French Tribal Policy, and the Nationalist Movement in Syria between Two World Wars," *Middle Eastern Studies* 18 (1982): 180–81; Lewis, *Nomads and Settlers*, 31.

54. Rogan, "Bringing the State Back," 47; id., *Frontiers of the State*, 81, 85–87; id., "Incorporating the Periphery: The Ottoman Extension of Direct Rule over Southeastern Syria (Transjordan), 1867–1914" (PhD diss., Harvard University, 1991), 143; Fischbach, *State, Society and Land*, 15; Lewis, *Nomads and Settlers*, 131.

55. Khoury, "Tribal Shaykh," 180–82; Lancaster, *Rwala Bedouin*, 84; Batatu, *Old Social Classes*, 73–86; Lewis, *Nomads and Settlers*, 31, 36; Jaussen, *Coutumes des arabes*, 163.

56. Hill, *With the Beduins*, 71–72; Lovell, *Scandalous Life*, 256.

57. Douglas Carruthers, *Arabian Adventure* (London: Witherby, 1935), 36.

58. Ibid., 37; Conder, *Heth and Moab*, 344.

59. Douglas Carruthers, "A Journey in North-Western Arabia," *Geographical Journal* 35, no. 3 (March 1910): 228; Lancaster, *Rwala Bedouin*, 74–75.

60. Irby and Mangles, *Travels in Egypt*, 145; Klein cited n. 23 above.

61. Tristram, *Land of Moab*, 168

62. Ibid.

63. On hospitality as a means to enhance political authority, see Andrew Shryock and Sally Howell, "'Ever a Guest in Our House': The Amir Abdullah, Shaykh Majid al-ʿAdwan and the Practice of Jordanian House Politics, as Remembered by Umm Sultan, the Widow of Majid," *International Journal of Middle East Studies* 33, no. 2 (2001): 247–69; Rogan, *Frontiers of the State*, 40–41, 188. Also see Conder, *Heth and Moab*, 322. On the notion of shaykhly reputation, see Lancaster, *Rwala Bedouin*, 81, 85–87.

64. Conder, *Heth and Moab*, 113–14.

65. Carruthers, *Arabian Adventure*, 36; Irby and Mangles, *Travels in Egypt*, 145; Conder, *Heth and Moab*, 113–14; Lovell, *Scandalous Life*, 156, 256; Jaussen, *Coutumes des arabes*, 137.

66. Al-Sawariyya, *ʿAmman wa-jiwaruha*, 165–69; Rogan, *Frontiers of the State*, 188.

67. Peake, *Taʾrikh Sharqi al-Urdunn*, 219.

68. For speculations as to the year of Mithqal's birth, see, e.g., Anselm Heyer, *Unter-*

gang des Morgenlandes (Berlin: Ullstein, 1966), 185 (suggesting 1875 as the year of his birth); USNA, Central Foreign Policy Files, 1967–1969, RG 59, Burns to State Department, Joint Weeka, April 12–18, April 19, 1967, Pol 2–1 Jordan, box 2252 (1877); Eliyahu Epstein, "Be-Artzot hamizrah," *Yarhon Ahdut ha-'Avoda* 13 (1931): 468 (1883); 'Awad Sayyah al-Mubarak al-Bakhit and 'Umar Muhammad Nazal al-'Armuti, *Sirat hayat al-shaykh Mithqal Sattam al-Fayiz shaykh mashayikh Bani Sakhr* (Amman: Matba'at al-Safir, [2012]), 52, 56–57 (1885).

69. Al-Bakhit and al-'Armuti, *Sirat hayat al-shaykh*, 52; testimony of Hamud Khalaf al-Hindawi ibn Hazam in ibid., 373–74; Jaussen, *Coutumes des arabes*, 27.

70. Tristram, *Land of Moab*, 356.

71. Shryock, *Nationalism and the Genealogical Imagination*, 256. On tribal poetry, in addition to Shryock's book, see Heikki Palva, *Narratives and Poems from Hesbāan: Arabic Texts Recorded among the Semi-nomadic al-Aǧārma Tribe* (Göteborg, Sweden: Acta Universitatis Gothburgensis, 1978); id., *Artistic Colloquial Arabic: Traditional Narratives and Poems from al-Balqa' (Jordan): Transcription, Translation, Linguistic and Metrical Analysis* (Helsinki: Finnish Oriental Society, 1992); Michael E. Meeker, *Literature and Violence in North Arabia* (Cambridge: Cambridge University Press, 1979); Lila Abu-Lughod, *Veiled Sentiments: Honor and Poetry in a Bedouin Society* (Berkeley: University of California Press, 1986); Steven C. Caton, *"Peaks of Yemen I summon": Poetry as Cultural Practice in a North Yemeni Tribe* (Berkeley: University of California Press, 1990); Smadar Lavie, *The Poetics of Military Occupation: Mzeina Allegories of Bedouin Identity under Israeli and Egyptian Rule* (Berkeley: University of California Press, 1990); Clinton Bailey, *Bedouin Poetry from Sinai and the Negev: Mirror of a Culture* (Oxford: Clarendon Press, 1991); Marcel Kurpershoek, *Oral Poetry and Narratives from Central Arabia*, 5 vols. (Leiden: Brill, 1994–2005); Clive Holes and Said Salman Abu Athera, *Poetry and Politics in Contemporary Bedouin Society* (Reading, UK: Ithaca Press, 2009).

72. Lovell, *Scandalous Life*.

73. Interview with the Fayiz family, al-Mashatta, Jordan, August 2008; al-Bakhit and al-'Armuti, *Sirat hayat al-shaykh*, 55–56; testimony of Fawza Mithqal al-Fayiz, ibid., 334; Jaussen, *Coutumes des arabes*, 27. Jaussen says that Thaqba returned to her family's camp after Sattam's death.

74. Jaussen, *Coutumes des arabes*, 27; Musil, *Arabia Deserta*, 6–9.

75. Al-Bakhit and al-'Armuti, *Sirat hayat al-shaykh*, 55; testimony of Hamud Khalaf al-Hindawi ibn Hazam, ibid., 373–74; testimony of Fawza Mithqal al-Fayiz, ibid., 334; testimony of Sami Mithqal al-Fayiz, ibid., 310.

76. According to a knowledgeable informant of the famous researcher Max von Oppenheim, among the nomads, the education process began when the boy turned ten: Hausarchiv des Bankhauses Sal. Oppenheim jr. & Cie., Köln [Cologne]. "Notizen von Dr. Azkoul / Kadri el Sattafi nr. 73, 1939," Nachlass Max von Oppenheim, Nr. 179.

77. On tribal law, or *'urf*, see esp. 'Awda Qasus, *Al-Qada' al-badawi* (Amman: n.p., 1936); Ahmed Saleh Suleiman Owidi, "Bedouin Justice in Jordan: The Customary Legal System of the Tribes and Its Integration into the Framework of State Policy from 1921 Onwards" (PhD diss., University of Cambridge, 1982); Muhammad Abu Hassan,

Al-Qada' al-'asha'iri fil-Urdunn (Amman: n.p., n.d.); Frank Stewart, "Customary Law among the Bedouin of the Middle East and North Africa," in *Nomadic Societies in the Middle East and North Africa: Entering the 21st Century*, ed. Dawn Chatty (Leiden: Brill, 2006), 239–79; Clinton Bailey, *Bedouin Law from Sinai and the Negev* (New Haven, CT: Yale University Press, 2009). See also chap. 4 above and the Epilogue in this book.

78. Tristram, *Land of Moab*, 103, 112.

79. Ibid., 206, 144–45, 168, 328.

80. Jaussen, *Coutumes des arabes*, 17, cites two cases of ten-year-old sons of shayks of the Bani Sakhr who took part in raiding. Fawwaz al-Sha'lan, the grandson of the leader of the Ruwala and a future leader of that tribal confederacy, could ride and shoot when he was eight: Carl R. Raswan, *The Black Tents of Arabia* (London: Hutchinson, 1935), 26.

81. Tristram, *Land of Moab*, 104, 328.

82. Blunt, *Pilgrimage to Nejd*, 9; Lovell, *Scandalous Life*, 155; Conder, *Heth and Moab*, 225.

83. Rogan, "Asiret Mektebi," 83–107; Selim Deringil, *The Well-Protected Domains: Ideology and the Legitimation of Power in the Ottoman Empire, 1876–1909* (London: I. B. Tauris, 1998), 101–4.

84. Al-Fayiz, *'Asha'ir Bani Sakhr*, 195.

85. Two exceptions are Mithqal's sister Tamam, who is mentioned in Ludwig Ferdinand Clauß, *Als Beduine unter Beduinen* (1933; 3rd ed., Freiburg im Breisgau: Herder, 1954), 94, and Dhahiba, who is remembered by the family: testimony of Sami Mithqal al-Fayiz in al-Bakhit and al-'Armuti, *Sirat hayat al-shaykh*, 310.

86. Alois Musil, *Palmyrena: A Topographical Itinerary* (New York: American Geographical Society, 1928), 17–18; Hill, *With the Beduins*, 251; Rogan, *Frontiers of the State*, 188; Conder, *Heth and Moab*, 317, 331–32; G. Robinson Lees, "Across Southern Bashan," *Geographical Journal* 5, no. 1 (January 1895): 5; Jaussen, *Coutumes des arabes*, 123.

87. Jaussen, *Coutumes des arabes*, 27; al-Bakhit and al-'Armuti, *Sirat hayat al-shaykh*, 301, 373–74.

CHAPTER 2: FROM MAVERICK TO POWERFUL SHAYKH

1. Miflih al-Nimr al-Fayiz, *'Asha'ir Bani Sakhr: Ta'rikh wa-mawaqif hata sanat 1950* (Amman: Matabi' al-Quwwat al-Musallaha, 1995), 199. I am grateful to Prof. Clive Holes for the translation.

2. Antonin Jaussen, *Coutumes des arabes au pays de Moab* (1907; facs. ed., Paris: Librairie d'Amerique et d'Orient, 1948), 27, 135.

3. Eliyahu Eilat, *Shivat Tzion va-'arav* (Tel Aviv: Dvir, 1971), 133.

4. UKNA, Kirkbride to Bevin, "Personalities in Transjordan," August 6, 1946, FO371/52945.

5. Norman Lewis, *Nomads and Settlers in Syria and Jordan, 1800–1980* (Cambridge: Cambridge University Press, 1987), 126; Nawfan Raja al-Hamud al-Sawariyya, *'Amman wa-jiwaruha khilal al-fatra 1864–1921* (Amman: Bank al-A'mal, 1996), 125–26.

6. Alois Musil, *Palmyrena: A Topographical Itinerary* (New York: American Geographical Society, 1928), 17–18; al-Sawariyya, *'Amman wa-jiwaruha*, 126–29.

7. Carlo Guarmani, *Northern Najd: A Journey from Jerusalem to Anaiza in Qasim* (1866; London: Argonaut Press, 1938), 124; H. B. Tristram, *The Land of Israel: A Journal of Travels in Palestine* (London: Society for Promoting Christian Knowledge, 1865), 470; Jaussen, *Coutumes des arabes*, 41.

8. John Zeller, "The Bedawin," *Palestine Exploration Fund Quarterly Statement* 33 (1901): 199.

9. Ibid.; Gray Hill, *With the Beduins* (London: Fisher, 1891), 249; al-Fayiz, *'Asha'ir Bani Sakhr*, 195. Even in the late 1990s, Andrew Shryock was told by 'Adwani tribes-people that poison was the reason for the death in 1946 of Majid al-'Adwan, the shaykh of shaykhs of the Balqa' alliance. Shryock, *Nationalism and the Genealogical Imagination: Oral History and Textual Authority in Tribal Jordan* (Berkeley: University of California Press, 1997), 309.

10. I owe this observation to Andrew Shryock.

11. Raouf Sa'd Abujaber, *Pioneers over Jordan: The Frontier of Settlement in Transjordan, 1850–1914* (London: I. B. Tauris, 1989), 74–75.

12. Eugene L. Rogan, *Frontiers of the State in the Late Ottoman Empire: Transjordan, 1850–1921* (Cambridge: Cambridge University Press, 1999), 193–200. Although Rogan's analysis of the Karak revolt makes no mention of the Bani Sakhr involvement, Muhammad Kurd 'Ali gives a detailed account of these tribes' role. Muhammad Kurd 'Ali, *Al-Rihla al-Anwariyya ila al-Asqa' al-Hijaziyya wal-Shamiyya*, vol. 3 (Beirut: Al-Matba'a al-'Ilmiyya, 1916), 113. It seems that only two small sections of the Bani Sakhr, the Ka'abna and Salit, actually took part in the revolt after the Ottomans tried to register them. Nawfan Raja al-Sawariyya and Muhammad Salim al-Tarawna, *Idha'at jadida 'ala Thawrat al-Karak* (Karak: Dar Rand lil-Nashr, 1999), 36–37, 64–65. See also Sa'd Abu Diyya, *Fil-'Alaqat al-'Arabiyya al-'Uthmaniyya: Thawrat al-Karak 'am 1910* (Amman: Mu'assasat Rum, 1992).

13. Al-Sawariyya, *'Amman wa-jiwaruha*, 128–30; *Al-Qabas* (Damascus), October 11, 1913. I am grateful to Munira Khayyat and her assistant Annabel Turner for providing me with this document from the library of the American University in Beirut.

14. Abujaber, *Pioneers over Jordan*, 75.

15. Al-Sawariyya, *'Amman wa-jiwaruha*, 247, 264–65.

16. *Al-Qabas* (Damascus), October 11, 1913. The warrior was Dirdah bin al-Bakhit.

17. "Personalities of South Syria," vol. 2: "Trans-Jordan," 12, UK, Sudan Archive, Durham University, Reginald Wingate Papers, SAD 206/5/2; Yigal Sheffy, *British Military Intelligence in the Palestine Campaign, 1914–1918* (London: Routledge, 2014), 135.

18. Rogan, *Frontiers of the State*, 223; Douglas Carruthers, *Arabian Adventure* (London: Witherby, 1935), 42; Fawwaz's speech is cited in Yusuf Salim al-Shuwayhat al-'Uzayzat, *Al-'Uzayzat fi Madaba* (no further details), 109.

19. Joseph Kostiner, "The Hashemite 'Tribal Confederacy' of the Arab Revolt, 1916–1917," in *National and International Politics in the Middle East: Essays in Honour of Elie Kedourie*, ed. E. Ingram (London: Frank Cass, 1986), 126–43; Joshua Teitelbaum, *The Rise and Fall of the Hashemite Kingdom of Arabia* (London: Hurst, 2001).

20. Rogan, *Frontiers of the State*, 227–29; 'Awda Qasus, "Mudhakkirat" [Memoirs] (MS), 110–11.

21. Rogan, *Frontiers of the State*, 229–31; Qasus, "Mudhakkirat," 111; al-Fayiz, *'Asha'ir Bani Sakhr*, 118–19; Mustafa Talas, *Al-Thawra al-'Arabiyya al-Kubra* (Damascus: Majallat al-Fikr al-'Askari, 1978), 385–87; Muhammad 'Ali al-'Ajluni, *Dhikrayat 'an al-Thawra al-'Arabiyya al-Kubra* (2nd ed., Amman: Dar al-Karmil, 2002), 32, 57, 80; *Arab Bulletin*, no. 71 (November 27, 1917): 473; ibid., no. 73 (December 16, 1917): 500, 502; ibid., no. 76 (January 13, 1918): 15; ibid., no. 79 (February 18, 1918): 52.

22. Eilat, *Shivat Tzion*, 127; al-Fayiz, *'Asha'ir Bani Sakhr*, 117; *Arab Bulletin*, no. 17 (August 30, 1916): 194–95; ibid., no. 37 (January 4, 1917): 4; ibid., no. 38 (January 19, 1917): 29; ibid., no. 64 (September 27, 1917): 393; ibid., no. 65 (October 8, 1917): 398–99; Jeremy Wilson, *Lawrence of Arabia: The Authorized Biography of T. E. Lawrence* (New York: Atheneum, 1990), 415.

23. *Arab Bulletin*, no. 57 (July 24, 1917): 308.

24. *Arab Bulletin*, no. 64 (September 27, 1917): 393; Eilat, *Shivat Tzion*, 127–28; al-Fayiz, *'Asha'ir Bani Sakhr*, 195–96.

25. I owe this point to Andrew Shryock.

26. Eilat, *Shivat Tzion*, 127–28; F. G. Peake, "History of Transjordan" (draft), 52, IWM, Peake Papers; ISA, "Notes on Beni Sakr Tribe" (two surviving pages from a report that was probably written in 1919 or 1920 by British Intelligence), 65 3221/23.

27. ISA, Eliyahu Epstein [Eilat], "Hamatzav ha-nochehi be-'Ever ha-Yarden," February 1931, 160, 2105/16; Eilat, *Shivat Tzion*, 127–28; *Arab Bulletin*, no. 64 (September 27, 1917): 393; ibid., no. 90 (May 24, 1918): 170; ibid., no. 93 (June 18, 1918): 206; Peake, "History of Transjordan," 53.

28. Oral testimony of Hajj Salih Mustafa Abu Hamur, April 28, 1987, cited in Ahmad 'Uwaydi al-'Abbadi, *Fi Rubu' al-Urdunn*, vol. 1 (Amman: Dar al-Fikr, 1987), 441; Ihsan al-Nimr, *Ta'rikh Jabal Nablus wal-Balqa'*, vol. 3 (Nablus: n.p., 1974), 142. On the Salt battle and refugee problem, see Rogan, *Frontiers of the State*, 235–37. For an interesting oral story with a somewhat different take on the issue, see Shryock, *Nationalism and the Genealogical Imagination*, 171–72.

29. Rogan, *Frontiers of the State*, 237; id., *The Fall of the Ottomans: The Great War in the Middle East* (New York: Basic Books, 2015), 368–69.

30. Matthew Hughes, *Allenby and British Strategy in the Middle East, 1917–1919* (London: Frank Cass, 1999), 85; Wilson, *Lawrence of Arabia*, 499; Hubert Young, *The Independent Arab* (London: John Murray, 1933), 176–78; *Arab Bulletin*, no. 87 (April 30, 1918): 142; al-Fayiz, *'Asha'ir Bani Sakhr*, 271.

31. Rogan, *Frontiers of the State*, 238; id., *Fall of the Ottomans*, 369. I am grateful to Yigal Sheffy who referred my attention to the Bani Sakhr's role in the battle and provided me with some of the relevant sources.

32. Mithqal's testimony cited in al-Nimr, *Ta'rikh Jabal Nablus*, 142.

33. *Arab Bulletin*, no. 92 (June 11, 1918): 185; Rogan, *Frontiers of the State*, 238–39; id., *Fall of the Ottomans*, 365–67, 370.

34. Rogan, *Frontiers of the State*, 240.

35. Al-Nimr, *Ta'rikh Jabal Nablus*, 142; Eliyahu Epstein [Eilat], "Be-Artzot hamizrah," *Yarhon Ahdut ha-'Avoda* 13 (1931): 468.

36. Epstein, "Be-Artzot hamizrah," 468; ISA, "Notes on Beni Sakr Tribe," 65 3221/23.

37. Rogan, *Frontiers of the State*, 242–45; Yoav Alon, *The Making of Jordan: Tribes, Colonialism and the Modern State* (London: I. B. Tauris, 2007), 14–16.

38. *Ahdath al-Thawra al-Suriyya al-Kubra kama saradaha qa'iduha al-'amm Sultan Basha al-Atrash, 1925–1927,* ed. Mustafa Talas (Damascus: Dar Talas, 2007), 54–55.

39. Epstein, "Be-Artzot hamizrah," 468; *Arab Bulletin*, no. 92 (June 11, 1918): 185; Rogan, *Frontiers of the State*, 239, 242–43; Qasus, "Mudhakkirat," 130–33; Philip S. Khoury, "The Tribal Shaykh, French Tribal Policy, and the Nationalist Movement in Syria between Two World Wars," *Middle Eastern Studies* 18 (April 1982): 183.

40. Muhammad 'Abd al-Qadir Khrisat, *Al-Urdunniyyun wal-qadaya al-wataniyya wal-qawmiyya* (Amman: Al-Jami'a al-Urdunniyya, 1991), 18; Yoav Gelber, *Jewish-Transjordanian Relations, 1921–1948* (London: Frank Cass, 1997), 9–10; ISA, Major I. N. Camp, "Summary of Jericho Political Information," January 15, 1920, RG-2/50a; Munib al-Madi and Sulayman Musa, *Ta'rikh al-Urdunn fil-qarn al-'ishrin, 1900–1959* (2nd ed., Amman: Maktabat al-Muhtasib, 1988), 85–88; Qasus, "Mudhakkirat," 131; Alon, *Making of Jordan*, 16–17.

41. James L. Gelvin: *Divided Loyalties: Nationalism and Mass Politics in Syria at the Close of Empire* (Berkeley: University of California Press, 1998), 35–36, 87–88; Alon, *Making of Jordan*, 16–17.

42. Al-Fayiz, *'Asha'ir Bani Sakr*, 122; Khrisat, *Al-Urdunniyyun*, 15, 26; *Al-'Asima* (Damascus), December 4, 1919, cited in Khrisat, *Al-Urdunniyyun*, 24. On the committees, see Gelvin, *Divided Loyalties*, 125–35.

43. ISA, I. N. Camp to GHQ, Cairo, "Conditions at Kerak," December 23, 1919, "News from Salt," January 5, 1920, and "Summary of Jericho Political Information," January 9 and 15, 1920, RG-2/50a; HA, Levi Schneurson Papers, reports dated January 20–25 and 26, 1920, 80/145/15.

44. Gelvin, *Divided Loyalties*, 45.

45. Rogan, *Frontiers of the State*, 243–44; HA, Schneurson Papers, "Trans-Jordania," February 2 and March 9, 1920, and "French Propaganda in Palestine and Transjordan," February 8, 1920; Mary C. Wilson, *King Abdullah, Britain and the Making of Jordan* (Cambridge: Cambridge University Press, 1987), 44–45; I. N. Camp, February 19, 1920, ISA, RG-2/1, cited by Wilson, ibid., 225.

46. Madi and Musa, *Ta'rikh al-Urdunn*, 95; HA, Schneurson Papers, reports dated April 2 and 25 and May 25, 1920, 80/145/15.

47. HA, Schneurson Papers, "Trans-Jordania," March 9, 1920, and L[evi] S[chneurson] to Eder, May 5, 1920; see also Gelber, *Jewish-Transjordanian Relations*, 12.

48. ISA, I. N. Camp to CID, OETA South, February 19, 1920, RG-2/50a.

49. HA, Schneurson Papers, "Trans-Jordania," March 9, 1920.

50. Wilson, *King Abdullah*, 45–48; ISA, high commissioner to Prodrome (the Foreign Office's telegraph address), August 3, 1920, I. N. Camp, "Notes on Southern Part of Trans-Jordania," July 27, 1920, and Colonel Ronald Storrs to Sir Herbert Samuel, August 21, 1920, RG-2/50a.

51. Uriel Dann, *Studies in the History of Transjordan, 1920–1949: The Making of a State* (Boulder, CO: Westview Press, 1984), 18–20.

52. MEC, Monckton Papers, Captain R. F. P. Monckton to district governor, August 23, 1920; ISA, Sir Herbert Samuel to Prodrome, August 22, 1920, I. N. Camp to civil secretary, August 23, 1920, and Mithqal, Mashhur, and Sayil to high commissioner, August 30, 1920, RG-2/50a.

53. Shauket Mufti (Habjoka), *Heroes and Emperors in Circassian History* (Beirut: Librairie du Liban, 1972), 275–76.

54. MEC, Brunton Papers, Captain C. D. Brunton, political report, October 3, 1920.

55. Dann, *Studies in the History*, 21, 23; ISA, I. N. Camp to civil secretary, memorandum on political situation, Salt-Amman area, September 22, 1920, RG-2/50a.

56. MEC, Brunton Papers, C. D. Brunton, political report, October 14, 1920.

57. ISA, I. N. Camp to civil secretary, memorandum on political situation, Salt-Amman area, September 22, 1920, RG-2/50a.

58. ISA, I. N. Camp to Wyndham Deedes, September 23, 1920, RG-2/50a.

59. ISA, civil secretary to I. N. Camp, September 23, 1920, RG-2/50a.

60. Dann, *Studies in the History*, 21–23; Muhammad Khayr Haghanduqa, *Mirza Basha Wasfi: Kitab watha'iqi* (Amman: Al-Jam'iyya al-'Ilmiyya al-Malakiyya, 1985), 24, 31, 47–64.

61. MEC, Brunton Papers, C. D. Brunton, political report, October 9, 1920.

62. Ibid.

63. Ibid., Brunton, political report, October 14, 1920.

64. Ibid., Brunton to the civil secretary, political report, October 23, 1920.

65. Ibid.

66. Ibid.

67. Ibid.

68. ISA, I. N. Camp, résumé of Salt and Amman reports, October 23–November 3, 1920, RG-2/50a.

69. IWM, F. G. Peake Papers, autobiographical essay on Peake's activities in Trans-Jordan during the decade after 1918, 12–14; C. S. Jarvis, *Arab Command: The Biography of Lieutenant Colonel F. W.* [sic] *Peake Pasha* (London: Hutchinson, 1942), 73–74.

70. MEC, Brunton Papers, C. D. Brunton, political report, October 3, 1920.

71. Peake, autobiographical essay cited in n. 69 above, 12–14; Jarvis, *Arab Command*, 73–74. According to Khayr al-Din Zirikli, *'Aman fi 'Amman* (Cairo: Al-Matba'a al-'Arabiyya, 1925), 7–8, however, Mithqal released Peake only after the intervention of Sharif 'Ali al-Harithi, Abdullah's agent in Transjordan.

72. Zirikli, *'Aman fi 'Amman*, 7–8; 'Ajluni, *Dhikrayat 'an al-Thawra*, 119.

CHAPTER 3: THE DECADE OF POWER AND GLORY

1. Mary C. Wilson, *King Abdullah, Britain and the Making of Jordan* (Cambridge: Cambridge University Press, 1987), 36–38, 42–44; Muhammad 'Ali al-'Ajluni, *Dhikrayat 'an al-Thawra al-'Arabiyya al-Kubra* (2nd ed., Amman: Dar al-Karmil, 2002), 83.

2. Sulayman Musa, *Imarat Sharq al-Urdunn: Nasha'tuha wa-tatawwuruha fi rub'*

qarn, 1921–1946 (Amman: Lajnat Ta'rikh al-Urdunn, 1990), 84, 93; al-'Ajluni, *Dhikrayat 'an al-Thawra*, 118.

3. 'Akif al-Fayiz, interview, Amman, March 1998.

4. Andrew Shryock, "Dynastic Modernism and Its Contradictions: Testing the Limits of Pluralism, Tribalism, and King Hussein's Example in Hashemite Jordan," *Arab Studies Quarterly* 22, no. 3 (Summer 2000): 57–79; Betty S. Anderson, *Nationalist Voices in Jordan: The Street and the State* (Austin: University of Texas Press, 2005), chap. 9.

5. Sa'id al-Mufti, "Sa'id al-Mufti yatadhakkaru," *Al-Dustur* (Amman), February 22, 1976; UKNA, Sir Herbert Samuel to Lord Curzon, December 30, 1920, FO141/440.

6. See chap. 2 above.

7. Abdullah to Mashhur, January 7, 1921, reproduced in Miflih al-Nimr al-Fayiz, *'Asha'ir Bani Sakhr: Ta'rikh wa-mawaqif hata sanat 1950* (Amman: Matabi' al-Quwwat al-Musallaha, 1995), 123.

8. Aaron S. Klieman, *Foundations of British Policy in the Arab World: The Cairo Conference of 1921* (Baltimore: Johns Hopkins Press, 1970), 75–76; Musa, *Imarat Sharq al-Urdunn*, 85–86; UKNA, report by F. G. Peake forwarded to the British Residency in Egypt, January 14, 1921, FO141/440.

9. Peake's report cited in the preceding note; Musa, *Imarat Sharq al-Urdunn*, 89; Khayr al-Din Zirikli, *'Aman fi 'Amman* (Cairo: Al-Matba'a al-'Arabiyya, 1925), 8.

10. Al-'Ajluni, *Dhikrayat 'an al-Thawra*, 119; Musa, *Imarat Sharq al-Urdunn*, 89; UKNA, report on the political situation in Palestine and Trans-Jordania, February 1921, and Sir Herbert Samuel to Colonial Secretary Winston Churchill, March 3, 1921, CO733/1.

11. Samuel to Churchill, March 3, 1921, and report in CO733/1 cited in the preceding note; Klieman, *Foundations of British Policy*, 206; MEC, Monckton Papers, revised record of conversation between R. F. C. Monckton and the ISA archivist P. A. Alsberg, September 1968.

12. Musa, *Imarat Sharq al-Urdunn*, 95; Alec Seath Kirkbride, *A Crackle of Thorns* (London: John Murray, 1956), 26–27; 'Abdullah bin Husayn, *Al-Athar al-kamila lil-Malik 'Abdullah bin Husayn* (2nd ed., Beirut: Al-Dar al-Muttahida lil-Nashr, 1979), 161; Zirikli, *'Aman fi 'Amman*, 27; Amin Muhammad Sa'id, *Muluk al-muslimin al-mu'asirin wa-duwaluhum* (Cairo: n.p., 1933), 319; MEC, Fitzroy Somerset Papers, report by L. L. Bright, March 13, 1921.

13. On the Cairo Conference, see Klieman, *Foundations of British Policy*, 105–38; Wilson, *King Abdullah*, 51–53.

14. Wilson, *King Abdullah*, 51–53.

15. See, e.g., ibid., 58–59; Joseph A. Massad, *Colonial Effects: The Making of National Identity in Jordan* (New York: Columbia University Press, 2001), 27; D. K. Fieldhouse, *Western Imperialism in the Middle East, 1914–1958* (Oxford: Oxford University Press, 2006), 224.

16. Wilson, *King Abdullah*, 55; Yoav Alon, *The Making of Jordan: Tribes, Colonialism and the Making of the Modern State* (London: I. B. Tauris, 2007), 40; 'Uthman Qasim to Shakir bin Zayd, August 23, 1922 (courtesy of Sulayman Musa).

17. Alon, *Making of Jordan*, 40–41.

18. UKNA, Albert Abramson, chief British representative, Trans-Jordania, reports nos. 1 and 2, April 21 and May 15, 1921, and Abdullah to Abramson, April 30, 1921, enclosed with report no. 2, CO733/3.

19. Wilson, *King Abdullah*, 64–65; UKNA, Abramson to Sir Herbert Samuel, 9 June 1921, CO733/3.

20. UKNA, "Situation in Transjordania," July 21–31, 1921, CO733/13.

21. Wilson, *King Abdullah*, 242.

22. Raouf Sa'd Abujaber, *Pioneers over Jordan: The Frontier of Settlement in Transjordan, 1850–1914* (London: I. B. Tauris, 1989), 189; W. B. Seabrook, *Adventures in Arabia among the Bedouins, Druses, Whirling Dervishes and Yezidee Devil-Worshippers* (1927; London: George G. Harrap, 1928), 89–91.

23. UKNA, Bertram Thomas, acting British representative, "Trans-Jordan," September 30, 1923, CO733/67.

24. This information is courtesy of Muhammad Yunis al-'Abbadi. See, too, "Intilaq musabaqat Mithqal al-Fayiz al-yawm," *Wikalat Anba' 'Arar*, May 1, 2010; 'Awad Sayyah al-Mubarak al-Bakhit and 'Umar Muhammad Nazal al-'Armuti, *Sirat hayat al-shaykh Mithqal Sattam al-Fayiz shaykh mashayikh Bani Sakhr* (Amman: Matba'at al-Safir, [2012]), 147–49.

25. UKNA, chief British representative, Trans-Jordania, July 1, 1921, CO733/4; Abujaber, *Pioneers over Jordan*, 76.

26. MEC, St John Philby Papers, Harry St John Philby, "Stepping Stones" (MS), 116–17.

27. UKNA, monthly report on Transjordan, December 1923, FO371/10106; Peake to Henry Cox, May 11, 1924, CO733/68.

28. UKNA, chief British representative, Trans-Jordania, report no. 2, May 15, 1921, CO733/3; Seabrook, *Adventures in Arabia*, 132; Ludwig Ferdinand Clauß, *Als Beduine unter Beduinen* (1933; 3rd ed., Freiburg im Breisgau: Herder, 1954), 77.

29. 'Amir Jadallah Musa, "Al-'Alaqat al-Urdunniyya-al-Su'udiyya ma bayna 1921–1928" (BA diss., University of Jordan, 1977), 168–70; Philby, "Stepping Stones" (MS cited n. 26 above), 225, 138.

30. MEC, St John Philby Papers, Harry St John Philby, diary entry, April 27, 1922.

31. *Sumuhu al-karim* in the Arabic text: *Al-Sharq al-'Arabi* (Amman), April 13, 1925.

32. Joseph Kostiner, "On Instruments and Their Designers: The Ikhwan of Najd and the Formation of the Saudi State," *Middle Eastern Studies* 21 (1985): 298–323.

33. H. St J. B. Philby, "Jauf and the North Arabian Desert," *Geographical Journal* 62, no. 4 (October 1923): 241–43, 246, 250, 256; UKNA, Sir Herbert Samuel to Colonial Secretary Winston Churchill, February 21, 1922, CO733/19; Philby to Samuel, May 9, 1922, CO733/22; Abdullah to Samuel enclosed in Samuel to Churchill, July 30, 1922, CO733/23.

34. Zirikli, *'Aman fi 'Amman*, 192; C. S. Jarvis, *Arab Command: The Biography of Lieutenant Colonel F. W. [sic] Peake Pasha* (London: Hutchinson, 1942), 101; Musa, *Imarat Sharq al-Urdunn*, 147–48; Jadallah Musa, "Al-'Alaqat," 11–14; MEC, St John Philby Papers, Harry St John Philby, diary entry, August 18, 1922.

35. Zirikli, *'Aman fi 'Amman*, 192. The original of the line reads: "Wa-liyuhya aqwam Mithqal fa-qad wazanu min al-rijal bi-mithqal qanatira."

36. Cited in al-Fayiz, *'Asha'ir Bani Sakhr*, 199. I am grateful to Prof. Clive Holes for the translation.

37. Seabrook, *Adventures in Arabia*, 90.

38. IWM, F. G. Peake Papers, Peake, draft of autobiography, 79–80.

39. Philby, "Stepping Stones" (MS cited n. 26 above), 16, 19, 24, 28.

40. Ibid., 130–33, 141.

41. UKNA, Acting high commissioner to secretary of state, August 1, 1923, CO733/48; *Al-Sharq al-'Arabi* (Amman), June 18, 1923 and August 25, 1924.

42. Jadallah Musa, "Al-'Alaqat," 168–70; *Al-Sharq al-'Arabi* (Amman), August 18, 1924; *Report by His Britannic Majesty's Government on the Administration under Mandate of Palestine and Transjordan for the Year 1924*, 69.

43. UKNA, acting high commissioner to secretary of state, August 1, 1923, CO733/48; *Al-Sharq al-'Arabi* (Amman), June 18, 1923, and August 25, 1924.

44. Thomas cited n. 23 above.

45. The following account is based on Yoav Alon, "The Balqa' Revolt: Tribes and Early State-Building in Transjordan," *Die Welt des Islams* 46, no. 1 (2006): 7–42.

46. *Al-Sharq al-'Arabi* (Amman), January 28 and February 11, 1924, reproduced in Muhammad Yunis al-'Abbadi, *Al-Rihla al-mulukiyya al-Hashimiyya* (Amman: Wizarat al-Thaqafa, 1997), 68, 70; Philby, "Stepping Stones" (MS cited n. 26 above), 148; 'Awda Qasus, "Mudhakkirat" [Memoirs] (MS), 190–91; Wilson, *King Abdullah*, 78. On the 'Adwani very different contemporary interpretation, see Andrew Shryock, *Nationalism and the Genealogical Imagination: Oral History and Textual Authority in Tribal Jordan* (Berkeley: University of California Press, 1997), 88–92.

47. UKNA, reports on Trans-Jordan, January 1–February 25, 1925, CO733/91, and July 1–31, 1925, CO733/96; situation report for the last quarter of 1927, CO831/1/2; Peter Gubser, *Politics and Change in Al-Karak, Jordan* (London: Oxford University Press, 1973), 21.

48. *Al-Sharq al-'Arabi* (Amman), October 20 and November 3, 1924, December 15, 1926.

49. UKNA, Cox, report on Trans-Jordan, September 1–October 31, 1924, CO733/75.

50. UKNA, Wauchope to Cunliffe-Lister, May 24, 1934, CO831/28/3.

51. *Al-Sharq al-'Arabi* (Amman), June 1, 1927; UKNA, Wauchope to Cunliffe-Lister, May 24, 1934, CO831/28/3; situation report for April 1–June 30, 1927, FO371/12272.

52. The Hadda Agreement, Appendix to *Report by His Britannic Majesty's Government on the Administration under Mandate of Palestine and Transjordan for the Year 1926*, 75–78; Wilson, *King Abdullah*, 99–100; Riccardo Bocco and Tariq M. M. Tell, "Pax Britannica in the Steppe: British Policy and the Transjordan Bedouin," in *Village, Steppe and State: The Social Origins of Modern Jordan*, ed. Eugene L. Rogan and Tariq M. M. Tell (London: British Academic Press, 1994), 111, 114; Bocco and Tell, "Frontière, tribus et Etat(s) en Jordanie orientale à l'époque du mandate," *Maghreb-Machrek* 147 (1995): 26–47.

53. Ma'an Abu-Nowar, *The History of the Hashemite Kingdom of Jordan*, vol. 1: *The Creation and Development of Transjordan, 1920–29* (Oxford: Ithaca Press, 1989), 173–75; UKNA, Plumer to Amery, May 18, 1926, and situation report for period ending May 31, 1926, CO733/114; situation report for period ending June 30, 1926, CO733/129; situation report for April 1–June 31, 1928, CO831/1/2. For an interesting study that examines British desert policy in the Middle East, see Robert S. G. Fletcher, *British Imperialism and the 'Tribal Question': Desert Administration and Nomadic Societies in the Middle East, 1919–1936* (Oxford: Oxford University Press, 2015). Fletcher convincingly shows that the enhanced British intervention in the desert characterized not only Transjordan but also Iraq and Egypt.

54. UKNA, Cox to Symes, January 13, 1927, CO733/133/8; Cox to Plumer, May 23, 1928, CO831/3/1.

55. *Al-Sharq al-'Arabi* (Amman), June 11, 1926; UKNA, Plumer to Amery, May 18, 1926, and situation report for period ending May 31, 1926, CO733/114.

56. Transjordan, minister of justice to prime minister, August 21, 1929, reproduced in *Al-Watha'iq al-Hashimiyya, awraq 'Abdullah bin al-Husayn*: vol. 10: *Al-'Alaqat al-Urdunniyya-al-Su'udiyya, 1925–1951*, ed. Muhammad 'Adnan al-Bakhit et al. (Amman: Jami'at Al al-Bayt, 1997), pt. 2, 159; UKNA, high commissioner to British consul, Jedda [Jidda], December 28, 1926, CO733/133/8; situation reports for January 1–March 31 and April 1–June 30, 1928, CO831/1/2. On the tribal practice of partial payment, see Dale F. Eickelman, *The Middle East and Central Asia: An Anthropological Approach* (1981; 3rd ed., Upper Saddle River, NJ: Prentice-Hall, 1998), 131–32.

57. Philip S. Khoury, "A Reinterpretation of the Origins and Aims of the Great Syrian Revolt of 1925–27," in *Arab Civilization: Challenges and Responses. Studies in Honor of Constantine K. Zurayk*, ed. George N. Atiyeh and Ibrahim M. Oweiss (Albany: State University of New York Press, 1988), 241–71; Michael Provence, *The Great Syrian Revolt and the Rise of Arab Nationalism* (Austin: University of Texas Press, 2005).

58. Wilson, *King Abdullah*, 89; Abu-Nowar, *History of the Hashemite Kingdom of Jordan*, 1: 152; 'Abd al-Rahman al-Shahbandar, *Mudhakkirat al-duktur 'Abd al-Rahman al-Shahbandar* (Beirut: Dar al-Irshad, 1968), 213–14; *Ahdath al-Thawra al-Suriyya al-Kubra kama saradaha qa'iduha al-'amm Sultan Basha al-Atrash, 1925–1927*, ed. Mustafa Talas (Damascus: Dar Talas, 2007), 291, 302; Eliyahu Eilat, *Shivat Tzion va-'arav* (Tel Aviv: Dvir, 1971), 130.

59. Joseph Kostiner, *The Making of Saudi Arabia, 1916–1936: From Chieftaincy to Monarchical State* (New York: Oxford University Press, 1993), chap. 2; Bocco and Tell, "Pax Britannica," 112–15.

60. UKNA, situation reports for January 1–March 31, April 1–June 30, and July 1–September 30, 1928, CO831/1/2; Abdullah to Plumer, February 16 and April 24, 1928, reproduced in *Al-Watha'iq al-Hashimiyya*, ed. Muhammad 'Adnan al-Bakhit, vol. 10, pt. 1, 273–85; Plumer to Amery, May 16, 1928, CO831/2/6; *Report by His Britannic Majesty's Government on the Administration under Mandate of Palestine and Transjordan for the Year 1928*, 95; Bocco and Tell, "Pax Britannica," 115–16; Alon, *Making of Jordan*, 84–87.

61. UKNA, Kirkbride, report on visit to tribes east of the Hejaz Railway, Decem-

ber 27, 1928, CO831/5/1; Chancellor to Amery, February 5, 1929, J. Chancellor Papers, Rhodes House Library, Oxford.

62. UKNA, Cox to Abdullah, April 9, 1929, cited in Musa, *Imarat Sharq al-Urdunn*, 323–24; Cox to OC RAF Trans-Jordan and Palestine, May 21, 1929, situation report April 1–June 30, 1929, and Stafford to Cox, May 28, 1929, CO831/5/9; Chancellor to Amery, May 31, 1929, CO831/5/1.

63. Abu-Nowar, *History of the Hashemite Kingdom of Jordan*, 1: 193–94; MEC, 'Arif al-'Arif Papers, 'Arif al-'Arif's diary, July 25 and 21, 1927; UKNA, Plumer to high commissioner for Syria and Lebanon, May 18, 1928, CO831/2/6; situation report for January 1–March 31, 1929, CO831/5/9.

64. Clauß, *Als Beduine*, 107.

65. Alon, *Making of Jordan*, 70, 73; MEC, Glubb Papers, John Glubb, "A Monthly Report on Events in the Deserts of Transjordan—October 1937."

66. Wilson, *King Abdullah*, 97–98; *Al-Sharq al-'Arabi* (Amman), June 20, 1928; *Al-Jarida al-Rasmiyya*, January 28, 1929; Musa, *Imarat Sharq al-Urdunn*, 203.

67. *Filastin* (Jaffa), June 18, 1929.

68. Ibid. And see also ibid., July 23 and August 6 and 13, 1929.

69. Avraham Sela, "The 'Wailing Wall' Riots (1929) as a Watershed in the Palestine Conflict," *Muslim World* 84, no. 1–2 (January–April 1994): 60–94; Hillel Cohen, *Year Zero of the Arab-Israeli Conflict, 1929* (2013), trans. Haim Watzman (Lebanon, NH: Brandeis University Press, 2015).

70. UKNA, Brigadier W. G. Dobbie, "Palestine Emergency: Narrative of Operations between 24th August and 12th September 1929," October 7, 1929, CO733/175/3; CZA, list of short biographies, n.d. (ca. 1931), S25/10654; Eilat, *Shivat Tzion*, 132.

71. Ludwig Ferdinand Clauß, *Als Beduine*, 77; id., *Semiten der Wüste unter sich: Miterlebnisse eines Rassenforschers* (Berlin: Büchergilde Gutenberg, 1937), 75.

72. CZA, N. Paper, "The Problems of Transjordania," March 31, 1931, S25/3509.

CHAPTER 4: BETWEEN TENT, CAMP, AND HOUSE

1. W. B. Seabrook, *Adventures in Arabia among the Bedouins, Druses, Whirling Dervishes and Yezidee Devil-Worshippers* (1927; London: George G. Harrap, 1928), 28.

2. Ibid., 13, 33, 136. On Emir Amin Arslan's rapport with the inhabitants of Transjordan, see Eugene L. Rogan, *Frontiers of the State in the Late Ottoman Empire: Transjordan, 1850–1921* (Cambridge: Cambridge University Press, 1999), 56.

3. Seabrook, *Adventures in Arabia*, 109, 111. Seabrook's descriptions of Mithqal are rich and perceptive and therefore invaluable for this biography. At the same time some of them are puzzling, at times resembling fantasy rather than fact. Given that his work is of a literary rather than scholarly nature, it is not surprising that he took liberties in his writing and often exaggerated and dramatized events to cater to the taste of his Western readers. Still, it is my impression that he did not invent them altogether. The credibility of this source is further supported by the fact that it is often cited by Jordanian researchers. In using it I have taken particular care to examine it cautiously and to qualify when needed, although it was not always possible to weigh Seabrook's account against other sources.

4. Ludwig Ferdinand Clauß, *Als Beduine unter Beduinen* (1933; 3rd ed., Freiburg im Breisgau: Herder, 1954), 77.

5. Ibid., xi. See also Ludwig Ferdinand Clauß, *Semiten der Wüste unter sich: Miterlebnisse eines Rassenforschers* (Berlin: Büchergilde Gutenberg, 1937).

6. Eliyahu Eilat, *Shivat Tzion va-'arav* (Tel Aviv: Dvir, 1971), 132.

7. Seabrook, *Adventures in Arabia*, 26.

8. Ibid., 31.

9. MEC, St John Philby Papers, Harry St John Philby, "Stepping Stones" (MS), 138; Seabrook, *Adventures in Arabia*, 36.

10. Seabrook, *Adventures in Arabia*, 42.

11. Clauß, *Als Beduine*, 106.

12. Seabrook, *Adventures in Arabia*, 42.

13. Ibid., 33–34.

14. Ibid., 35–36, 69; Clauß, *Als Beduine*, 106–7. On coffee paraphernalia and their symbolic meaning, see Linda L. Layne, *Home and Homeland: The Dialogics of Tribal and National Identities in Jordan* (Princeton, NJ: Princeton University Press, 1994); Andrew Shryock and Sally Howell, "'Ever a Guest in Our House': The Amir Abdullah, Shaykh Majid al-'Adwan, and the Practice of Jordanian House Politics, as Remembered by Umm Sultan, the Widow of Majid," *International Journal of Middle East Studies* 33, no. 2 (2001): 247–69.

15. Seabrook, *Adventures in Arabia*, 54; Mithqal owned "thousands of camels" according to Clauß, *Semiten der Wüste*, 80–81.

16. Seabrook, *Adventures in Arabia*, 54–55.

17. Alois Musil, *Arabia Deserta: A Topographical Itinerary*, vol. 2 (New York: American Geographical Society, 1927), 5, 10, 104, 106; Norman Lewis, *Nomads and Settlers in Syria and Jordan, 1800–1980* (Cambridge: Cambridge University Press, 1987), 5.

18. Douglas Carruthers, *Arabian Adventure: To the Great Nafud in Quest of the Oryx* (London: H. F. & G. Witherby, 1935), 44–45.

19. Seabrook says that Mithqal's mother lived in Umm al-'Amad, too, but according to a report cited in chap. 1, Mithqal left the Ruwala camp and joined the Bani Sakhr after his mother's death.

20. Seabrook, *Adventures in Arabia*, 40–41, 74.

21. Clauß, *Als Beduine*, 41.

22. Ibid., 79–80.

23. For a brilliant analysis of shaykhs' practice to impress their non-tribal guests, see William Lancaster, *The Rwala Bedouin Today* (Cambridge: Cambridge University Press, 1981), 82–84.

24. Seabrook, *Adventures in Arabia*, 133.

25. Ibid., 132–33.

26. Clauß, *Als Beduine*, 83, 126.

27. Ibid., 87.

28. ISA, [Eliyahu Epstein], "The Current Situation in Transjordan—Report of a Visit in February 1931," 160/2105/16.

29. Ibid.; Eilat, *Shivat Tzion*, 130, 135–36.

30. Clauß, *Als Beduine*, 102–4.

31. Carl R. Raswan, *The Black Tents of Arabia* (London: Hutchinson, 1935), 55, 113.

32. Seabrook, *Adventures in Arabia*, 68, 74; Clauß, *Als Beduine*, 86–87.

33. Interview with 'Akif al-Fayiz, *Al-Dustur* (Amman), June 6, 1994.

34. CZA, [Avira], "At the house of Mithqal Fayiz Pasha," June 15, 1941, S25/3504; interview with Tayil Mithqal al-Fayiz and Faysal al-Fayiz at the family farm in al-Mashatta, Jordan, August 5, 2008.

35. Interview with Tayil Mithqal al-Fayiz at the family farm in al-Mashatta, August 5, 2008. Tayil said he heard this story from his father.

36. Interviews with Sami Mithqal al-Fayiz, October 20, 2008, and July 11, 2009, Zizya, Jordan; interview with Faysal al-Fayiz and Tayil Mithqal al-Fayiz at the family farm in al-Mashatta, August 5, 2008; Clauß, *Als Beduine*, 105; Eliyau Eilat, "Maga'im ishiyim 'im beduyey 'Ever ha-Yarden bi-shnot ha-shloshim," in *Reshimot be-noshe ha-beduyim*, no. 9, ed. Yitzhak Bailey (Sde Boker, Israel: Midreshet Sde Boker, 1978), 8.

37. Clauß, *Als Beduine*, 91, 108–9, 112, 133–34; CZA, [Avira], "At the House of Mithqal Fayiz Pasha," June 15, 1941, S25/3504; interviews with Sami Mithqal al-Fayiz, October 20, 2008, and July 11, 2009, Zizya; testimony of Mamduh Sultan al-Fayiz in 'Awad Sayyah al-Mubarak al-Bakhit and 'Umar Muhammad Nazal al-'Armuti, *Sirat hayat al-shaykh Mithqal Sattam al-Fayiz shaykh mashayikh Bani Sakhr* (Amman: Matba'at al-Safir, [2012]), 306.

38. Eilat, *Shivat Tzion*, 135; MEC, Glubb Papers, John Glubb, "A Monthly Report on the Administration of the Desert, August–October 1934."

39. Interview with Faysal al-Fayiz and Tayil Mithqal al-Fayiz at the family farm in al-Mashatta, August 5, 2008; testimony of Fawza Mithqal al-Fayiz in al-Bakhit and al-'Armuti, *Sirat hayat al-shaykh*, 333–35; testimony of Muslim Khalaf al-Qtifan, ibid., 344–45; testimony of Muhammad Hamdan Marji al-Dabayba, ibid., 353.

40. CZA, [Avira], "At the House of Mithqal Fayiz Pasha," June 15, 1941, S25/3504.

41. Ibid.; Eilat, *Shivat Tzion*, 135.

42. Interview with 'Akif al-Fayiz, *Al-Dustur* (Amman), June 6, 1994; Eilat, *Shivat Tzion*, 135.

43. Clauß, *Als Beduine*, 87.

44. Interview with Faysal al-Fayiz and Tayil Mithqal al-Fayiz at the family farm in al-Mashatta, August 5, 2008; Mithqal's daughter in law also reported Mithqal's preference to 'Adul: testimony of Wajid Sulayman al-Jam'ani cited in al-Bakhit and al-'Armuti, *Sirat hayat al-shaykh*, 273–75.

45. Interview with Faysal al-Fayiz and Tayil Mithqal al-Fayiz at the family farm in al-Mashatta, August 5, 2008; Clauß, *Semiten der Wüste*, 89.

46. See chap. 1 above.

47. Clauß, *Semiten der Wüste*, 137.

48. Clauß, *Als Beduine*, 86–88, 93–95, 102; id., *Semiten der Wüste*, 88–90, 97.

49. Seabrook, *Adventures in Arabia*, 36–37; ISA, [Eliyahu Epstein], "The Current Situation in Transjordan—Report of a Visit in February 1931," 160/2105/16.

50. Seabrook, *Adventures in Arabia*, 30–31, 132.

51. Ibid., 89–91; Clauß, *Als Beduine*, 80–81; E. Epstein, *Ukhlusey 'Ever ha-Yarden ve-hayehem* (Tel Aviv: Omanut, 1933), 15, 39.

52. UKNA, Sir Herbert Samuel to Thomas, "A Note on Slavery in Palestine and Trans-Jordan," April 24, 1924, CO733/67; Carl R. Raswan, *Escape from Baghdad* (Hildesheim, Germany: Georg Olms, 1978), 85; Nachlass Max von Oppenheim, Nr. 180, Hausarchiv des Bankhauses Sal. Oppenheim jr. & Cie., Köln [Cologne], "Antwort von Dr. Azkoul nr. 60, Anlage zum Brief von Max von Oppenheim an Fischer, 12 November 1941."

53. Alois Musil, *The Manners and Customs of the Rwala Bedouins* (New York: American Geographical Society, 1928), 276–78; Raswan, *Escape from Baghdad*, 84–85. On slavery in the Middle East, see Ehud R. Toledano, *Slavery and Abolition in the Ottoman Middle East* (Seattle: University of Washington Press, 1998), and id., *As If Silent and Absent: Bonds of Enslavement in the Islamic Middle East* (New Haven, CT: Yale University Press, 2007).

54. UKNA, Sir Herbert Samuel to Thomas, "A Note on Slavery in Palestine and Trans-Jordan," April 24, 1924, CO733/67. Similar observations can be found in Epstein, *Ukhlusey 'Ever ha-Yarden*, 38–39.

55. Toledano, *Slavery and Abolition*, 4.

56. Seabrook, *Adventures in Arabia*, 89.

57. Ibid., 70–71; Clauß, *Als Beduine*, 101; CZA, Avira to Gershon, March 4, 1941, S25/3504.

58. The earliest available document with Mithqal's signature is from 1934: *Al-Watha'iq al-Hashimiyya, awraq 'Abdullah bin al-Husayn*: vol. 16 [*Al-'Asha'ir al-Urdunniyya, 1921–1951*], pt. 3: *Qararat lajnat al-ishraf 'ala al-badu, 1931–1949*, ed. Muhammad 'Adnan al-Bakhit et al. (Amman: Jami'at Al al-Bayt, 2003), 244.

59. Seabrook, *Adventures in Arabia*, 36–37, 69; Epstein, *Ukhlusey 'Ever ha-Yarden*, 30, 42.

60. Seabrook, *Adventures in Arabia*, 33–34, 36–38, 69–70.

61. Ibid., 34.

62. Clauß, *Als Beduine*, 86.

63. Seabrook, *Adventures in Arabia*, 74.

64. Clauß, *Als Beduine*, 100–101; id., *Semiten der Wüste*, 97. On a similar custom among the Ruwala, see Raswan, *Black Tents*, 144–45.

65. Seabrook, *Adventures in Arabia*, 68.

66. Ibid., 37–39, 68–69; Clauß and Epstein recounted a similar procedure: Clauß, *Als Beduine*, 82; Epstein, *Ukhlusey 'Ever ha-Yarden*, 15–17.

67. Clauß, *Semiten der Wüste*, 105.

68. Seabrook, *Adventures in Arabia*, 39.

69. The following account is based on Seabrook, *Adventures in Arabia*, 120–31. Raswan, *Black Tents*, 53–65, describes a raiding expedition that ended without any actual raiding.

70. Seabrook, *Adventures in Arabia*, 129.

71. Ibid., 126. On the strict rules of raiding, see Great Britain, *A Handbook of Syria*

(including Palestine) (London: HMSO, 1919–20), 229–30. For a study dedicated to theorizing raids, see Louise E. Sweet, "Camel Raiding of North Arabian Bedouin: A Mechanism of Ecological Adaptation," *American Anthropologist* 67 (1965): 1132–50.

72. Godfrey Lias, *Glubb's Legion* (London: Evans Bros., 1956), 74–76.

73. Cited in ibid., 75.

74. Clauß, *Als Beduine*, 104; Eilat, *Shivat Tzion*, 133; ISA, [Eliyahu Epstein], "The Current Situation in Transjordan—Report of a Visit in February 1931," 160/2105/16.

75. [Epstein], "Current Situation," cited in preceding note.

76. The following account is based on Seabrook, *Adventures in Arabia*, 63–67.

77. Ibid., 66–67. Italics and gloss in square brackets in original.

78. Ibid., 67.

79. Ibid., 42–43. This assertion has not been corroborated in other sources.

80. William Young, "'The Bedouin': Discursive Identity or Sociological Category? A Case Study from Jordan," *Journal of Mediterranean Studies* 9, no. 2 (1999): 280–81.

81. Seabrook, *Adventures in Arabia*, 46.

82. Ibid., 46–48.

83. Testimony of Fawza Mithqal al-Fayiz in al-Bakhit and al-'Armuti, *Sirat hayat al-shaykh*, 336.

84. CZA, Cna'ani [Avira's code name], "At the House of Mithqal Fayiz," July 9, 1941, S25/3504.

CHAPTER 5: TIMES OF CRISIS

1. E. Epstein, *Ukhlusey 'Ever ha-Yarden ve-hayehem* (Tel Aviv: Omanut, 1933), 33–34; testimony of Muslim Khalaf al-Qtifan in 'Awad Sayyah al-Mubarak al-Bakhit and 'Umar Muhammad Nazal al-'Armuti, *Sirat hayat al-shaykh Mithqal Sattam al-Fayiz shaykh mashayikh Bani Sakhr* (Amman: Matba'at al-Safir, [2012]), 338–39.

2. Riccardo Bocco and Tariq M. M. Tell, "*Pax Britannica* in the Steppe: British Policy and the Transjordan Bedouin," in *Village, Steppe and State: The Social Origins of Modern Jordan*, ed. Eugene L. Rogan and Tariq M. M. Tell (London: British Academic Press, 1994), 117–18.

3. UKNA, Cox to high commissioner, August 28, 1930, CO831/7/8.

4. The following section is based on Yoav Alon, *The Making of Jordan: Tribes, Colonialism and the Modern State* (London: I. B. Tauris, 2007), chap. 4. See also Bocco and Tell, "*Pax Britannica*," 108–27; Joseph A. Massad, *Colonial Effects: The Making of National Identity in Jordan* (New York: Columbia University Press, 2001), chap. 3; Sa'd Abu Diyya and 'Abd al-Majid Mahdi, *Al-Jaysh al-'Arabi wa-diblumasiyyat al-sahra* (Amman: Mudiriyyat al-Matabi' al-'Askariyya, 1987).

5. UKNA, John Glubb, "Note on the Situation on the Southern Frontier of Trans-Jordan" (n.d. [November–December 1930]), CO831/11/1; Bocco and Tell, "*Pax Britannica*," 118– 21.

6. UKNA, Burnett to Shuckburgh, February 11, 1931, CO831/11/1; Glubb to Peake, "Situation on the Nejd Frontier" (n.d. [ca. October–November 1931]), CO831/13/3.

7. Bocco and Tell, "*Pax Britannica*," 120–22; id., "Frontière, tribus et Etat(s) en Jor-

danie orientale à l'époque du mandate," *Maghreb-Machrek* 147 (1995): 26–47; Norman Lewis, *Nomads and Settlers in Syria and Jordan, 1800–1980* (Cambridge: Cambridge University Press, 1987), 134–35; MEC, Glubb Papers, John Glubb, "A Monthly Report on Events in the Deserts of Transjordan" (hereafter cited as "Glubb's report"). This information was gathered from several reports during 1932–36.

8. Glubb's reports, November 1932 and July 1935; Eliyahu Epstein [Eilat], "Be-Artzot hamizrah," *Yarhon Ahdut ha-'Avoda* 13 (1931): 473.

9. Glubb's reports, November 1932 and January 1933; UKNA, Kirkbride to Cox, "Notes on Inspection of Southern Trans-Jordan, 29.2.32 to 6.3.32," CO831/19/8.

10. Glubb's reports, December 1933 and August–October 1934 cited in Bocco and Tell, "*Pax Britannica,*" 121; Tariq Moraiwed Tell, *The Social and Economic Origins of Monarchy in Jordan* (New York: Palgrave Macmillan, 2013), 86.

11. UKNA, Glubb's report, June 1936, CO831/37/3; MEC, Glubb's reports, January 1934 and January 1935.

12. Epstein, *Ukhlusey 'Ever ha-Yarden,* 50; *Al-Jarida al-Rasmiyya,* January 28, 1929 and January 16, 1932.

13. Glubb's report, October 1937.

14. UKNA, Kirkbride, report on the political situation, June 1942, CO831/58/3; CZA, Aharon Haim Cohen, secretary of the Jewish Agency's Political Department's Arab Bureau, "Report on Visit to Amman, August 4–5, 1932," August 10, 1932, S25/6313.

15. *Report by His Britannic Majesty's Government on the Administration under Mandate of Palestine and Transjordan for the Year 1929,* 138; UKNA, Cox to Wauchope, March 25, 1932, and Treasury to CO, May 25, 1932, CO831/18/1; Epstein, *Ukhlusey 'Ever ha-Yarden,* 53.

16. Epstein, *Ukhlusey 'Ever ha-Yarden,* 73; CZA, N. Paper, "Agricultural Overview of the Vicinity of Amman-Madaba," April 11, 1930, S25/3505; id., "The Problems of Transjordania," March 31, 1931, S25/3509.

17. Aharon Cohen, "Report" cited n. 14 above.

18. *Al-Watha'iq al-Hashimiyya, awraq 'Abdullah bin al-Husayn*: vol. 16: [*Al-'Asha'ir al-Urdunniyya, 1921–1951*], pt. 2: *Mahadir wa-jalasat lajnat al-ishraf 'ala al-badu, 1931–1949,* ed. Muhammad 'Adnan al-Bakhit et al. (Amman: Jami'at Al al-Bayt, 2001), 138; IWM, F. G. Peake Papers, Peake to Warham, February 17, 1928; *Al-Jarida al-Rasmiyya,* February 1 and August 16, 1929.

19. Mary C. Wilson, *King Abdullah, Britain and the Making of Jordan* (Cambridge: Cambridge University Press, 1987), 242; Ludwig Ferdinand Clauß, *Als Beduine unter Beduinen* (1933; 3rd ed., Freiburg im Breisgau: Herder, 1954), 90.

20. ISA, [Eliyahu Epstein], "The Current Situation in Transjordan—Report of a Visit in February 1931," 160/2105/16; CZA, Mithqal to Hasidoff, July 28, 1932, S25/3491; *Filastin* (Jaffa), July 26, 1932. By 1943, Mithqal owed the government over £4,500, about half of this going back to 1930–31 (UKNA, "Political Situation for July 1943," CO831/60/2).

21. *Al-Sharq al-'Arabi* (Amman), October 20 and November 3, 1924, December 15, 1926, April 1, 1927, and January 15, 1928; *Al-Jarida al-Rasmiyya,* May 16, 1933.

22. *Al-Majlis al-Tashri'i,* December 22, 1930.

23. See, e.g., *Al-Majlis al-Tashri'i*, November 22, 1931; UKNA, Alec and Alen Kirkbride, "Note on Inspection of the Ajloun District, 30 April 1932," CO831/19/8, and id. to Cox, July 3, 1934, CO831/27/1.

24. *Al-Majlis al-Tashri'i*, December 28, 1931.

25. Ibid.

26. Alon, *Making of Jordan*, 103–7; Lewis, *Nomads and Settlers*, 133, 135; Hatem A. Sarairah, "A British Actor on the Bedouin Stage: Glubb's Career in Jordan, 1930–1956" (PhD diss., Indiana University, 1989), 124.

27. *Al-Jarida al-Rasmiyya*, March 24 and 27, 1931; Aharon Cohen, "Report" cited n. 14 above.

28. UKNA, Glubb's report, June 1936, CO831/37/3. Mithqal's sons Tayil and Talal described Glubb's relations with their father similarly (interview at the family farm in al-Mashatta, Jordan, August 5, 2008).

29. Muhammad 'Abd al-Qadir Khrisat, *Al-Urdunniyyun wal-qadaya al-wataniyya wal-qawmiyya* (Amman: Al-Jami'a al-Urdunniyya, 1991), 108–9; *Al-Urdunn* (Amman), October 8, 1930.

30. This account is based in part on Mithqal's testimony in CZA, Aharon Cohen, "Report on My Visit to Amman, December 13–19, 1933," December 24, 1933, S25/10122; see also UKNA, Kirkbride, situation report, December 1933, CO831/23/11.

31. CZA, Nahum Paper to Frederick Kisch, March 16, 1931, S25/3509.

32. Eliyahu Eilat, *Shivat Tzion va-'arav* (Tel Aviv: Dvir, 1971), 133.

33. *Al-Majlis al-Tashri'i*, November 16 and December 22, 1930.

34. Yoav Alon, "Tribal Shaykhs and the Limits of British Imperial Rule," *Journal of Imperial and Commonwealth History* 32, no. 1 (2004): 69–92; Michael Fischbach, *State, Society and Land in Jordan* (Leiden: Brill, 2000), 95–97.

35. *Al-Majlis al-Tashri'i*, February 9, 1931.

36. Ibid., January 2, 1935.

37. UKNA, colonial secretary to high commissioner, November 29, 1934, CO831/27/2; CZA, Aharon Cohen, "A Conversation with Mithqal Pasha al-Fayiz at the House of M. Shertok, 3 September, 1934," September 4, 1934, S25/10122; protocol of a joint meeting of the executives of the Jewish Agency, the Jewish National Fund, and the Palestine Land Development Company, December 6, 1934, KKL5/7110.

38. UKNA, acting high commissioner to colonial secretary, October 20, 1934, CO831/27/2.

39. On the land reform, see Fischbach, *State, Society and Land.*

40. UKNA, high commissioner to colonial secretary, November 2, 1934, CO831/27/2.

41. UKNA, colonial secretary to high commissioner, November 29, 1934, CO831/27/2; Resident Henry Cox to the high commissioner, July 6, 1936 (attached to Glubb's June 1936 report), CO831/37/3.

42. *Filastin* (Jaffa), August 9 and 17, 1932.

43. On the common practice of bribery in the Arab press, see Ami Ayalon, *The Press in the Arab Middle East* (New York: Oxford University Press, 1995), 122–26, 211–12.

44. *Batal al-'uruba* in the original text: *Filastin* (Jaffa), September 27, 1931.

45. See, e.g., *Filastin* (Jaffa), May 21 and August 9 and 30, 1932, October 30, 1937; *Al-Karmil* (Haifa), August 27, 1932.

46. Khrisat, *Al-Urdunniyyun*, 172; CZA, "Information of the Arab Bureau: al-Hayat, Jerusalem, August 25, 1931," S25/3567; T. Ashkenazi, October 28, 1930, S25/3161, and list of short biographies (n.d. [ca. 1931]), S25/10654.

47. *Filastin* (Jaffa), October 18, 1931.

48. *Al-Ahram* (Cairo), September 11 and 16, 1931; *Filastin* (Jaffa), September 10, 12, 16, 19, 22, 23, 27, and 29, 1931.

49. *Filastin* (Jaffa), September 16 and 30, October 18, 1931; CZA, Nathan Kaplan's report on the negotiations with Rufayfan al-Majali, September 29, 1932, A264/18.

50. For examples of how Mithqal's relationship with the Zionists has been portrayed in the scholarly literature, focusing exclusively on the economic dimension, see Kenneth W. Stein, *The Land Question in Palestine, 1917–1939* (Chapel Hill: University of North Carolina Press, 1984), 194; Wilson, *King Abdullah*, 106–7, 110; Lewis, *Nomads and Settlers*, 139; Avi Shlaim, *Collusion across the Jordan* (Oxford: Oxford University Press, 1988), 52; Joseph Nevo, *King Abdallah and Palestine: A Territorial Ambition* (Basingstoke, UK: Macmillan, 1996), 22; Yoav Gelber, *Jewish-Transjordanian Relations, 1921–1948* (London: Frank Cass, 1997), 37; Fischbach, *State, Society and Land*, 166, 180–81; Philip Robins, *A History of Jordan* (Cambridge: Cambridge University Press, 2004), 50; Tancred Bradshaw, *Britain and Jordan: Imperial Strategy, King Abdullah I and the Zionist Movement* (London: I. B. Tauris, 2012), 63; Khrisat, *Al-Urdunniyyun*, 138; and Zvi Ilan, *Ha-Kmiha le-hityashvut yehudim be-'Ever ha-Yarden, 1871–1947* (Jerusalem: Yad Ben Zvi, 1985), 372.

51. The literature on the relations between the Zionist movement and Transjordan is quite extensive. See, e.g., Shlaim, *Collusion across the Jordan*; Nevo, *King Abdallah and Palestine*; Gelber, *Jewish-Transjordanian Relations*; Bradshaw, *Britain and Jordan*; Yoav Alon, "Friends Indeed or Accomplices in Need? The Jewish Agency, Emir Abdullah and the Shaykhs of Transjordan, 1922–39," in *Israel's Clandestine Diplomacies*, ed. Clive Jones and Tore T. Petersen (London: Hurst, 2013), 31–48.

52. CZA, N. Paper to Kisch, March 16, 1931, S25/3509; Gelber, *Jewish-Transjordanian Relations*, 37.

53. CZA, N. Paper to Kisch, March 16, 1931, and id., "The Problems of Transjordania," March 30, 1931, S25/3509. See also Gelber, *Jewish-Transjordanian Relations*, 37; Wilson, *King Abdullah*, 106–7.

54. Gelber, *Jewish-Transjordanian Relations*, 37.

55. CZA, Joint Bureau's report, August 12, 1931, and Hason to Medzini, October 12, 1931, J105/25; Kalwariski to Arlosoroff, September 29, 1931, S25/4142, cited in Gelber, *Jewish-Transjordanian Relations*, 37–38.

56. Gelber, *Jewish-Transjordanian Relations*, 37.

57 Ibid., 40; *Filastin* (Jaffa), March 17 and 19, 1932; *Davar* (Tel Aviv), October 11, 1932 (reporting from *Filastin*).

58. CZA, Mithqal to Hasidoff, July 28, 1932, and Moshe Shertok, "Conversation with Mithqal Pasha al-Fayiz on August 16, 1932 at the House of Mr. Hasidoff in Jerusalem," August 29, 1932, S25/3491.

59. CZA, Hilmi al-Shalabi al-Samiri to Moshe Shertok, January 16, 1932, J105/10; Gelber, *Jewish-Transjordanian Relations*, 41.

60. Yehuda Edelstein, *Avraham Shapira*, vol. 2 (Tel Aviv: Yedidim, 1939), 502–5.

61. CZA, Aharon Cohen, "Gad's [code name of Taysir al-Dawji, the Jewish Agency's principal agent in Transjordan] Information," May 3, 1932, J105/25.

62. CZA, Aharon Cohen, "Conversation with Mithqal Pasha al-Fayiz on August 16, 1932 at the House of Mr. Hasidoff in Jerusalem," August 29, 1932, S25/3491; "Conversation with T.D. Regarding His Mission in Amman," February 28, 1932, J105/25; "The Visit of Mithqal at the House of Y. Ben Zvi, August 24, 1933," August 30, 1933, S25/3485; and his reports cited nn. 14 and 30 above.

63. For examples of some of the first reports, see *Filastin* (Jaffa), July 26, August 9, and October 14, 1932.

64. *Filastin* (Jaffa), August 9, 1932.

65. CZA, *Al-Karmil* (Haifa), November 9, 1932, from Hebrew trans., "In the Arab Press," November 15, 1932, S25/22005.

66. Surah al-Baqarah 2: 65–66.

67. CZA, Haim Arlosoroff to members of the Jewish Agency Executive, December 6, 1932, S25/3492; Gelber, *Jewish-Transjordanian Relations*, 42–43; Wilson, *King Abdullah*, 107; Sulayman Bashir, *Judhur al-wisaya al-Urduniyya* (Jerusalem: n.p., 1980), 11–18, 22–24. Among the dignitaries who approached the Jewish Agency were several of the Majali and Tarawna shaykhs of Karak, Sultan al-'Adwan, the leader of the Balqa' tribal alliance, shaykh Rashid al-Khuza'i, the leader of Jabal 'Ajlun, Sa'id Abujaber, a large Christian landowner and merchant, shaykh Muhammad abu Taya of the Huwaytat, and Muhammad al-Muhaysan, the governor of 'Ajlun and owner of land in Tafila: CZA, Aharon Cohen, "Report from the Visit at the Emir's palace, December 12, 1934," December 13, 1934, S25/3505; Moshe Shertok, March 16, 1933 [handwritten note], S25/3507; Cohen, "Report from the Visit to Amman, 7–8 March 1933," March 10, 1933, S25/6313.

68. CZA, Emanuel Neuman to the members of the Zionist Executive, February 23, 1933, Z4/4118; Aharon Cohen, "Report from the Visit to Amman, 7–8 March 1933," S25/6313. For a more detailed account of British reactions and policy towards Jewish penetration into Transjordan, see Gelber, *Jewish-Transjordanian Relations*, chap. 3 (esp. 38–42, 47–53) and 67, 70.

69. CZA, Haim Arlosoroff to the members of the Jewish Agency Executive, December 6, 1932, S25/3492.

70. CZA, meeting between Mithqal Pasha al-Fayiz and the president of the Jewish Agency, January 2, 1933, S25/3491.

71. Ibid.

72. Ernest Gellner, *Nations and Nationalism* (Ithaca, NY: Cornell University Press, 1983); Eric Hobsbawm, *Nations and Nationalism since 1870* (Cambridge: Cambridge University Press, 1983); Anthony D. Smith, *The Ethnic Origins of Nations* (Oxford: Blackwell, 1986); Benedict Anderson, *Imagined Communities: Reflections on the Rise and Spread of Nationalism* (1983; 2nd ed., London: Verso, 1991). In the Middle Eastern con-

text, see esp. *Rethinking Nationalism in the Arab Middle East*, ed. Israel Gershoni and James Jankowski (New York: Columbia University Press, 1997). For excellent discussions of the interplay between nationalism and tribalism, as well as the recent developments in Jordan, see Andrew Shryock, *Nationalism and the Genealogical Imagination: Oral History and Textual Authority in Tribal Jordan* (Berkeley: University of California Press, 1997), esp. chap. 8, and Linda L. Layne, *Home and Homeland: The Dialogics of Tribal and National Identities in Jordan* (Princeton, NJ: Princeton University Press, 1994).

73. Alon, *Making of Jordan*, 29, 41, 64.

74. In the comparison between premodern tribal societies and modern national ones, I was inspired by the concepts of *Gemeinschaft* and *Gesellschaft* and imagined communities. See Ferdinand Tönnies, *Gemeinschaft und Gesellschaft: Abhandlung des Communismus und des Socialismus als empirischer Culturformen* (Leipzig: Fues, 1887), trans. and ed. Charles Price Loomis as *Community and Society* (East Lansing: Michigan State University Press, 1957) and Anderson, *Imagined Communities*.

75. Cox to high commissioner, July 6, 1936 (cited n. 41 above).

76. *Al-Ahram* (Cairo), March 16, 1932, and January 18, 1933; *Filastin* (Jaffa), January 20, 1933; Gelber, *Jewish-Transjordanian Relations*, 45. On the Ghawr al-Kibd deal, see Anita Shapira, "The Option on Ghaur al-Kibd: Contacts between Emir Abdallah and the Zionist Executive, 1932–1935," *Studies in Zionism* 1, no. 2 (1980): 239–83; Wilson, *King Abdullah*, 107–10; Shlaim, *Collusion across the Jordan*, 50–54; Gelber, *Jewish-Transjordanian Relations*, 43–47.

77. CZA, Aharon Cohen, "Information from Mithqal Pasha on Ghawr al-Kibd," January 25–26, 1933, S25/4143; id., "Report on My Visit to Emir Abdullah," January 12, 1934, S25/3487.

78. CZA, S[hertok], meeting with Mithqal al-Fayiz, December 21–23, 1932, S25/3491.

79. CZA, S[hertok], meetings with Mithqal al-Fayiz, January 12 and 23, 1933, S25/3491.

80. CZA, original mortgage certificate, April 13, 1933, S25/3491; Aharon Cohen, "From the Activities of the Arab Bureau," January 18, 1937, S25/3642; id., "Report on the Visit to Amman, January 16, 1933," S25/6313.

81. *Filastin* (Jaffa), February 5, 1932.

82. CZA, Aharon Cohen, reports on visits to Amman, January 20 and February 15, 1933, S25/6313; Mithqal to Arlozoroff, February 3, 1933, S25/3491.

83. CZA, Aharon Cohen, reports on visits to Amman, January 20 and February 15, 1933, S25/6313; *Filastin* (Jaffa), January 18, 1933.

84. The present author heard an echo of the case in 1998, while conducting an interview with Muslih Sa'd al-Halahla, a 96-year-old member of the 'Ajarma tribe (Umm al-Basatin, Jordan, July 1998). See also *Filastin*'s report on Abdullah's visit to Jerusalem escorted by Mithqal, January 18, 1933; UKNA, Cox, situation report, January 1933, CO831/23/11.

85. *Palestine Post* (Jerusalem), April 2, 1933; CZA, Aharon Cohen, "Report from the Visit to Amman," March 10, 1933, S25/6313; Cohen, "From the Activities of the Arab Bureau," January 18, 1937, S25/3642; id., report cited n. 30 above.

86. UKNA, Resident Henry Cox, report on the administration of Trans-Jordan for the quarter ending September 30, 1933, FO684/6. The Political Department kept a copy of the party's constitution, which stated general goals such as loyalty to Abdullah, defending the political, economic, and social rights of the country's people, and promoting solidarity among its inhabitants: CZA, "Al-Nizham al-asasi li-Hizb al-Tadammun al-Urdunni," March 24, 1933, S25/3491.

87. *Filastin* (Jaffa), May 26, 1933. See also UKNA, Kirkbride, situation report, July 1933, CO831/23/1.

88. CZA, Aharon Cohen, "Gad's Information, May 3, 1933," May 4, 1933, S25/4143; UKNA, chief secretary to Parkinson, May 5, 1933, CO831/22/10.

89. CZA, Aharon Cohen, "Echo from the Party with the Leaders of Transjordan," April 16, 1933, S25/3510. The other delegates were Shaykh Rashid al-Khuza'i from 'Ajlun, Shaykh Salim abu al-Ghanim, the leader of the Ghunaymat tribes, Shams al-Din al-Shami, a Circassian leader and a former member of the Legislative Council, and Mitri Zurayqat, Christian tribal leader from Karak and a member of the council.

90. Khrisat, *Al-Urdunniyyun*, 136–37; *Filastin* (Jaffa), April 13 and May 26, 1933.

91. Cohen cited n. 89 above.

92. CZA, Mithqal to Mrs. Arlosoroff, June 21, 1933, S25/3491; Sa'id al-Mufti, "Sa'id al-Mufti yatadhakkaru," *Al-Dustur* (Amman), May 8, 1976; and see also, e.g., *Filastin* (Jaffa), May 28 and 31, June 3, 8, and 21, 1933.

93. *Filastin* (Jaffa), June 30 and July 1, 1933. In a conversation with one Zionist official, Mithqal claimed that although the Agency had helped him financially to organize the conference, he was left £60 in the red: CZA, Aharon Cohen, "The Visit of Mithqal at the House of Y. Ben Zvi, August 24, 1933," August 30, 1933, S25/3485.

94. CZA, Aharon Cohen, "Report from the Visit at the Emir's Palace, December 12, 1934," December 13, 1934, S25/3505; "Nida' ila al-'alam al-'arabi . . . " July 1933, S25/3515 ; *Filastin* (Jaffa), July 1, 1933; *Al-Ahram* (Cairo), July 1, 1933; Khrisat, *Al-Urdunniyyun*, 139.

95. *Filastin* (Jaffa), June 29, 1933.

96. Khrisat, *Al-Urdunniyyun*, 129; On the rivalry between the two shaykhs, see Gelber, *Jewish-Transjordanian Relations*, 138; CZA, Aharon Cohen, "A Conversation with M.U., August 2, 1938," S25/22189.

97. *Filastin* (Jaffa), August 12, 1933.

98. Khrisat, *Al-Urdunniyyun*, 129. For a typical, extremely gingerly treatment in English of the affair by a Jordanian historian, see Ma'an Abu-Nowar, *The Development of Trans-Jordan, 1929–1939* (Reading, UK: Ithaca Press, 2006), 156–61. For a different treatment, see Tell, *Social and Economic Origins*, 96–97.

99. Cohen, report cited n. 30 above.

100. UKNA, "Extracts from the Report on the Political Situation for the Month of October 1933," CO831/22/10; CZA, Aharon Cohen, "The Visit of Mithqal at the House of Y. Ben Zvi, August 24, 1933," August 30, 1933, S25/3485; id., report cited n. 30 above.

101. Gelber, *Jewish-Transjordanian Relations*, 51.

102. CZA, Moshe Shertok, "Note on Visit to Amman," April 24, 1934, S25/3515; Cohen, conversation cited n. 37 above.

103. *Davar* (Tel Aviv), April 12, May 11, and August 7, 1934; *Palestine Post* (Jerusalem), April 11, 1934.

104. Interview with Aharon Cohen's daughter, Arlozora Bloch, Herzliya, Israel, May 26, 2012, and Skype conversation with his youngest son, Doron Cohen, October 2012. I am grateful to Doron Cohen for his help.

105. I am grateful to Andrew Shryock for suggesting this fascinating interpretation.

106. For another example of Mithqal's charming his Zionist acquaintances, see the account of Rachel Yanait Ben Zvi in her *Darki siparti* (Jerusalem: Kiryat Sefer, 1971), 107.

107. Cohen, report cited n. 30 above.

108. Ibid.; CZA, Hasidoff to Shertok, October 27, 1937, S25/3513.

109. CZA, Yitzhak Cohen to Mithqal al-Fayiz, December 12, 1935, S25/3491.

110. UKNA, colonial secretary to high commissioner, November 29, 1934, CO831/27/2; Cox to high commissioner, July 6, 1936 (cited n. 41 above); Glubb's report, June 1936, CO831/37/3.

111. CZA, Aharon Cohen "From the Activities of the Arab Bureau," January 18, 1937, S25/3642.

112. Moshe Sharett, *Yoman medini, 1936* (Tel Aviv: 'Am 'Oved and Zionist Library, 1976), 52; HA, entry for February 11, 1936, in the Political Department diary, Ben Zvi files, no. 8, cited in Gelber, *Jewish-Transjordanian Relations*, 74.

113. *Al-Majlis al-Tashri'i*, February 20, 1936. See also February 23 and March 26, 1936.

114. Ibid., February 26, 1936 (the Legislative Council meeting was held on January 13, 1936).

115. The literature on the revolt is extensive. For a useful summary, see a good account in Baruch Kimmerling and Joel S. Migdal, *Palestinians: The Making of a People* (Cambridge, MA: Harvard University Press, 1993).

116. UKNA, Glubb's report, June 1936, CO831/37/3.

117. CZA, Aharon Cohen to Shertok and Ben Zvi, May 18, 1936, S25/3539.

118. CZA, Eliyahu Sasson, "Information of the Arab Bureau," May 11 and June 14, 1936, S25/3240.

119. CZA, Aharon Cohen's report on his meeting with Unsi, July 9, 1936, S25/22233.

120. UKNA, Glubb's reports, May and June 1936, and Cox to high commissioner, July 6, 1936 (cited n. 41 above).

121. UKNA, Glubb's report, July 1936, CO831/37/3.

122. *Al-Difa'* (Jaffa), July 10, 1936, reproduced in Khrisat, *Al-Urdunniyyun*, 318.

123. CZA, Eliyahu Sasson, "Conversation with Mithqal Pasha al-Fayiz, the head of the Bani Sakhr tribe, October 27, 1936," October 28, 1936, S25/3491; Khrisat, *Al-Urdunniyyun*, 187.

124. Gelber, *Jewish-Transjordanian Relations*, 99; Akram Zu'aytar, *Yawmiyyat Akram Zu'aytar: Al-Haraka al-wataniyya al-Filastiniyya, 1935–1939* (Beirut: Mu'assasat al-Dirasat al-Filastiniyya, 1980), 226.

125. UKNA, Glubb's reports, March and June 1937, CO831/41/11.

126. MEC, Glubb's report, March 1940, Glubb Papers.

127. UKNA, Wauchope to Ormsby-Gore, August 31, 1936, CO831/39/14; CZA,

Sasson, "Information of the Arab Bureau," August 25, 1936, S25/3240; Aharon Cohen's report on his meeting with Unsi, July 9, 1936, S25/22233.

128. Sasson, conversation cited n. 123 above; HA, Aharon Cohen's report on his meeting with Mithqal Pasha, October 27, 1936, Ben-Zvi's files, no. 18, cited in Gelber, *Jewish-Transjordanian Relations*, 105; CZA, Cohen, "From the Activities of the Arab Bureau," January 18, 1937, S25/3642; id., "Conversation at the House of Dr. B. Joseph, April 15, 1937," April 21, 1937, S25/3485.

129. I am grateful to Andrew Shryock for making this important point.

130. UKNA, Glubb's report, August 1937, CO831/41/11.

131. Testimony of Sa'ud al-Dhiyab al-Fayiz in al-Bakhit and al-'Armuti, *Sirat hayat al-shaykh*, 287–88; testimony of 'Issam al-Sharbaji in ibid., 377; Sultan al-Hattab, "Sami Mithqal al-Fayiz—wida'an," *Al-Ra'y* (Amman), December 1, 2012, www.alrai.com/article /554204.html (accessed November 20, 2015); Sasson, conversation cited n. 123 above; CZA, [Yitzhak Avira], "At the House of Mithqal Fayiz Pasha," June 15, 1941, S25/3504.

132. CZA, Aharon Cohen, "Visit in the House of M.U. in Shuna, 8 December 1937," December 10, 1937, S25/3491; 'Abd al-Hamid Shuman, *Al-'Issami: Sirat 'Abd al-Hamid Shuman* (no further details), reproduced in al-Bakhit and al-'Armuti, *Sirat hayat al-shaykh*, 396–99; testimony of Muslim Khalaf al-Qtifan cited in ibid., 339, 343.

133. UKNA, report by Lash (Glubb's aide) for the month of May 1937, CO831/41/11.

134. CZA, Cohen, "Visit in the house of M.U. in Shuna, December 8, 1937," December 10, 1937, S25/3491; id., "A Letter from Transjordan, December 9, 1937" and "A Letter from Transjordan, December 15, 1937," S25/3539.

135. UKNA, Cox, "Report on the Political Situation for the Month of December 1937," January 3, 1938, CO831/41/8.

136. CZA, Cohen, letters cited n. 134 above; UKNA, Cox, "Report on the Political Situation for the Month of December 1937," January 3, 1938, CO831/41/8.

137. CZA, "Political Information about the Arabs, January 1, 1939," S25/3541 (courtesy of Harel Chorev).

138. Gelber, *Jewish-Transjordanian Relations*, 138; Cohen, conversation cited n. 96 above.

139. CZA, Avira to Gershon, March 4, 1941, S25/3504.

CHAPTER 6: DISGRUNTLED ACCOMMODATION

1. Yoav Alon, *The Making of Jordan: Tribes, Colonialism and the Modern State* (London: I. B. Tauris, 2007), 131; Tariq Moraiwed Tell, *The Social and Economic Origins of Monarchy in Jordan* (New York: Palgrave Macmillan, 2013), 98–99; Ma'an Abu-Nowar, *The Development of Trans-Jordan, 1929–1939* (Reading, UK: Ithaca Press, 2006), 296.

2. UKNA, situation report for the month of February 1940, CO831/55/8; CZA, Avira to Gershon, March 4, 1941, S25/3504.

3. Abu-Nowar, *Development of Trans-Jordan*, 295–96; MEC, Glubb Papers, John Glubb, "A Monthly Report on Events in the Deserts of Transjordan" (hereafter cited as "Glubb's report"), April 1940, and Dr. S. A. Jones, "Nutrition of the Trans-Jordan Bedouin," appendix to Glubb's report, March 1940; CZA, Avira to Gershon, March 4, 1941, S25/3504.

4. Bashar Muhammad Abu Nusayr al-Masarwa, *'Asha'ir Masarwa al-Jiza min 1864–1958* (Madaba, Jordan: n.p., 2000), 41, 44, 85; 'Abd al-Ra'uf al-Rawabda, *Mu'jam al-'asha'ir al-Urdunniyya* (Amman: Matabi' al-Mu'assasa al-Suhufiyya al-Urdunniyya, 2010), 49–50.

5. Testimonies of Tayil Mithqal al-Fayiz and Sami Mithqal al-Fayiz cited in 'Awad Sayyah al-Mubarak al-Bakhit and 'Umar Muhammad Nazal al-'Armuti, *Sirat hayat al-shaykh Mithqal Sattam al-Fayiz shaykh mashayikh Bani Sakhr* (Amman: Matba'at al-Safir, [2012]), 309, 318; CZA, Avira to Gershon, March 4, 1941, S25/3504.

6. IWM, F. G. Peake Papers, Peake to Cox, August 12, 1938.

7. MEC, Sir Herbert Stewart, "Agricultural Conditions and Possibilities in Transjordan and Arab Palestine," June 20, 1949, Middle East Development Division, box 1 . Although anachronistic, this description serves to illustrate Mithqal's farm in the late 1930s.

8. IWM, F. G. Peake Papers, Peake to Cox, August 12, 1938; MEC, Glubb's report, March 1940.

9. CZA, unsigned report titled "My Journey to Amman," December 25, 1940, S25/8005 ; [Yitzhak Avira], "At the house of Mithqal Fayiz Pasha," June 15, 1941, S25/3504. On the relations between Abdullah and Talal, see Mary C. Wilson, *King Abdullah, Britain and the Making of Jordan* (Cambridge: Cambridge University Press, 1987), 92–93.

10. Glubb's report, March 1940.

11. IWM, F. G. Peake Papers, F. C. Ogdan to Moody, July 28, 1938, and Peake to Cox, August 12, 1938; HA, CID Files, intelligence summary no. 56/39, August 18, 1939, 47/91 (courtesy of Yoni Furas).

12. Max Adrian Simon Oppenheim, *Die Beduinen*, vol. 2 (Leipzig: O. Harrassowitz, 1943), 234; *Al-Urdunn* (Amman), June 1, 1939; testimony of Muslim Khalaf al-Qtifan in al-Bakhit and al-'Armuti, *Sirat hayat al-shaykh*, 342; *Palestine Post* (Jerusalem), March 24, 1940; *Al-Urdunn* (Amman), November 3, 1940.

13. CZA, Arye Kimchi to Moshe Shertok, June 17, 1938, and notes exchanged between Shertok and Aharon Cohen, June 19–20, 1938, S25/3491, cited in Yoav Gelber, *Jewish-Transjordanian Relations, 1921–1948* (London: Frank Cass, 1997), 145; Cohen to Kimchi, June 21, 1938, S25/3491, cited in Sulayman Bashir, *Judhur al-wisaya al-Urduniyya* (Jerusalem: n.p., 1980), 53–54; interview with Arlozora Bloch (Cohen's daughter), Herzliya, Israel, May 26, 2012.

14. Glubb's reports, November 1938 and March 1940.

15. Glubb's report, March 1940.

16. UKNA, Sir Harold MacMichael to Viscount Cranborne, June 8, 1942, CO831/59/5; political report, July 1942, CO831/58/3.

17. UKNA, political report, November 1939, CO831/51/8.

18. UKNA, Kirkbride, "Report on the political situation for the month of April 1940," CO831/55/8.

19. Ibid.

20. HA, Sahari, September 20, 1940, 105/378 (courtesy of Roy Marom).

21. UKNA, Kirkbride, "Report on the political situation for the month of November 1940," CO831/55/8.

22. CZA, Muhammad Mustafa al-Shibli's answers to Sasson's questionnaire,

December 16, 1940, S25/3505; testimony of Fahd Maqbul al-Ghabin cited in al-Bakhit and al-'Armuti, *Sirat hayat al-shaykh*, 368.

23. *Al-Urdunn* (Amman), December 18, and September 29, 1940.

24. Ibid., September 22 and 29, 1940.

25. CZA, Avira to Gershon, March 4, 1941, S25/3504.

26. Ibid.

27. The following account is based on CZA, Avira to Gershon, March 4, 1941, [Avira], "At the house of Mithqal Fayiz Pasha," June 15, 1941, and Cna'ani [Avira's code name] "At the House of Mithqal Fayiz," July 9, 1941, S25/3504.

28. This gendered architectural feature is still commonplace in Jordan and other parts of the Arab world, especially among societies that underwent processes of sedentarization. For an illuminating analysis of the correlation between tribal culture and modern architecture in Jordan, see Linda L. Layne, *Home and Homeland: The Dialogics of Tribal and National Identities in Jordan* (Princeton, NJ: Princeton University Press, 1994), chap. 3; Abu-Lughod points out the effects that the move from tent to stone house had on the growing segregation of the women in formerly nomadic societies: Lila Abu-Lughod, *Veiled Sentiments: Honor and Poetry in a Bedouin Society* (Berkeley: California University Press, 1988), 72–74.

29. It is not clear if the mother of these two sons was Tarfa, mentioned in chap. 4, or a different wife.

30. Riccardo Bocco and Tariq M. M. Tell, "*Pax Britannica* in the Steppe: British Policy and the Transjordan Bedouin," in *Village, Steppe and State: The Social Origins of Modern Jordan*, ed. Eugene L. Rogan and Tariq M. M. Tell (London: British Academic Press, 1994), 125–26.

31. CZA, Cna'ani [Avira's code name], "At the House of Mithqal Fayiz," July 9, 1941, S25/3504.

32. Ibid., June 15, 1941.

33. Ibid., July 9, 1941.

34. UKNA, telegram to Sir Miles Lampson, June 9, 1941 enclosed with MacMichael to Lord Moyne, June 18, 1941, and high commissioner to HM ambassador in Cairo, June 14, 1941, CO831/59/11. On the Ruwala in Syria, see Philip S. Khoury, "The Tribal Shaykh, French Tribal Policy, and the Nationalist Movement in Syria between Two World Wars," *Middle Eastern Studies* 18 (April 1982), 180–93.

35. CZA, Sasson to Shertok, "Two Conversations with Mithqal al-Fayiz," August 13, 1941, S25/3504; [Avira], "At the House of Mithqal Fayiz Pasha," June 15, 1941, S25/3504. And see also Gelber, *Jewish-Transjordanian Relations*, 169.

36. CZA, Sasson to Shertok, "A Meeting with the Emir Mujahim al-Sha'lan," September 4, 1941, S25/3140/I.

37. UKNA, Kirkbride, "Report on the Political Situation for the Month of September 1941," CO831/58/2; Kirkbride to MacMichael, September 9, 1941, CO831/58/2; CZA, Avira, "The Affair of Negotiations to Purchase a Tractor in Transjordan," October 4, 1941, S25/3504; Mithqal's version is corroborated by a Zionist observer: CZA, Dov, "At Mithqal's House," October 9, 1941, S25/8005.

38. UKNA, Kirkbride to MacMichael, September 9, 1941, CO831/58/2.

39. Ibid.; CZA, Avira, "The Affair of Negotiations to Purchase a Tractor in Transjordan," October 4, 1941, S25/3504; Dov, "At Mithqal's House," October 9, 1941, S25/8005.

40. CZA, Dov, "At Mithqal's House," October 9, 1941, S25/8005.

41. UKNA, high commissioner to secretary of state, July 9, 1942, CO831/59/16; Kirkbride, "Report on the Political Situation for the Month of June 1942," CO831/58/3; *Al-Urdunn* (Amman), April 11, 1943.

42. UKNA, Kirkbride, "Report[s] on the Political Situation for the Months of June and July 1943," CO831/60/2.

43. UKNA, MacMichael to Viscount Cranborne, June 8, 1942, CO831/59/5.

44. UKNA, Kirkbride, "Report[s] on the Political Situation for the Months of June and July 1943," CO831/60/2.

45. Interview with Salih Kni'an al-Fayiz, Manja, Jordan, July 31, 1998; CZA, Yirmiyahu to Yehoshu'a, July 27, 1943, S25/22670.

46. CZA, Yehoshu'a Hankin to Jewish National Fund, February 11, 1944, and Yosef Weitz to Hankin, February 17, 1944, KKL5/13672; Yosef Weitz, "Ha-Masa wu-matan 'im sheykh ha-sheykhim be-'Ever ha-Yarden," *Ma'ariv* (Tel Aviv), October 18, 1967; testimony of Mut'ab Dirdah al-Bakhit cited in al-Bakhit and al-'Armuti, *Sirat hayat al-shaykh*, 298.

47. UKNA, Kirkbride to Bevin, "Personalities in Transjordan," August 6, 1946, FO371/52945.

48. Michael Fischbach, *State, Society and Land in Jordan* (Leiden: Brill, 2000), 87–88, 97.

49. Jordanian National Library, Prime Ministry Files, Glubb to prime minister of Transjordan, May 17, 1939, file *Shakawi al-'asha'ir*.

50. The text is reproduced in Ahmad 'Uwaydi al-'Abbadi, *Al-Jara'im al-sughra 'ind al-'asha'ir al-Urdunniyya* (Amman: Dar al-Fikr, 1987), 369–72.

51. Ibid., 370.

52. Aqwal al-Shaykh Mithqal al-Fayiz, August 15, 1953, reproduced in Ahmad 'Uwaydi al-'Abbadi, *Muqaddima li-dirasat al- 'asha'ir al-Urdunniyya* (2nd ed., Amman: Al-Dar al-'Arabiyya lil-Nashr, 1985), 292–93.

53. Testimony of Fahd Maqbul al-Ghabin cited in al-Bakhit and al-'Armuti, *Sirat hayat al-shaykh*, 360–63; interview with 'Akif al-Fayiz, *Al-Dustur* (Amman), June 6, 1994; Jum'a Hammad, "Mithqal al-Fayiz!" ibid., April 16, 1967; *Al-Urdunn* (Amman), September 7, 1957.

54. Testimony of 'Awad Sayyah al-Mubarak al-Bakhit cited in al-Bakhit and al-'Armuti, *Sirat hayat al-shaykh*, 71–74.

55. Ibrahim Abu-Lughod, *Resistance, Exile and Return* (Birzeit, Palestine: Birzeit University, 2003), 50–51. Avira met the uncle when he accompanied Mithqal in Jaffa and reported his earlier services to Mithqal and their great friendship: CZA, Avira to Gershon, March 4, 1941 S25/3504.

56. CZA, "Information from Transjordan," June 5, 1947, S25/9037; UKNA, monthly situation reports for Transjordan for the months of September and October 1947, FO371/62206.

57. USNA, RG 59, Talcott W. Seelye, "Syrian Support of Nation Party," July 6, 1954, 785.00/7–654; *Filastin* (Jerusalem), October 3, 1954.

58. CZA, Hankin to Jewish National Fund, August 6, 1943, KKL5/13535; Hankin to id., February 11, 1944, and Weitz to Hankin, February 17, 1944, KKL5/13672. Yosef Weitz, "Ha-Masa wu-matan 'im sheykh ha-sheykhim be-'Ever ha-Yarden," *Ma'ariv* (Tel Aviv), October 18, 1967. On the transfer idea, see Benny Morris, "Revisiting the Palestinian Exodus of 1948," in *The War for Palestine: Rewriting the History of 1948*, ed. Eugene L. Rogan and Avi Shlaim (Cambridge: Cambridge University Press, 2001), 39–48.

59. CZA, translation from *Filastin* (Jaffa), September 5, 1944, S25/22113; UKNA, monthly situation report for Transjordan for the month of February 1947, FO371/62206.

60. *Al-Jarida al-Rasmiyya*, August 1, 1946; *Al-Urdunn* (Amman), March 8 and 20, 1949.

61. Testimony of Darwish Dilan al-Bakhit cited in al-Bakhit and al-'Armuti, *Sirat hayat al-shaykh*, 332.

62. Interview with 'Akif al-Fayiz, *Al-Dustur* (Amman), June 6, 1994; Sulayman Musa, *Ayam la tunsa: Al-Urdunn fi harb 1948* (2nd ed., Amman: Matabi' al-Quwwat al-Musallaha, 1998), 50–51; Bassam 'Id Qaqish, *Al-Mu'assasa al-'askariyya al-Urdunniyya wa-tatawwuruha, 1946–1967* (Amman: Matba'at al-Quwwat al-Musallaha al-Urdunniyya, 1998), 148; Ronen Yitzhak, *Shutafut ve-'oynut: 'Abdallah, ha-Ligyon ha-'Arvi ve-milhemet 1948* (Jerusalem: Misrad ha-Bitahon, 2006), 22.

63. CZA, "Information from Transjordan," July 4, [1947], S25/9038.

64. *Al-Urdunn* (Amman), April 15, 1949; Alon, *Making of Jordan*, 120.

65. *Al-Jarida al-Rasmiyya*, September 1, 1946.

66. Evidence of the intimacy in their relations can be found in the testimony of 'Issam al-Sharbaji in al-Bakhit and al-'Armuti, *Sirat hayat al-shaykh*, 379.

67. Interview with 'Akif al-Fayiz, *Al-Dustur* (Amman), June 6, 1994.

68. Ibid.

69. *Al-Urdunn* (Amman), September 21, 1943.

70. Yosef Weitz, "Ha-Masa wu-matan 'im sheykh ha-sheykhim be-'Ever ha-Yarden," *Ma'ariv* (Tel Aviv), October 18, 1967.

71. UKNA, political report, July 1942, CO831/58/3.

72. Interview with 'Akif al-Fayiz, *Al-Dustur* (Amman), June 6, 1994.

73. Ibid.; *Al-Urdunn* (Amman), December 6, 1950, January 30, August 3, and November 20, 1951; *Filastin* (Jerusalem), October 2 and 3, 1954; Uriel Dann, *King Hussein and the Challenge of Arab Radicalism: Jordan, 1955–1967* (Oxford: Oxford University Press, 1989), 38; Philip Robins, *A History of Jordan* (Cambridge: Cambridge University Press, 2004), 95.

74. Dann, *King Hussein*, 21–67; Betty S. Anderson, *Nationalist Voices in Jordan: The Street and the State* (Austin: University of Texas Press, 2005), chaps. 7 and 8; Robert B. Satloff, *From Abdullah to Hussein: Jordan in Transition* (New York: Oxford University Press, 1994), chaps. 7, 8, and 9; Robins, *History of Jordan*, 91–102; Avi Shlaim, *Lion of Jordan: The Life of King Hussein in War and Peace* (London: Allen Lane, 2007), chaps. 4, 5, 6, and 7; Nigel Ashton, *King Hussein of Jordan: A Poitical Life* (New Haven, CT: Yale University Press, 2008), chaps. 2, 3, and 4.

75. Dann, *King Hussein*, 64; Lawrence Tal, *Politics, the Military and National Secu-*

rity in Jordan, 1955–1967 (Basingstoke, UK: Palgrave Macmillan, 2002), 48; *Filastin* (Jerusalem), July 28 and August 4, 1957; MEC, Slade-Baker Papers, John Slade-Baker, diary entry for April 23, 1957.

76. Dann, *King Hussein*, 64; Satloff, *From Abdullah to Hussein*, 171; Khalid Musa al-Zu'bi, *'Akif al-Fayiz: Sirat hayah siyasiyya wa-barlamaniyya* (Amman: Markaz al-Dirasat al-Barlamaniyya, 2007).

77. See, e.g., *Filastin* (Jerusalem), October 6, 1964, January 1, August 28, and December 3, 1965. U.S. and British reports likewise stopped associating 'Akif with Mithqal, the sole exception being "Pre-election Atmosphere in Jordan," April 3, 1967, USNA, Central Foreign Policy Files, 1967–1969, RG 59, box 2523, Pol 14 Jordan.

78. *Filastin* (Jerusalem), November 14, 1957.

79. USNA, RG 59, Robert Keeley, "Causes of Disaffection with Rifa'i Regime," September 3, 1958, 785 00/9–358; Tal, *Politics, the Military and National Security*, 69, 76, 83, 93.

80. Testimony of Wajid Sulayman al-Jam'ani cited in al-Bakhit and al-'Armuti, *Sirat hayat al-shaykh*, 273.

81. Anselm Heyer, *Untergang des Morgenlandes* (Berlin: Ullstein, 1966), 48–49.

82. See USNA, RG59, Robert Keeley, "Causes of Disaffection with Rifa'i Regime," September 3, 1958, 785 00/9–358.

83. Jordanian National Library, Mithqal bin Fayiz to (Jordanian) prime minister, November 7, 1963, 225/12/2/27, http://opac.nl.gov.jo/adlibweb/detail.aspx?parentpriref =901139218# (accessed November 21, 2015).

84. Ya'akov Yaniv, *Hatzo'nim bi-Yhuda uvi-Yrushalayim* (Jerusalem: Ariel, 1980), 26.

85. Interview with Faysal al-Fayiz and Tayil Mithqal al-Fayiz at the family farm in al-Mashatta, Jordan, August 5, 2008; testimony of Wajid Sulayman al-Jam'ani cited in al-Bakhit and al-'Armuti, *Sirat hayat al-shaykh*, 276.

86. *Filastin* (Jerusalem), October 6, 1964, January 1, August 28, and December 3, 1965; UKNA, P. C. H. Holmer minutes, April 22, 1958, FO371/134091.

87. *Al-Dustur* (Amman), April 16, 1967.

88. USNA, Central Foreign Policy Files, 1967–1969, RG 59, Burns to State Department, Joint Weeka, April 12–18, April 19, 1967, Pol 2–1 Jordan, box 2252.

89. Eliyahu Eilat, "Met sheykh ha-sheykhim be-'Ever ha-Yarden," *Ma'ariv* (Tel Aviv), September 8, 1967.

90. Asher Susser, *Both Banks of the Jordan: A Political Biography of Wasfi al-Tall* (Ilford, UK: Frank Cass, 1994), 117; UKNA, A. B. Urwick to A. C. Goodison, October 12, 1966, FO371/186549; J. P. Tripp, "Jordan General Elections," April 5, 1967, FCO17/210; USNA, Central Foreign Policy Files, 1967–1969, RG 59, "Jordan Elections," April 19, 1967, Pol 14 Jordan, box 2253.

EPILOGUE: JORDAN AFTER MITHQAL

1. Testimonies of Tayil Mithqal al-Fayiz and Sami Mithqal al-Fayiz cited in 'Awad Sayyah al-Mubarak al-Bakhit and 'Umar Muhammad Nazal al-'Armuti, *Sirat hayat al-shaykh Mithqal Sattam al-Fayiz shaykh mashayikh Bani Sakhr* (Amman: Matba'at al-Safir, [2012]), 309, 318.

2. Norman Lewis, *Nomads and Settlers in Syria and Jordan, 1800–1980* (Cambridge: Cambridge University Press, 1987), 147.

3. Khalid Musa al-Zuʻbi, *ʻAkif al-Fayiz: Sirat hayah siyasiyya wa-barlamaniyya* (Amman: Markaz al-Dirasat al-Barlamaniyya, 2007); interview with ʻAkif al-Fayiz, *Al-Dustur* (Amman), June 7, 1994.

4. Linda L. Layne, *Home and Homeland: The Dialogics of Tribal and National Identities in Jordan* (Princeton, NJ: Princeton University Press, 1994); Andrew Shryock, *Nationalism and the Genealogical Imagination: Oral History and Textual Authority in Tribal Jordan* (Berkeley: University of California Press, 1997).

5. Layne, *Home and Homeland*; Shryock, *Nationalism and the Genealogical Imagination*. See also Ahmad ʻUwaydi Al-ʻAbbadi, *ʻAshaʼir al-Urdunn: Jawlat maydaniyya wa-tahlilat* (Amman: Al-Ahliyya lil-Nashr wal-Tawziʻ, 2005).

6. Shryock, *Nationalism and the Genealogical Imagination*, 70; Richard T. Antoun, "Civil Society, Tribal Process, and Change in Jordan: An Anthropological View," *International Journal of Middle East Studies* 32, no. 4 (November 2000): 441–63; Jessica Watkins, "Seeking Justice: Tribal Dispute Resolution and Societal Transformation in Jordan," ibid., 46, no. 1 (February 2014): 31–49. For recent examples, see "Government Seeks Religious Leaders' Support as It Drafts Tribal Law," *Jordan Times* (Amman), August 10, 2015, http://www.jordantimes.com/news/local/gov%E2%80%99t-seeks-religious-leaders%E2%80%99-support-it-drafts-tribal-law, and "Salt Tribal Leaders Agree Limitations on 'Jalwa,'" ibid., October 13, 2015, http://www.jordantimes.com/news/local/salt-tribal-leaders-agree-limitations-jalwa%E2%80%99 (both accessed November 20, 2015).

7. Layne, *Home and Homeland*.

8. On Mithqal's arrest of Peake, see, e.g., Abd al-Hadi Raji Al-Majali, "Lawih bi-idak, lawih bi-idak," *Al-Raʼy* (Amman), October 21, 2012.

9. Al-Bakhit and al-ʻArmuti, *Sirat hayat al-shaykh*.

10. Various Jordanian newspapers, April 1998.

11. Interview with Sami Mithqal al-Fayiz, Zizya, Jordan, July 11, 2009.

12. Yoav Alon, "From Abdullah (I) to Abdullah (II): The Monarchy, the Tribes and the Shaykhly Families in Jordan, 1920–2012," in *Tribes and States in a Changing Middle East*, ed. Uzi Rabi (London: Hurst, forthcoming).

BIBLIOGRAPHY

ARCHIVES AND PRIVATE PAPERS

Jordan
The National Library, Amman
　Prime Ministry Files
　Al-Sharq al-'Arabi [The Arab East], 1923–28, renamed *Al-Jarida al-Rasmiyya li-Hukumat Sharq al-Urdunn* [The Official Gazette], 1929–46
The Library, Jordanian Parliament, Amman
　Mudhakkirat al-Majlis al-Tashri'i [Minutes of the Legislative Council], 1930–46

Israel
Israel State Archives (ISA), Jerusalem
　RG-2 (Chief Secretary)
　65 (Collections of abandoned Arab documents)
　160 (Yitzhak Ben Zvi collection)
Central Zionist Archives (CZA), Jerusalem
　A264 (Felix Frankfurter Papers)
　J105 (Joint Bureau Files)
　KKL5 (Jewish National Fund)
　S25 (Jewish Agency's Political Department)
　Z4 (Zionist Organization, Central Office, London)
Hagana Archives (HA), Tel Aviv
　CID Files
　Levi Schneurson Papers

United Kingdom
National Archives, London (UKNA; formerly the Public Records Office)
　CO733 (Colonial Office, Palestine)
　CO831 (Colonial Office, Transjordan)
　FCO17 (Foreign Office, Eastern Department and successors)
　FO141 (Foreign Office and Foreign and Commonwealth Office: Embassy and Consulates, Egypt: General Correspondence)
　FO371 (Foreign Office: Political Departments: General Correspondence from 1906 to 1966)
　FO684 (Foreign Office, Damascus Consulate)

Middle East Centre (MEC), St Antony's College, Oxford, Private Papers Collection
  'Arif al-'Arif
  C. D. Brunton
  John Glubb
  Middle East Development Division
  R. F. P. Monckton
  Harry St John Philby
  J. B. Slade-Baker
  Fitzroy Richard Somerset
Church Missionary Society (CMS) Archives, Birmingham
  Rev Frederick Klein
Imperial War Museum, London
  F. G. Peake Papers
Rhodes House Library, Oxford
  J. Chancellor Papers
Sudan Archive, Durham University, Durham
  Reginald Wingate Papers

United States
National Archives, College Park, Maryland (USNA)
  RG 59 (General Records of the Department of State)

Germany
Hausarchiv des Bankhauses Sal. Oppenheim jr. & Cie., Köln [Cologne]
  Nachlass Max von Oppenheim

NEWSPAPERS

Al-Ahram (Cairo)
Daily Star (Beirut)
Davar (Tel Aviv)
Al-Dustur (Amman)
Filastin (Jaffa and from 1948 Jerusalem)
Jordan Times (Amman)
Al-Karmil (Haifa)
Ma'ariv (Tel Aviv)
New York Review of Books
Palestine Post (Jerusalem)
Al-Qabas (Damascus)
Al-Ra'y (Amman)
Time Magazine (New York)
Al-Urdunn (Amman)

INTERVIEWS

'Akif al-Fayiz, Amman, March 1998
Salih Kni'an al-Fayiz, Manja, Jordan, July 1998
Muslih Sa'd al-Halahla, Umm al-Basatin, Jordan, July 1998
Tayil Mithqal al-Fayiz, al-Mashatta, Jordan, August 2008
Faysal al-Fayiz, al-Mashatta, August 2008
Talal Mithqal al-Fayiz, al-Mashatta, August 2008
Sami Mithqal al-Fayiz, Zizya, Jordan, October 2008 and July 2009
Arlozora Bloch, Herzliya, Israel, May 2012
Doron Cohen, via Skype, October 2012

WEB SITES

Al-Monitor: http://www.al-monitor.com
Al-Jazeera (English): http://www.aljazeera.com
Hoqook: https://hoqook.wordpress.com/
Open Democracy: https://www.opendemocracy.net
Reuters: http://www.reuters.com
Today's Zaman: http://www.todayszaman.com
Wikalat 'Ammun: http://www.ammonnews.net
Wikalat Anba' 'Arar: http://www.sha3erjordan.net

BRITISH OFFICIAL ISSUANCE

Cairo Intelligence Department [World War I], Arab Bureau. *Arab Bulletin*.

DISSERTATIONS

Hamarneh, Mustafa. "Social and Economic Transformation of Trans-Jordan, 1921–1946."
    PhD diss., Georgetown University, 1985.
Musa, 'Amir Jadallah. "Al-'Alaqat al-Urdunniyya-al-Su'udiyya ma bayna 1921–1928." BA
    diss., University of Jordan, 1977.
Owidi, Ahmed Saleh Suleiman. "Bedouin Justice in Jordan: The Customary Legal Sys-
    tem of the Tribes and its Integration into the Framework of State Policy from 1921
    onwards." PhD diss., University of Cambridge, 1982.
Rogan, Eugene L. "Incorporating the Periphery: The Ottoman Extension of Direct Rule
    over Southeastern Syria (Transjordan), 1867–1914." PhD diss., Harvard University, 1991.
Sarairah, Hatem A. "A British Actor on the Bedouin Stage: Glubb's Career in Jordan,
    1930–1956." PhD, diss. Indiana University, 1989.

UNPUBLISHED

Qasus, 'Awda. "Mudhakkirat" (Memoirs).

PUBLISHED SOURCES

Al-'Abbadi, Ahmad 'Uwaydi. *Muqaddima li-dirasat al-'asha'ir al-Urdunniyya*. 2nd ed.
    Amman: Al-Dar al-'Arabiyya lil-Nashr, 1985.

——. *Al-Jara'im al-sughra 'ind al-'asha'ir al-Urdunniyya.* Amman: Dar al-Fikr, 1987.

——. *Fi Rubu' al-Urdunn.* Vol. 1. Amman: Dar al-Fikr, 1987.

——. *'Asha'ir al-Urdunn: Jawlat maydaniyya wa-tahlilat.* Amman: Al-Ahliyya lil-Nashr wal-Tawzi', 2005.

Al-'Abbadi, Muhammad Yunis. *Al-Rihla al-mulukiyya al-Hashimiyya.* Amman: Wizarat al-Thaqafa, 1997.

Abu Diyya, Sa'd. *Fil-'Alaqat al-'Arabiyya al-'Uthmaniyya: Thawrat al-Karak 'amm 1910.* Amman: Mu'assasat Rum, 1992.

Abu Diyya, Sa'd, and 'Abd al-Majid Mahdi. *Al-Jaysh al-'Arabi wa-diblumasiyyat al-sahra.* Amman: Mudiriyyat al-Matabi' al-'Askariyya, 1987.

Abu Hassan, Muhammad. *Al-Qada' al-'asha'iri fil-Urdunn.* Amman: n.p., n.d.

Abujaber, Raouf Sa'd. *Pioneers over Jordan: The Frontier of Settlement in Transjordan, 1850–1914.* London: I. B. Tauris, 1989.

Abu-Lughod, Ibrahim. *Resistance, Exile and Return.* Birzeit, Palestine: Birzeit University, 2003.

Abu-Lughod, Lila. *Veiled Sentiments: Honor and Poetry in a Bedouin Society.* Berkeley: University of California Press, 1988.

Abu-Nowar, Ma'an. *The History of the Hashemite Kingdom of Jordan:* vol. 1: *The Creation and Development of Transjordan, 1920–29.* Oxford: Ithaca Press, 1989.

——. *The Development of Trans-Jordan, 1929–1939.* Reading, U.K.: Ithaca Press, 2006.

Al-'Ajluni, Muhammad 'Ali. *Dhikrayat 'an al-Thawra al-'Arabiyya al-Kubra.* 2nd ed. Amman: Dar al-Karmil, 2002.

Alon, Yoav. "Tribal Shaykhs and the Limits of British Imperial Rule." *Journal of Imperial and Commonwealth History* 32, no. 1 (2004): 69–92.

——. "The Balqa' Revolt: Tribes and Early State-Building in Transjordan." *Die Welt des Islams* 46, no. 1 (2006): 7–42.

——. *The Making of Jordan: Tribes, Colonialism and the Modern State.* London: I. B. Tauris, 2007.

——. "'Heart-Beguiling Araby' on the Frontier of Empire: Early Anglo-Arab Relations in Transjordan." *British Journal of Middle Eastern Studies* 36, no. 1 (2009): 55–72.

——. "Friends Indeed or Accomplices in Need? The Jewish Agency, Emir Abdullah and the Shaykhs of Transjordan, 1922–39." In *Israel's Clandestine Diplomacies,* ed. Clive Jones and Tore T. Petersen, 31–48. London: Hurst, 2013.

——. "From Abdullah (I) to Abdullah (II): The Monarchy, the Tribes and the Shaykhly Families in Jordan, 1920–2012." In *Tribes and States in a Changing Middle East,* ed. Uzi Rabi. London: Hurst, forthcoming.

Anderson, Benedict. *Imagined Communities: Reflections on the Rise and Spread of Nationalism.* 1983. 2nd ed. London: Verso, 1991.

Anderson, Betty S. *Nationalist Voices in Jordan: The Street and the State.* Austin: University of Texas Press, 2005.

Antoun, Richard T. "Civil Society, Tribal Process, and Change in Jordan: An Anthropological View." *International Journal of Middle Eastern Studies* 32, no. 4 (November 2000): 441–63.

Ashton, Nigel. *King Hussein of Jordan: A Poitical Life.* New Haven, CT: Yale University Press, 2008.

Ayalon, Amy. *The Press in the Arab Middle East.* New York: Oxford University Press, 1995.

Ayubi, Nazih N. *Over-stating the Arab State: Politics and Society in the Middle East.* London: I. B. Tauris, 1995.

Bailey, Clinton. *Bedouin Poetry from Sinai and the Negev: Mirror of a Culture.* Oxford: Clarendon Press, 1991.

———. *Bedouin Law from Sinai and the Negev.* New Haven, CT: Yale University Press, 2009.

Al-Bakhit, 'Awad Sayyah al-Mubarak and 'Umar Muhammad Nazal al-'Armuti. *Sirat hayat al-shaykh Mithqal Sattam al-Fayiz shaykh mashayikh Bani Sakhr.* Amman: Matba'at al-Safir, [2012].

Al-Bakhit, Muhammad 'Adnan et al., eds. *Al-Watha'iq al-Hashimiyya, awraq 'Abdullah bin al-Husayn:* vol. 10: *Al-'Alaqat al-Urdunniyya-al-Su'udiyya, 1925–1951.* 2 parts. Amman: Jami'at Al al-Bayt, 1997.

———, eds. *Al-Watha'iq al-Hashimiyya, awraq 'Abdullah bin al-Husayn:* vol. 16: [*Al-'Asha'ir al-Urdunniyya, 1921–1951*], part 2: *Mahadir wa-jalasat lajnat al-ishraf 'ala al-badu, 1931–1949.* Amman: Jami'at Al al-Bayt, 2001.

———, eds. *Al-Watha'iq al-Hashimiyya, awraq 'Abdullah bin al-Husayn:* vol. 16: [*Al-'Asha'ir al-Urdunniyya, 1921–1951*], part. 3: *Qararat lajnat al-ishraf 'ala al-badu, 1931–1949.* Amman: Jami'at Al al-Bayt, 2003.

Baram, Amatzia. "Neo-Tribalism in Iraq: Saddam Hussein's Tribal Policies, 1991–6." *International Journal of Middle East Studies* 29, no. 1 (1997): 1–31.

Bashir, Sulayman. *Judhur al-wisaya al-Urduniyya.* Jerusalem: n.p., 1980.

Batatu, Hanna. *The Old Social Classes and the Revolutionary Movements of Iraq.* Princeton, NJ: Princeton University Press, 1978.

Ben Zvi, Rachel Yanait. *Darki siparti.* Jerusalem: Kiryat Sefer, 1971.

Bin Husayn, 'Abdullah. *Al-Athar al-kamila lil-Malik 'Abdullah bin Husayn.* 2nd ed. Beirut: Al-Dar al-Muttahida lil-Nashr, 1979.

Blunt, Anne. *A Pilgrimage to Nejd.* 2 vols. 2nd ed. London: John Murray, 1881.

Bocco, Riccardo, and Tariq M. M. Tell. "*Pax Britannica* in the Steppe: British Policy and the Transjordan Bedouin." In *Village, Steppe and State: The Social Origins of Modern Jordan*, ed. Eugene L. Rogan and Tariq M. M. Tell, 108–27. London: British Academic Press, 1994.

———. "Frontière, tribus et Etat(s) en Jordanie orientale à l'époque du mandate." *Maghreb-Machrek* 147 (1995): 26–47.

Bradshow, Tancred. *Britain and Jordan: Imperial Strategy, King Abdullah I and the Zionist Movement.* London: I. B. Tauris, 2012.

Büssow, Johann. *Hamidian Palestine: Politics and Society in the District of Jerusalem, 1872–1908.* Leiden: Brill, 2011.

Carruthers, Douglas. "A Journey in North-Western Arabia." *Geographical Journal* 35, no. 3 (March 1910): 225–45.

——. *Arabian Adventure: To the Great Nafud in Quest of the Oryx*. London: H. F. & G. Witherby, 1935.

Caton, Steven C. *"Peaks of Yemen I summon": Poetry as Cultural Practice in a North Yemeni Tribe*. Berkeley: University of California Press, 1990.

Clauß, Ludwig Ferdinand. *Semiten der Wüste unter sich: Miterlebnisse eines Rassenforschers*. Berlin: Büchergilde Gutenberg, 1937.

——. *Als Beduine unter Beduinen*. 1933. 3rd ed. Freiburg im Breisgau: Herder, 1954.

Cohen, Amnon. *Palestine in the 18th Century*. Jerusalem: Magnes Press, 1973.

Cohen, Hillel. *Year Zero of the Arab-Israeli Conflict, 1929*. 2013. Translated by Haim Watzman. Lebanon NH: Brandeis University Press, 2015.

Conder, Claude R. *Heth and Moab: Explorations in Syria in 1881 and 1882*. 1883. 3rd ed. London: Watt, 1892.

Dann, Uriel. *Studies in the History of Transjordan, 1920–1949: The Making of a State*. Boulder, CO: Westview Press, 1984.

——. *King Hussein and the Challenge of Arab Radicalism: Jordan, 1955–1967*. Oxford: Oxford University Press, 1989.

David, Assaf. *Jordan Update: October 2012*. Tel Aviv: Economic Cooperation Foundation, 2012.

——. *Jordan Update: November 2012*. Tel Aviv: Economic Cooperation Foundation, 2012.

Deringil, Selim. *The Well-Protected Domains: Ideology and the Legitimation of Power in the Ottoman Empire, 1876–1909*. London: I. B. Tauris, 1998.

——. "'They Live in a State of Nomadism and Savagery': The Late Ottoman Empire and the Post-Colonial Debate." *Comparative Studies in Society and History* 45 (2003): 311–42.

Dodge, Toby. *Inventing Iraq: The Failure of Nation-Building and a History Denied*. New York: Columbia University Press, 2003.

Doughty, Charles Montagu. *Travels in Arabia Deserta*. 1888. London: Cape, 1926.

Dresch, Paul. "The Position of Shaykhs among the Northern Tribes of Yemen." *Man* 19, no. 1 (March 1984): 31–49.

——. *Tribes, Government, and History in Yemen*. Oxford: Oxford University Press, 1989.

Edelstein, Yehuda. *Avraham Shapira*. Vol. 2. Tel Aviv: Yedidim, 1939.

Efrati, Noga. *Women in Iraq: Past Meets Present*. New York: Columbia University Press, 2012.

Eickelman, Dale F. *Knowledge and Power in Morocco: The Education of a Twentieth-Century Notable*. Princeton, NJ: Princeton University Press, 1985.

——. *The Middle East and Central Asia: An Anthropological Approach*. 1981. 3rd ed., Upper Saddle River, NJ: Prentice-Hall, 1998; 4th ed., 2002.

Eilat, Eliyahu [see also under Epstein below]. *Shivat Tzion va-'arav*. Tel Aviv: Dvir, 1971.

——. "Maga'im ishiyim 'im beduyey 'Ever ha-Yarden bi-shnot ha-shloshim." In *Reshimot be-noshe ha-beduyim*, no. 9, ed. Yitzhak Bailey. Sde Boker, Israel: Midreshet Sde Boker, 1978.

Eisenstadt, Michael. "Iraq: Tribal Engagement Lessons Learned." *Military Review*, September–October 2007: 16–31.

Epstein, Eliyahu [see also under Eilat above]. "Be-Artzot hamizrah." *Yarhon Ahdut ha-'Avoda* 13, (1931): 117–19, 467–74.

———. *Ukhlusey 'Ever ha-Yarden ve-hayehem*. Tel Aviv: Omanut, 1933.

Al-Fayiz, Miflih al-Nimr. *'Asha'ir Bani Sakhr: Ta'rikh wa-mawaqif hata sanat 1950*. Amman: Matabi' al-Quwwat al-Musallaha, 1995.

Faroqhi, Suraiya. *Pilgrims and Sultans: The Hajj under the Ottomans, 1517–1683*. London: I. B. Tauris, 1994.

Farouk-Sluglett, Marion and Peter Sluglett. "The Transformation of Land Tenure and Rural Social Structure in Central and Southern Iraq c. 1870–1958." *International Journal of Middle East Studies* 15, no. 4 (1983): 491–505.

Fieldhouse, D. K. *Western Imperialism in the Middle East, 1914–1958*. Oxford: Oxford University Press, 2006.

Fischbach, Michael. *State, Society and Land in Jordan*. Leiden: Brill, 2000.

Fletcher, Robert S. G. *British Imperialism and the 'Tribal Question': Desert Administration and Nomadic Societies in the Middle East, 1919–1936*. Oxford: Oxford University Press, 2015.

Geertz, Clifford. *The Social History of an Indonesian Town*. Cambridge: Cambridge University Press, 1965.

Gelber, Yoav. *Jewish-Transjordanian Relations, 1921–1948*. London: Frank Cass, 1997.

Gellner, Ernest. *Nations and Nationalism*. Ithaca, NY: Cornell University Press, 1983.

Gelvin, James L. *Divided Loyalties: Nationalism and Mass Politics in Syria at the Close of Empire*. Berkeley: University of California Press, 1998.

Gershoni, Israel, and James Jankowski, eds. *Rethinking Nationalism in the Arab Middle East*. New York: Columbia University Press, 1997.

Great Britain. Admiralty. Naval Intelligence Division. Geographical Section. *A Handbook of Syria (including Palestine)*. London: HMSO, 1919–20.

———. Colonial Office. *Report by His Britannic Majesty's Government to the Council of the League of Nations on the Administration of Palestine and Transjordan for the Years 1923–38*. London: HMSO, 1924–39.

Guarmani, Carlo. *Northern Najd: A Journey from Jerusalem to Anaiza in Qasim*. Translated by Lady Muriel Capel-Cure. Edited by Douglas Carruthers. 1866. London: Argonaut Press, 1938.

Gubser, Peter. *Politics and Change in Al-Karak, Jordan*. London: Oxford University Press, 1973.

Haghanduqa, Muhammad Khayr. *Mirza Basha Wasfi: Kitab watha'iqi*. Amman: Al-Jam'iyya al-'Ilmiyya al-Malakiyya, 1985.

Al-Hallaq, Ahmad al-Budayri. *Hawadith Dimashq al-yawmiyya, 1154–1175h / 1741–1762m*. Cairo: Al-Jam'iyya al-Misriyya lil-Dirasat al-Ta'rikhiyya, 1959.

Heyer, Anselm. *Untergang des Morgenlandes*. Berlin: Ullstein, 1966.

Hill, Gray. *With the Beduins*. London: Fisher, 1891.

———. "A Journey East of the Jordan and the Dead Sea, 1895." *Palestine Exploration Fund Quarterly Statement* 28 (1896): 24–46.

———. "A Journey to Petra—1896." *Palestine Exploration Fund Quarterly Statement* 29 (1897): 35–44.

Hobsbawm, Eric. *Nations and Nationalism since 1870.* Cambridge: Cambridge University Press, 1983.

Holes, Clive, and Said Salman Abu Athera. *Poetry and Politics in Contemporary Bedouin Society.* Reading, U.K.: Ithaca Press, 2009.

Hughes, Matthew. *Allenby and British Strategy in the Middle East, 1917–1919.* London: Frank Cass, 1999.

Hütteroth, W. D., and K. Abdulfattah. *Historical Geography of Palestine, Transjordan and Southern Syria in the Late 16th Century.* Erlangen: Frankische Geographische Gesellschaft, 1977.

Ilan, Zvi. *Ha-Kmiha le-hityashvut yehudim be-'Ever ha-Yarden, 1871–1947.* Jerusalem: Yad Ben Zvi, 1985.

Irby, Charles Leonard, and James Mangles. *Travels in Egypt and Nubia, Syria and Asia Minor during the Years 1817 & 1818.* 1823. 2nd ed. London: John Murray, 1845.

Jabar, Falah. "Sheikhs and Ideologues: Deconstruction and Reconstruction of Tribes under Patrimonial Totalitarianism in Iraq, 1968–1998." In *Tribes and Power: Nationalism and Ethnicity in the Middle East,* ed. Falah Jabar and Hosham Dawod, 69–109. London: Saqi, 2003.

Jarvis, C. S. *Arab Command: The Biography of Lieutenant-Colonel F. W. [sic] Peake Pasha, C.M.G., C.B.E.* London: Hutchinson, 1942.

Jaussen, Antonin. *Coutumes des arabes au pays de Moab.* 1907. Facsimile ed. Paris: Librairie d'Amerique et d'Orient, 1948.

Kasaba, Resat. *A Moveable Empire: Ottoman Nomads, Migrants and Refugees.* Seattle: University of Washington Press, 2009.

El-Katiri, Mohammed. *State-Building Challenges in a Post-Revolution Libya.* Carlisle, PA: Strategic Studies Institute, U.S. Army War College, 2012.

Khoury, Philip S. "The Tribal Shaykh, French Tribal Policy, and the Nationalist Movement in Syria between Two World Wars." *Middle Eastern Studies* 18 (1982): 180–93.

———. "A Reinterpretation of the Origins and Aims of the Great Syrian Revolt of 1925–27." In *Arab Civilization: Challenges and Responses. Studies in Honor of Constantine K. Zurayk,* ed. George N. Atiyeh and Ibrahim M. Oweiss, 241–71. Albany: State University of New York Press, 1988.

Khoury, Philip S., and Joseph Kostiner. "Introduction: Tribes and the Complexities of State Formation in the Middle East." In *Tribes and State Formation in the Middle East,* ed. Philip S. Khoury and Joseph Kostiner, 1–22. Berkeley: University of California Press, 1990. London: I. B. Tauris, 1991.

Khrisat, Muhammad 'Abd al-Qadir. *Al-Urdunniyyun wal-qadaya al-wataniyya wal-qawmiyya.* Amman: Al-Jami'a al-Urdunniyya, 1991.

Kimmerling, Baruch, and Joel S. Migdal. *Palestinians: The Making of a People.* Cambridge, MA: Harvard University Press, 1993.

Kirkbride, Alec Seath. *A Crackle of Thorns*. London: John Murray, 1956.

Klein, Frederick. "The Original Discovery of the Moabite Stone." *Palestine Exploration Fund Quarterly Statement* 1–2 (March 31 to June 30, 1870): 281–83.

Klieman, Aaron S. *Foundations of British Policy in the Arab World: The Cairo Conference of 1921*. Baltimore: Johns Hopkins Press, 1970.

Kostiner, Joseph. "On Instruments and Their Designers: The Ikhwan of Najd and the Formation of the Saudi State." *Middle Eastern Studies* 21 (1985): 298–323.

———. "The Hashemite 'Tribal Confederacy' of the Arab Revolt." In *National and International Politics in the Middle East: Essays in Honour of Elie Kedourie*, ed. Edward Ingram, 126–43. London: Frank Cass, 1986.

———. *The Making of Saudi Arabia, 1916–1936: From Chieftaincy to Monarchical State*. New York: Oxford University Press, 1993.

Kurd 'Ali, Muhammad. *Al-Rihla al-Anwariyya ila al-asqa' al-Hijaziyya wal-Shamiyya*. Vol. 3. Beirut: Al-Matba'a al-'Ilmiyya, 1916.

Kurpershoek, Marcel P. *Oral Poetry and Narratives from Central Arabia*. 5 vols. Leiden: Brill, 1994–2005.

Lancaster, William. *The Rwala Bedouin Today*. Cambridge: Cambridge University Press, 1981.

Landau, Jacob M. *The Hejaz Railway and the Muslim Pilgrimage*. Detroit: Wayne State University Press, 1971.

Lavie, Smadar. *The Poetics of Military Occupation: Mzeina Allegories of Bedouin Identity under Israeli and Egyptian Rule*. Berkeley: University of California Press, 1990.

Layne, Linda L. *Home and Homeland: The Dialogics of Tribal and National Identities in Jordan*. Princeton, NJ: Princeton University Press, 1994.

Lees, G. Robinson. "Across Southern Bashan." *Geographical Journal* 5, no. 1 (January 1895): 1–27.

Lewis, Norman. *Nomads and Settlers in Syria and Jordan, 1800–1980*. Cambridge: Cambridge University Press, 1987.

Lias, Godfrey. *Glubb's Legion*. London: Evans Bros., 1956.

Littmann, Enno. "Eine amtliche Liste der Beduinenstämme des Ostjordanlandes." *Zeitschrift des Deutschen Palästina-Vereins* 24 (1901): 26–31.

Lovell, Mary S. *A Scandalous Life: The Biography of Jane Digby*. 1995. Paperback ed. London: Fourth Estate, 2010.

Al-Madi, Munib, and Sulayman Musa. *Ta'rikh al-Urdunn fil-qarn al-'ishrin, 1900–1959*. 2nd ed. Amman: Maktabat al-Muhtasib, 1988.

Marr, Phebe. *The Modern History of Iraq*. Boulder, CO: Westview Press, 1985.

Marx, Emanuel. "The Tribe as a Unit of Subsistence: Nomadic Pastoralism in the Middle East." *American Anthropologist* 79 (1977): 343–63.

———. "The Political Economy of Middle Eastern and North African Pastoral Nomads." In *Nomadic Societies in the Middle East and North Africa: Entering the 21st Century*, ed. Dawn Chatty, 78–97. Leiden: Brill, 2006.

Al-Masarwa, Bashar Muhammad Abu Nusayr. *'Asha'ir Masarwa al-Jiza min 1864–1958*. Madaba, Jordan: n.p., 2000.

Massad, Joseph A. *Colonial Effects: The Making of National Identity in Jordan*. New York: Columbia University Press, 2001.

Meeker, Michael E. *Literature and Violence in North Arabia*. Cambridge: Cambridge University Press, 1979.

Minawi, Mostafa. *The Ottoman Scramble for Africa*. Stanford: Stanford University Press, 2016.

Morris, Benny. "Revisiting the Palestinian Exodus of 1948." In *The War for Palestine: Rewriting the History of 1948*, ed. Eugene L. Rogan and Avi Shlaim, 37–59. Cambridge: Cambridge University Press, 2001.

Mufti (Habjoka), Shauket. *Heroes and Emperors in Circassian History*. Beirut: Librairie du Liban, 1972.

Musa, Sulayman. *Imarat Sharq al-Urdunn: Nasha'tuha wa-tatawwuruha fi rub' qarn, 1921–1946*. Amman: Lajnat Ta'rikh al-Urdunn, 1990.

———. *Ayam la tunsa: Al-Urdunn fi harb 1948*. 2nd ed. Amman: Matabi' al-Quwwat al-Musallaha, 1998.

Musil, Alois. *Arabia Deserta: A Topographical Itinerary*. Vol. 2. New York: American Geographical Society, 1927.

———. *Palmyrena: A Topographical Itinerary*. New York: American Geographical Society, 1928.

Nakash, Yitzhak. *The Shi'is of Iraq*. Princeton, NJ: Princeton University Press, 1994.

Nevo, Joseph. *King Abdallah and Palestine: A Territorial Ambition*. Basingstoke, U.K.: Macmillan, 1996.

Al-Nimr, Ihsan. *Ta'rikh Jabal Nablus wal-Balqa'*. Vol. 3. Nablus: n.p., 1974.

Northey, A. E. "Expedition to the East of Jordan." *Palestine Exploration Fund Quarterly Statement* 4 (1872): 57–72.

Oppenheim, Max Adrian Simon. *Die Beduinen*. Vol. 2. Leipzig: Otto Harrassowitz, 1943.

Palva, Heikki. *Narratives and Poems from Hesbāan: Arabic Texts Recorded among the Seminomadic al-Aĝaarma Tribe*. Göteborg, Sweden: Acta Universitatis Gothburgensis, 1978.

———. *Artistic Colloquial Arabic: Traditional Narratives and Poems from al-Balqa' (Jordan): Transcription, Translation, Linguistic and Metrical Analysis*. Helsinki: Finnish Oriental Society, 1992.

Peake, F. G. *Ta'rikh Sharqi al-Urdunn wa-qaba'iliha*. Jerusalem: Matba'at Dar al-Aytam al-Islamiyya, 1935.

Peters, F. E. *The Hajj: The Muslim Pilgrimage to Mecca and the Holy Places*. Princeton, NJ: Princeton University Press, 1994.

Philby, H. St J. B. "Jauf and the North Arabian Desert." *Geographical Journal* 62, no. 4 (October 1923): 241–59.

Provence, Michael. *The Great Syrian Revolt and the Rise of Arab Nationalism*. Austin: University of Texas Press, 2005.

Al-Qalqashandi, Abi al-'Abbas Ahmad b. 'Ali. *Qala'id al-juman fil-ta'rif bi-qaba'il 'Arab al-zaman*. Edited by Ibrahim al-Abyari. 2nd ed. Cairo: Dar al-Kutub al-Islamiyya, 1982.

Qaqish, Bassam 'Id. *Al-Mu'assasa al-'askariyya al-Urdunniyya wa-tatawwuruha, 1946–1967*. Amman: Matba'at al-Quwwat al-Musallaha al-Urdunniyya, 1998.

Qasus, 'Awda. *Al-Qada' al-badawi*. Amman: n.p., 1936.

Rafeq, Abdul-Karim. *The Province of Damascus, 1723–1783*. Beirut: Khayats, 1966.

Raswan, Carl R. *The Black Tents of Arabia*. London: Hutchinson, 1935.

———. *Escape from Baghdad*. Hildesheim, Germany: Georg Olms, 1978.

Al-Rawabda, 'Abd al-Ra'uf. *Mu'jam al-'asha'ir al-Urdunniyya*. Amman: Matabi' al-Mu'assasa al-Suhufiyya al-Urdunniyya, 2010.

Robins, Philip. *A History of Jordan*. Cambridge: Cambridge University Press, 2004.

Rogan, Eugene L. "Bringing the State Back: The Limits of Ottoman Rule in Jordan, 1840–1910." In *Village, Steppe and State: The Social Origins of Modern Jordan*, ed. Eugene L. Rogan and Tariq Tell, 32–57. London: British Academic Press, 1994.

———. "Asiret Mektebi: Abdülhamid II's School for Tribes (1892–1907)." *International Journal of Middle East Studies* 28, no. 1 (1996): 83–107.

———. *Frontiers of the State in the Late Ottoman Empire: Transjordan, 1850–1921*. Cambridge: Cambridge University Press, 1999.

———. *The Fall of the Ottomans: The Great War in the Middle East*. New York: Basic Books, 2015.

Sa'id, Amin Muhammad. *Muluk al-muslimin al-mu'asirin wa-duwaluhum*. Cairo: n.p., 1933.

Salzman, Philip Carl. "Hierarchical Image and Reality: The Construction of a Tribal Chiefship." *Comparative Studies in Society and History* 42 (2000): 49–66.

Satloff, Robert B. *From Abdullah to Hussein: Jordan in Transition*. New York: Oxford University Press, 1994.

Al-Sawariyya, Nawfan Raja al-Hamud. *'Amman wa-jiwaruha khilal al-fatra 1864–1921*. Amman: Bank al-A'mal, 1996.

Al-Sawariyya, Nawfan Raja, and Muhammad Salim al-Tarawna. *Idha'at jadida 'ala Thawrat al-Karak*. Karak, Jordan: Dar Rand lil-Nashr, 1999.

Seabrook, W. B. *Adventures in Arabia among the Bedouins, Druses, Whirling Dervishes and Yezidee Devil-Worshippers*. New York: Harcourt, Brace, 1927. London: George G. Harrap, 1928.

Sela, Avraham. "The 'Wailing Wall' Riots (1929) as a Watershed in the Palestine Conflict." *Muslim World* 84, no. 1–2 (January–April 1994): 60–94.

Al-Shahbandar, 'Abd al-Rahman. *Mudhakkirat al-duktur 'Abd al-Rahman al-Shahbandar*. Beirut: Dar al-Irshad, 1968.

Shapira, Anita. "The Option on Ghaur al-Kibd: Contacts between Emir Abdallah and the Zionist Executive, 1932–1935." *Studies in Zionism* 1, no. 2 (1980): 239–83.

Sharett, Moshe. *Yoman medini, 1936*. Tel Aviv: 'Am 'Oved and Zionist Library, 1976.

Sheffy, Yigal. *British Military Intelligence in the Palestine Campaign, 1914–1918*. London: Routledge, 2014.

Shlaim, Avi. *Collusion across the Jordan*. Oxford: Oxford University Press, 1988.

———. *Lion of Jordan: The Life of King Hussein in War and Peace*. London: Allen Lane, 2007.

Shryock, Andrew. "The Rise of Nasir Al-Nims: A Tribal Commentary on Being and Becoming a Shaykh." *Journal of Anthropological Research* 46 (1990): 153–76.

———. *Nationalism and the Genealogical Imagination: Oral History and Textual Authority in Tribal Jordan*. Berkeley: University of California Press, 1997.

———. "Dynastic Modernism and its Contradictions: Testing the Limits of Pluralism, Tribalism, and King Hussein's Example in Hashemite Jordan." *Arab Studies Quarterly* 22, no. 3 (Summer 2000): 57–79.

Shryock, Andrew, and Sally Howell. "'Ever a Guest in Our House': The Amir Abdullah, Shaykh Majid al-'Adwan, and the Practice of Jordanian House Politics, as Remembered by Umm Sultan, the Widow of Majid." *International Journal of Middle East Studies* 33, no. 2 (2001): 247–69.

Sluglett, Peter. *Britain in Iraq: Contriving King and Country, 1914–1932*. New York: Columbia University Press, 2007.

Smith, Anthony D. *The Ethnic Origins of Nations*. Oxford: Blackwell, 1986.

Stein, Kenneth W. *The Land Question in Palestine, 1917–1939*. Chapel Hill: The University of North Carolina Press, 1984.

Stewart, Frank. "Customary Law among the Bedouin of the Middle East and North Africa." In *Nomadic Societies in the Middle East and North Africa: Entering the 21st Century*, ed. Dawn Chatty, 239–79. Leiden: Brill, 2006.

Susser, Asher. *Both Banks of the Jordan: A Political Biography of Wasfi al-Tall*. Ilford, U.K.: Frank Cass, 1994.

Sweet, Louise E. "Camel Raiding of North Arabian Bedouin: A Mechanism of Ecological Adaptation." *American Anthropologist* 67 (1965): 1132–50.

Sykes, Mark. "Narrative of a Journey East of Jebel Ed-Druse." *Palestine Exploration Fund Quarterly Statement* 31 (1899): 47–56.

Tal, Lawrence. *Politics, the Military and National Security in Jordan, 1955–1967*. Basingstoke, U.K.: Palgrave Macmillan, 2002.

Talas, Mustafa. *Al-Thawra al-'Arabiyya al-Kubra*. Damascus: Majallat al-Fikr al-'Askari, 1978.

———, ed. *Ahdath al-Thawra al-Suriyya al-Kubra kama saradaha qa'iduha al-'amm Sultan Basha al-Atrash, 1925–1927*. Damascus: Dar Talas, 2007.

Teitelbaum, Joshua. *The Rise and Fall of the Hashemite Kingdom of Arabia*. London: Hurst, 2001.

Tell, Tariq Moraiwed, *The Social and Economic Origins of Monarchy in Jordan*. New York: Palgrave Macmillan, 2013.

Tidrick, Kathryn. *Heart-Beguiling Araby*. Cambridge: Cambridge University Press, 1981.

Toledano, Ehud R. *Slavery and Abolition in the Ottoman Middle East*. Seattle: University of Washington Press, 1998.

———. *As If Silent and Absent: Bonds of Enslavement in the Islamic Middle East*. New Haven, CT: Yale University Press, 2007.

Tönnies, Ferdinand. *Gemeinschaft und Gesellschaft: Abhandlung des Communismus und des Socialismus als empirischer Culturformen*. Leipzig: Fues, 1887. Translated and edited by Charles Price Loomis as *Community and Society* (East Lansing: Michigan State University Press, 1957).

Tripp, Charles. *The History of Iraq*. Cambridge: Cambridge University Press, 2002.

Tristram, Henry Baker. *The Land of Israel: A Journal of Travels in Palestine*. London: Society for Promoting Christian Knowledge, 1865.

———. *The Land of Moab: Travels and Discoveries on the East Side of the Dead Sea and the Jordan*. London: John Murray, 1873.

Al-'Uzayzat, Yusuf Salim al-Shuwayhat. *Al-'Uzayzat fi Madaba* (no further details).

Warren, Charles. "Expedition to East of Jordan, July and August 1867." *Palestine Exploration Fund Quarterly Statement* 1–2 (March 31 to June 30, 1870): 284–306.

Watkins, Jessica. "Seeking Justice: Tribal Dispute Resolution and Societal Transformation in Jordan." *International Journal of Middle East Studies* 46, no. 1 (February 2014): 31–49.

Wilson, Jeremy. *Lawrence of Arabia: The Authorized Biography of T. E. Lawrence*. New York: Atheneum, 1990.

Wilson, Mary C. *King Abdullah, Britain and the Making of Jordan*. Cambridge: Cambridge University Press, 1987.

Yaniv, Ya'akov. *Hatzo'nim bi-Yhuda uvi-Yrushalayim*. Jerusalem: Ariel, 1980.

Yitzhak, Ronen. *Shutafut ve-'oynut: 'Abdallah, ha-Ligyon ha-'Arvi ve-milhemet 1948*. Jerusalem: Misrad ha-Bitahon, 2006.

Young, Hubert. *The Independent Arab*. London: John Murray, 1933.

Young, William. "'The Bedouin': Discursive Identity or Sociological Category? A Case Study from Jordan." *Journal of Mediterranean Studies* 9, no. 2 (1999): 275–99.

Zeller, John. "The Bedawin." *Palestine Exploration Fund Quarterly Statement* 33 (1901): 185–203.

Zirikli, Khayr al-Din. *'Aman fi 'Amman*. Cairo: Al-Matba'a al-'Arabiyya, 1925.

Zu'aytar, Akram. *Yawmiyyat Akram Zu'aytar: Al-Haraka al-wataniyya al-Filastiniyya, 1935–1939*. Beirut: Mu'assasat al-Dirasat al-Filastiniyya, 1980.

Al-Zu'bi, Khalid Musa. *'Akif al-Fayiz: Sirat hayah siyasiyya wa-barlamaniyya*. Amman: Markaz al-Dirasat al-Barlamaniyya, 2007.

INDEX

Note: "M" refers to Mithqal al-Fayiz. Page numbers in italic type indicate illustrations. Page numbers followed by "*m*" indicate maps.